Foreword

BY THE RT. HON. WILLIAM ROSS, M.P.

Secretary of State for Scotland

This memorandum, which replaces "The Primary School in Scotland", published in 1950, has been prepared by a committee representative of the teaching profession, colleges of education and Her Majesty's Inspectors of Schools. Its purpose is to provide mainly for teachers and trainee teachers, but also for education authorities, colleges of education and general readers, an up-to-date appraisal of the best practices in primary schools in Scotland and of the principles on which, in the view of those most closely associated with its development over the past decade, primary education should be based. It also contains much valuable information and advice on methods, facilities and organisation in the classroom and the school.

I hope that it will give a great many people the opportunity of seeing in proper perspective a part of our educational system which perhaps attracts less attention than it deserves but remains of fundamental importance for the later development of the abilities and character of our children. It is one in which striking advances have been made in recent years. I trust that the memorandum will lead to a wider appreciation of the work that is done in our primary schools; of the demands that are made on the patience, skill and enterprise of the teachers; of the triumphs and disappointments that all teachers experience; and of the great contribution that can be made by interested and helpful parents.

We have a great tradition in education and we owe it to our successors to keep our educational thinking and practice abreast of the needs of our day and to lay foundations on which they in their turn can build. In education as well as in industry, science, and the arts, progress depends on willingness to push beyond familiar horizons. To be a success, this publication should not only provide guidance and information for primary school teachers, students in training, and education authorities but it should also stimulate continuing thought and constant re-appraisal of our own work by those of us who have any measure of responsibility for primary education, whether as teachers or administrators. I commend it wholeheartedly both to these groups of readers and also to the wider public for its general interest and importance.

William Ross

Membership of the Committee

MR. J. SHANKS (*Chairman*), H.M. Chief Inspector, Scottish Education Department.

MR. J. BENNETT, MBE, H.M. Inspector, Scottish Education Department.

MISS A. B. BROCK, MA, Senior Lecturer in Methods, Jordanhill College of Education.

MISS J. D. BROWN, Lecturer in Methods, Moray House College of Education.

MISS J. T. DUNCANSON, H.M. Inspector, Scottish Education Department.

MR. N. FULLWOOD, H.M. Inspector, Scottish Education Department.

SISTER JULIE MARIE GILLESPIE, MBE, Head Teacher, St. Patrick's R.C. Primary School, Dumbarton.

MR. W. GILLIES, H.M. Inspector, Scottish Education Department.

MR. W. GRAY, MA, Head Teacher, Wishaw Primary School, Lanarkshire.
(Joined the Committee in November, 1962.)

MISS I. MCHAFFIE, Head Teacher, Kingswood Infant School, Aberdeen.

MR. K. E. MILLER, OBE, H.M. Inspector, Scottish Education Department.

MR. H. S. MISKIMMIN, MA, Head Teacher, Riverside Secondary School, Stirling.

MISS M. E. MITCHELL, Lecturer in Methods, Aberdeen College of Education.

MR. J. G. MORRIS, H.M. Inspector, Scottish Education Department.

MR. C. R. PEARCE, MA, JP, Head Teacher, Hyvots Bank Primary School, Edinburgh.

MR. J. F. SMITH, MA, First Assistant, Mosspark Primary School, Glasgow.

MR. T. SNEDDON, MA, FEIS, Head Teacher, Blacklaw Primary School, Dunfermline, Fife.

MR. D. M. WHYTE, Head Teacher, Forfar North and East Primary Schools, Angus.

MR. A. K. FORBES (*Secretary*), H.M. Inspector, Scottish Education Department.

The Committee began its deliberations in February, 1962, under the Chairmanship of MR. R. MACDONALD, H.M. Chief Inspector, who resigned in September, 1962, on his retiral. MR. W. GORDON, MA, Head Teacher, Clune Park Primary School, Port Glasgow, Renfrewshire, resigned from membership in August, 1962, and MR. J. ANDERSON, H.M. Inspector, was a member from November, 1962, to August, 1964.

The Committee take this opportunity of thanking all who helped them in any way and, in particular, acknowledge the invaluable service given them by their Secretary, Mr. A. K. Forbes, H.M. Inspector, not only in the routine of the secretaryship, but also in the quite arduous task of preparing and editing the text.

SCOTTISH EDUCATION DEPARTMENT

Primary Education in Scotland

EDINBURGH
HER MAJESTY'S STATIONERY OFFICE
1965

© *Crown copyright 1965*

Printed and Published by
HER MAJESTY'S STATIONERY OFFICE

To be purchased from
13a Castle Street, Edinburgh EH2 3AR
49 High Holborn, London WC1V 6HB
41 The Hayes, Cardiff CF1 1JW
Brazennose Street, Manchester M60 8AS
Southey House, Wine Street, Bristol BS1 2BQ
258 Broad Street, Birmingham B1 2HE
80 Chichester Street, Belfast BT1 4JY
or through booksellers

Printed in Scotland

First published 1965

Fourth impression 1975

ISBN 0 11 490313 1

Contents

Preface

"The Primary School in Scotland" was published in 1950, at a time when the Advisory Council's report "Primary Education" (1947) had aroused widespread interest by its fresh and challenging approach to educational problems. The purpose of the Department's publication, which was described as a memorandum on the curriculum, was to show how the principles enunciated by the Advisory Council could be translated into terms of classroom practice. Although both documents were published after the war, the essential work on them, other than editorial, was completed between the years 1942 and 1945. They dealt, therefore, with conditions as they existed in the schools some twenty years ago. To a certain extent, also, they suggested new ways of doing things and looked ahead to the changes which increasingly have influenced the work of teachers in recent years. It is because of the fundamental nature of these changes and of others that are taking place that a new memorandum has been produced.

In many schools nowadays, the whole atmosphere is different from what it was twenty years ago. The relationship between pupil and teacher is easier and friendlier. The physical environment is brighter and pleasanter, and facilities of all kinds for both pupils and teachers are greatly improved. The most fundamental changes, however, are those which have arisen from the growing acceptance by teachers of the principles underlying an education based on the needs and interests of the child and the nature of the world in which he is growing up. Through a wide range of experiences the pupil is given opportunities to participate actively in his own learning. As a result, his approach to what is to be learned is livelier and his final understanding deeper. In addition, his whole attitude to work may be so improved that he is anxious to continue learning. The new memorandum takes account of what is now regarded as the best practice in the schools, outlining the most significant developments in curriculum and methods, but at the same time offering scope to enterprising teachers to make their own contributions to progress.

The memorandum avoids prescription of either subject-matter or methods. It discusses the general principles governing primary education and provides, as fully as considerations of space permit, a source-book of suggestions on which schemes may be based, rather than the outline of any particular scheme. Some topics are discussed in greater detail than others. Where this has been done, as in drama, mathematics, and art and craft activities, it is because in these aspects of the curriculum there are new approaches with which many teachers may be unfamiliar and on which they would welcome exemplification and practical guidance.

The form of the memorandum differs in many respects from its predecessor. It was useful in 1950 to preserve a number of traditional features in the description of primary school courses. The treatment of "subjects" was based on the sub-divisions which generally appeared in the weekly time-tables exhibited in the classroom; the separate treatment, in each of the curricular chapters, of the infant classes reflected an acceptance of the differences between infant room methods and those used throughout the rest of the school. Under the particular headings employed, information could readily be obtained by the teacher about recommended methods of presentation, and about the proposed lightening of the curriculum, branch by branch, which was a very important feature of the memorandum. In view, however, of the progress since made by the schools in "eliminating wasteful methods and unnecessary processes", other considerations now outweigh the advantages of such an arrangement. The suggestions now being made are based on what is known of the growth and development of the child, and emphasis is laid on the importance of fashioning the curriculum according to his needs at the various stages of his development. Primary education is depicted as a gradual and continuing process, with no clear-cut divisions between subjects or stages. For these reasons, the memorandum deliberately avoids treating each "subject" of the curriculum as if it were a separate entity, or the infant classes as if they were something quite distinct from the rest of the primary school.

Part I of the new memorandum sets the scene for the suggestions that follow, by describing the primary school child, his nature and his needs, by discussing the world in which he is growing up and the type of environment which the school is expected to provide for him, and by outlining the general responsibilities of the head teacher and his staff. Part II, in addition to considering the curriculum in general, embraces matters of school and class organisation, assessment and method. In Part III the various branches of the curriculum are dealt with more fully, and those "subjects" which derive both their interest and their usefulness from what they have in common at least as much as from their differences are grouped together. Thus the chapter on "Language Arts" includes all the language skills; the title "Environmental Studies" is employed for all the activities which arise from the pupil's observation and investigation of his environment; "Art and Craft Activities" brings together a variety of creative activities which have hitherto been considered separately. Part IV contains chapters on a number of other topics which appear to merit separate consideration. The Index contains the cross references which are inevitable and indeed desirable in a document which emphasises the continuity of methods and the linking of the branches of the curriculum.

A good deal of thought has been given in recent years to the question of social training as a function of the primary school. The Committee entrusted with the preparation of the memorandum are convinced of the importance of social and moral education and accept the view that the school must share with the home the responsibility for it and that the tone and spirit of a school exercise a considerable influence on the behaviour and outlook of the pupils. Certain aspects of social training are treated in the chapters on "Health Education" and "Conduct and Discipline". Since, however, personal and social relations, the development of judgment and values, are matters which cannot be dissociated from the curriculum generally and all that goes on within the school and the classrooms, social training has not been treated in a separate chapter. References, however, to this aspect of the school's responsibility abound in the memorandum and are amply indexed.

It will be noted that there is no chapter on religious education. While the Committee were aware that religious education does not come within the responsibility of the Secretary of State, they did not feel debarred on this account from considering its place and purpose in the curriculum. They were conscious, however, that the composition of the Committee was such that they could not deal adequately with the principles and issues involved, and they believe that the consideration of religious education should be undertaken by an *ad hoc* body on which both teachers and denominational interests are represented.

It will also be noted that the memorandum makes no more than a passing reference to nursery education. The intention had been to include a chapter on the nursery school, but since at the present time essential developments in other fields of education prevent the improvement and expansion of nursery school provision it has not been considered opportune to do so. The Committee hope that when circumstances become more favourable a separate memorandum on nursery education will be issued by the Department.

IN this memorandum "Code" means the Schools (Scotland) Code, 1956, which embodies the Regulations governing the conduct of all public and grant-aided schools in Scotland.

The nomenclature of the Code is used in designating the yearly stages of the primary course. The course normally extends to seven years, from age five to about twelve. The numeral "I" is used for the stage which pupils enter when they become of school age, "VII" for the last stage. An infant class is a class at stage P I or stage P II.

For reasons of convenience, "she", "her", have been used of the teacher; "he", "him", "his" of the head teacher and of the pupil.

Second Impression - Amendments

THE last paragraph in the section "Growth and Development", pages 4 and 5, has been revised in the light of recent research and investigation, the results of which have become available since the first impression.

In addition, two minor amendments have been made: on page 17, line 4—"unquestioningly" for "unquestionably"; on page 166, last paragraph, line 8—"effect" for "effort".

Part 1

Chapter 1
The Child

IT is now generally accepted that the primary school is much more than a preparation for the secondary school: it is a stage of development in its own right. The pattern of education in the primary school years must, therefore, above all have regard for the nature of the child and for the way he grows and develops during this period. In recent years research has yielded a considerable amount of information on these very points, and if education at the primary level is to meet the child's needs and interests, this body of knowledge must exercise a decisive influence on the attitude and practice of teachers.

In this chapter an attempt is made to summarise for the teacher some of the most significant conclusions of research into child development, to give her a general picture of the child as he grows towards adolescence, and to indicate those of his needs which the primary school has to try to meet. It is not and cannot be a complete and systematic account applicable in all respects to all children; for children differ, in natural endowment, in the guidance given them in the home, and in the opportunities which their environment can afford them.

Growth and Development

From the information which is available about the child, four main conclusions can be drawn which have important implications for education. The first of these is that the sequences which growth and development follow are fairly similar for all children, and that there are many attainments and skills which children achieve spontaneously, and many things which they discover for themselves at stage in their development when they are ready to do so. The implication for the teacher in this is that she must appreciate the stages through which the child is passing in his development towards adulthood, and attempt to provide for him the environment, experiences and guidance which will stimulate progress along natural lines. By satisfying the needs of one stage she provides for development more efficiently than by trying to anticipate or prepare for the next. She must realise that the child is not an adult in miniature: he does not feel, or act, or think like an adult. It is her function to supply means of assisting his natural development, and not to distort it by adopting a logical approach or by insisting too early on adult standards for which the child is not yet ready.

The second fact about growth which must be recognised is that, since the natural endowment of children is not uniform, there is considerable variation from one child to another in the rate at which they develop and in the attainments which they eventually achieve. Throughout the primary school, therefore, children who are in the same class by reason of their chronological age may differ markedly in respect of their physical, emotional and intellectual development. A special instance of this, with which most teachers are familiar, is that girls are generally in advance of boys in most aspects of their development at all stages up to the age of puberty. It is vital that these individual differences should be recognised and catered for in all spheres of the child's activities in school. The teacher's methods and organisation should be sufficiently flexible to allow each child to progress at an appropriate pace, and to achieve satisfaction and success at his own level.

A third feature of growth and development which has important implications for education is that they are continuous. Children develop at different rates; they may grow more quickly in some respects and more slowly in others; their rate of development may be uneven; but there are no clear-cut divisions between the various stages which they pass through. The artificial nature of school organisation makes it inevitable that the child, as he grows, passes from teacher to teacher, from department to department, from school to school, but it is essential that the change from one to the other should not be abrupt. The continuous nature of the child's development must be catered for by continuity of organisation and methods as he passes through our schools, and the transition from one administrative stage to the next must be as smooth and as gradual as possible. Nowhere is this more true than at the end of what is traditionally called the "infant department", and at the stage of transfer to secondary education.

The fourth feature is that children appear to be maturing earlier. They are certainly taller and heavier on average than their parents were at a similar age, and signs of puberty are in evidence earlier. The causes of this acceleration of growth are not fully understood, and it is uncertain whether the trend will continue. At present about one girl in eight may be expected to reach puberty by her twelfth birthday; puberty among boys is about two years later on average than among girls. Thus, there may well be a need in a primary school for some elementary guidance for boys and girls on the nature of adolescence and its physical and emotional accompaniments. Social pressures also tend to produce an earlier maturity of outlook and behaviour. Pupils in the last years of the primary school may show changes in their attitude to school work and become less dependent in their relationship with the class teacher. Thus it may be advisable at this stage to make appropriate changes in teaching method, in the content of the curriculum and in the deployment of the staff, in recognition of the developing maturity of the pupils and of the need to ease their transition to secondary education.*

The Primary School Years

The primary school receives the five-year-old child at a time when a considerable amount of development has taken place, and assumes responsibility for his education for a period of seven years during which the process of growth and development continues. When the child first comes to school, he is usually already well developed physically, and though he has little control over his smaller muscles, he has achieved sufficient co-ordination to run, jump, throw a ball, and skip, he is able to move his limbs as quickly as his elders, and he is strong for his size. His power of close vision and his ability to perceive musical pitch are comparatively poor, but otherwise his senses are as acute as they will ever be. He is constantly active, and does not sit still for long. He is very much an individual, wishing to be involved in doing things, and in achieving satisfaction, for himself. He looks for relatively easy success, asks many questions, and requires short, definite answers. His span of attention may be brief, his interests short-lived. Emotion is more dominant than intellect, and his emotional reactions are violent, though of short duration. His characteristic mode of learning is play, in which reality and fantasy are still mingled, and through which he assimilates past experiences and approaches new ones. He has, as a rule, already achieved a proficiency in speech which is more or less adequate to his present needs; he has formed some idea of size, number, money, weight, and length; and the regular rhythm of daily living has given him a rudimentary understanding of time. He may also have a notion of the printed word as something which has meaning. His knowledge of the world and of people has been derived from his home environment, his family and his friends, and limited concepts of acceptable behaviour have been established from his experience of the behaviour pattern within the family group. He is already aware that certain actions have certain

See note on page x.

consequences. He imitates his elders, wishes to be accepted by them, and will appeal to them for help and appreciation, since he is as yet by no means self-sufficient. He responds readily to a sympathetic adult who is prepared to meet him on his own terms and to form an easy, give-and-take relationship with him. He enters enthusiastically into pursuits which interest him, but his enthusiasm can be killed by an adult who tries too insistently or overtly to direct his activities. His curiosity about the world around him, his desire to learn, and the delight and satisfaction which he derives from each fresh discovery make him willing to co-operate in his own education and ready to respond to the stimulus which can be provided in the classroom by a rich environment and an understanding teacher.

During his primary school life his development continues, physically, emotionally and intellectually, and his awareness of the world and of other people gradually increases and widens. It is a period of steady physical growth, when his proportions change, his legs lengthening in relation to his body and making him more proficient at running and jumping. Co-ordination of hand and eye improves and he can soon catch and hit a ball as well as throw it. Fairly soon he gains control of his finer muscles, and in consequence shows a marked increase in manual and bodily dexterity. Improvement in acuity of vision helps him to achieve the degree of visual discrimination which he requires for reading. All this time the girls are maturing more quickly than the boys, but the boys gradually develop a greater degree of muscular strength and endurance which is reflected in a divergence of interests between the sexes in the physical activities which they pursue. Both, however, slowly gain greater staying-power and can maintain activities over progressively longer periods. As has been already noted, many of the girls and some of the boys reach the stage of puberty before they have left the primary school.

As the child grows, emotionally he becomes less self-centred, and although his emotions vary in strength and duration, he gradually learns to control them. With the increase of his interests, activities and understanding, there come greater self-awareness and emotional stability, so that events which once worried him are now taken calmly. The process is a slow one, and as part of the whole process of maturation it continues far beyond the primary school years. In an atmosphere of security and affection, however, and in the hands of teachers who understand the developing pattern of his emotions, his increasing desire for independence, which occasionally reveals itself in hostility and rebelliousness against authority, can be diverted into rewarding channels, and used to motivate him in the pursuit of his own education.

During these years the child is also coming to a knowledge of the values held in esteem by society and learning to do what he ought rather than what he would like. Some five-year-olds are quite lacking in self-control, given to outbursts of temper, sulky, quarrelsome with other children, or afraid to associate with them. Usually, however, finding themselves as members of a small group, or of a class, with common interests, needs and desires, and wishing to stand well with this little community, they assimilate enough of the manners and customs of those around them to be accepted, and concepts of desirable social attitudes and actions begin to develop. Adult standards are slow to emerge, and the change from the self-centred attitude of the child to the objective, responsible outlook expected of the adult is a gradual one. The child learns from his experience of how others treat him, and from his observation of how his elders treat one another, and, although increasingly he seeks the approval of his companions rather than that of adults, at this time the influence of his teachers is particularly strong. The teacher who is patient and understanding in her treatment of him, and who herself sets an example of the standards of conduct and taste which she expects in her charges, makes a considerable contribution to his moral development. He comes eventually to see the need for simple rules of behaviour and to comply with them, and begins to play a responsible part in the community of his class and his school, sharing, co-operating, and perhaps even leading.

Along with his physical, emotional and social development go a marked growth of the child's intellectual powers, and consequently an increase in the skills which he can master and in his understanding of the world around him. Essentially he learns to think by doing things: for him active experience is the preliminary to thought. He learns best when he is actively participating in the process, and the more varied, the more "real", and the more meaningful his experiences, the more likely it is that learning will take place. His power of abstract reasoning proceeds directly from his experiments with the real and the concrete, and as he becomes capable of observing more than one aspect of a situation at a time, his thinking becomes more subtle and flexible. He progresses in his ability to relate and organise his knowledge, and can eventually appreciate simple logical relationships. His questions become more pertinent, his knowledge more definite. He will accept guidance towards further goals which he can see and appreciate, and he will respond to direction from an adult whom he trusts. His mental development is accompanied by an increase in skills. His developing mastery of language is an aid to his thought, and enables him to express himself

B

more and more proficiently in speech and in writing, and to use his skill in reading in the pursuit of information and pleasure. He shows a capacity for ingenious and original construction, and becomes more interested in a satisfactory end-product to his creative work than in his earlier years, when the process of creation was interest and satisfaction enough for him. His approach to his environment becomes more objective: he makes collections, wants to know how things work, is curious about what other people do and the tools that they use. His desire to be like his elders and to share their experiences eventually leads him to aim more and more at adult standards and to appreciate the need for technical skills. Towards the end of his primary school life his knowledge begins to sort itself out into categories, and an appreciation of the separate "subjects" of the curriculum emerges. He may develop an interest in one rather than in an other, and may pursue a chosen interest in more detail than before.

One of the most important aspects of intellectual development for the primary school is the formation of concepts. This process begins very early in the child's life, and continues long after the period of primary education, but it is during the primary school years that many basic and vital concepts are at least partially formed. As the child grows and develops, and his range of experience extends, he comes to apprehend that certain things which share common characteristics can be related in his mind, and that his knowledge can therefore be classified and labelled. In the young child, for example, it is possible to observe the emergence of the concept of "car" from the great variety of four-wheeled vehicles which he sees around him. In the primary school both first-hand and second-hand experience contribute to the formation and development of the child's concepts, and both are important for his intellectual progress at this stage. The more varied his experience, the more reliable his concepts are likely to be. The child who lives beside the upper reaches of the Clyde and the child in Glasgow, for example, will have concepts of "river" which are radically different unless both are provided with complementary experience.

It is important for the teacher to realise that there are times in the development of most children when specific concepts may be expected to become established, and that their establishment is dependent on the amount and variety of the children's experience. Some examples from the field of arithmetic may serve to illustrate this. Most children, for instance, are seven or eight years old before they achieve the concept of conversation of substance: that is, that equal amounts of material remain equivalent even when their shape and distribution are changed. The younger child, depending on his perception, believes that a long thin jar of water contains more— or less—than a short fat one, even after he is shown that they contain equal amounts of water. Much practical manipulation is necessary before children come to see that appearances are not everything. Concepts of weight are even later in developing than those of substance, and only after long experience of lifting, carrying, and weighing, does the child come to realise that size is not always a reliable indication of weight. It is probable that weight concepts are not fully developed till the child is at least nine or ten years old. Concepts of time are even slower in developing. In the early stages of school life, the child has only a rudimentary idea of time as it is related to his own personal experience. His unit of time is the day. and he first becomes aware of the timing of the normal events of the day as they effect his own daily living. As he grows older he gradually apprehends smaller and larger units, and by the time he is seven or eight he understands the conventional time words— hour, minute, week and month—he can tell the time from the clock, and can begin to read a calender. Subsequent development brings an extension of his understanding of the passage and duration of time, and eventually a grasp of historical time. This last concept, however, is very slow to establish itself, and may not be fully grasped by many pupils in the primary school. The lesson to be drawn from these illustrations is that, at all stages in the school, not only the way things are taught, but also the time at which they are introduced must have regard for the natural growth and development of the child.

Throughout the primary school years play is one of the activities which can engage the child's whole being, physical, mental, and emotional, and through which he can learn about his environment and adjust himself to it. It should not be regarded as the antithesis of work, since effort, intensity, concentration, and many of the other characteristics commonly attributed to work belong equally to play. It is through play that the child tests and becomes aware of his own physical powers. Often it seems to be merely muscular activity, with no apparent aim or shape, but it is beneficial in reducing surplus energy and renewing powers of concentration, as at "play-time" in school. Feelings of exasperation, rage and many other emotions may be "exploded" harmlessly by means of play. Frequently it is used as a repetition of experience, when the child spontaneously practises something that he has achieved and so obtains a sense of security and perhaps relief from anxiety. Play can also be a medium of imaginative expression for the child: he appropriates the materials which he finds to hand and invests them with imaginative qualities that make them a vehicle for the concepts, wishes and fantasies that fill his mind. Much of his play is imitative, especially of the activities of adults, and the skills which he observes in his elders come to him in large measure through his copying of their actions at work and at leisure.

In his early years at school his play is mainly self-centred and solitary. He is concerned with his own body, his own physical needs and demands, the material world of objects which surround him, his family, and the other human beings who care for him. Soon, however, as he gains fluency in speech and adjusts himself to his immediate environment, he extends his interests to other things and other people. He begins to watch others at play, and even to talk to older groups of children, though he still may not take part in their activities. He may play alongside others, intent on his own occupations, and perhaps may accept the participation of another, but without real co-operation. In this way he and his fellows may play in association, without rules, without division of labour, without hierarchy. Eventually, however, a capacity for co-operative play is attained, and common interests lead to the formation of groups. At first these are small, and frequently changing, but more formal groupings follow, with their own identity, their own loyalties, their own rights of entry. This is the age of the "gang", which is usually confined to one sex, since the interests of the boys and the girls have begun to diverge. It is a time, too, when the child's sense of purpose in play is increasing and he is beginning to show a greater degree of persistence and initiative. Certain children emerge as leaders, revealing an ability to organise the resources of their group towards known and desired ends. It is now that the child is ready to play his part in a team, keeping to the rules, subordinating his personal desires to the wishes of the group, obtaining emotional satisfaction from identification with others. The enlightened teacher can now use the group to foster both emotional and moral development.

The Needs of the Child

The task of education is two-fold: it must satisfy both the needs of the individual and the requirements of society. It must seek not only to develop each individual as fully as his capacity will allow, so that he may experience a satisfactory life as a person, but also to produce citizens who are skilful, knowledgeable, adaptable, capable of co-operation, and as far as possible of leadership, and who can therefore make a worthwhile contribution to the life and work of their community. Education must therefore have due regard both for the needs of the child as an individual with his own characteristics and tendencies, and also for the attainments, qualities and attitudes which society will expect of him as an adult. These are considerations which are important for all levels of education, but they are particularly relevant to the primary school, which assumes responsibility for the education of the child during a period in his life when he is acquiring the concepts, attitudes and skills which will be the basis of all his future development. The function of the primary school, therefore, is not merely to prepare him for secondary education or to teach him the basic skills, but to begin to prepare him for life. Consequently it must concern itself with the whole child, fashioning its organisation, its curriculum and its methods in such a way as to cater for every facet of his developing personality. The needs of the child which the primary school must try to meet if it is to accomplish this challenging and complex task are set out below.

The Need for Security

Most children, by the age of 12, have developed a considerable degree of self-reliance and independence, and derive delight and satisfaction from their increasing ability to do things for themselves and in their own way; but they still need, as they have needed throughout the primary school years, a sense of security. The term "security" is difficult to define, and perhaps liable to misinterpretation, but it implies that the child should be happy and contented and free from fear, frustrations, anxiety and bewilderment, yet not so protected that his initiative is curbed. The provision of an environment in which the child feels secure and sure of being understood is one of the teacher's most important responsibilities. The child needs to feel that he is accepted and liked, that he "belongs" to the class community, that the contributions he makes are appreciated by his teacher and his fellows. It is important to him that he should be valued as a personality, that his teacher should be interested in his activities and his progress, and that she should be appreciative of his efforts. He needs an adult whom he can trust, and to whom he can appeal for help in his difficulties, for commendation in his moments of discovery or success. He feels secure when what is asked of him is within his capacity, when he can understand what is going on round about him, when his life is governed by a familiar routine. This is not to say that he should never be asked to face any challenges or to experience any discomfiture; indeed, over-protection can be prejudicial to his development. Nevertheless the demands which the teacher makes should be such that the child can meet them successfully and his morale is not undermined by frequent failure.

The Need for Guidance

No child can learn for himself all the things that he needs to know, and in both his individual and his social development he is largely dependent on the help and guidance of adults. In other words, there are things that he has to be taught, not only in the intellectual sphere, but also in order that his emotional, moral and social development may follow a pattern which will make him acceptable to the society in which he will live as an adult. The amount of guidance which the teacher gives, however, the form that it takes, and the time when she gives it should be determined by what she knows of each individual child, and her approach should be constructive rather than prescriptive. The teacher who tells her pupils everything, and leaves them no opportunities to exercise their own responsibility and initiative in discovering things for themselves, is preventing the development of the qualities which are of most value to them in the continuation of their own education.

The Need for Freedom

It follows from what has been said about guidance that an element of freedom in children's education is essential. The value of play as a spontaneous expression of the child's interests and as his natural way of learning has already been stressed in an earlier paragraph; but it is unfortunately true that although play has been given its place in some of our schools in the younger classes, it has received little recognition as an important part of the learning process at subsequent stages. The primary school child has a natural curiosity and a desire to learn which make him capable of seriously and deliberately pursuing his own education on lines of his own choice. He needs and should be given opportunities to explore and investigate his environment, to make his own discoveries and draw his own conclusions, to observe, to experiment, to collect, to construct, to read and to record. Furthermore, his abundance of energy and his need for physical activity demand that he should be allowed some freedom of movement, in the classroom as well as out of it. It is important, therefore, that school life should not impose on him too great a degree of immobility, or keep him engaged for too long on sedentary occupations. It is also vital that he should be given freedom to experiment with language, both in speech and in writing. His ability to express himself and to communicate with others can only be hampered by the imposition in the classroom of an unnatural silence and by a too early insistence on conventional correctness.

The Need to Understand

Understanding is a primary aim of learning and a prerequisite of further progress. Wherever possible, the child should be helped to see a purpose in what he is asked to do and in the rules he is asked to keep; the skills which he acquires and the processes which he learns to perform should as far as possible arise from his own experience of concrete situations and problems, and not just as a result of unquestioning memorisation. There may be occasions when, for practical and utilitarian reasons, it is convenient to postpone understanding in favour of mechanical skill, and it is true that there is a time in their development when children enjoy mechanical and repetitive work; but rote learning without understanding should be avoided. Children should not be expected to achieve symbolic, abstract thinking before they are ready for it, and the work they are asked to do should not be for them a mere meaningless manipulation of verbal and other symbols.

The Need for the " Real " and the " Concrete "

It has already been noted that the child is a constructive thinker, and that the concepts he forms, and the ability for abstract thought which he achieves, are dependent upon the extent and the variety of his active experiences. Consequently one of the teacher's tasks is to provide him with an environment which is as rich as her imagination and the resources at her disposal will allow, and through this to give him a wide range of experiences and activities which will enable him to learn in a context of reality by seeing, doing, and talking. Frequently real life has to be supplemented within the classroom, and learning has to take place at second-hand through structured apparatus, books, aural and visual aids, and all the great variety of educational material which is now available to schools. Ideally, however, experience should be first-hand. When in the child's eyes his work in the school is clearly related to the real world, he generally approaches it with greater interest and enthusiasm. Teachers, therefore, should be prepared, in the quest for "real life" experience for their pupils, to break out of the confines of the classroom and to exploit other areas within the school and its grounds or beyond the bounds of the school altogether.

Chapter 2

The Environment

The Child in a Changing World

IN determining the type of education which is appropriate in the primary school, it has to be appreciated that the child grows up in an environment of which school is only a part, and that he is exposed to the influence of a great variety of elements—people, places, events and things—which, both before and during his period of primary schooling, constitute the major part of his waking life. No less important for the teacher than an understanding of the nature of the child and of his growth and development is a knowledge of the environment from which he comes to school each morning, and to which he returns each afternoon. Education cannot hope to be relevant to the needs of the child, or to the world in which he lives, unless it takes his environment into account, using whatever positive contribution can be derived from it, and endeavouring to compensate for what it lacks.

In the past, educationists and sociologists, when studying the environment and the pressures it may exercise, have often found it convenient to divide so vast a field into three parts—the home, the school and the wider world beyond—and to deal with each part separately. Nowadays, however, through a variety of agencies, not least television and sound broadcasting, the wider world may impinge so directly upon both the home and the school as to make it difficult to treat these three aspects of the child's environment separately.

Nevertheless, in time sequence the home comes first, and during one of the most critical periods in the child's life it constitutes virtually the whole of his environment. The influence of the home, therefore, is very strong. During the pre-school years and after, not only the child's physical and intellectual development, but also his behaviour and attitudes depend largely on the extent to which the conditions and atmosphere in the home are propitious for the successful nurturing of his capabilities. For example, his attitude to work and the inner drive to achieve success in what he undertakes may be a direct consequence of things seen, said or done at home. Even his developing view of himself as "good" or "bad", "clever" or "stupid", reflects in large part the approval, tacit or expressed, of his parents. If there is parental indifference or neglect he may never have gained confidence in himself, and if he is over-indulged

15

he may have aquired an undue sense of his own importance. His experience of affection and discipline and his relations with others at home also affect his ability to adjust to other people, whether they be children of his own age, older children, or adults. Children who have been allowed a high degree of freedom at home often take it for granted that a similar freedom will be permitted in school. If, however, they have been accustomed at home to receive a rational explanation for any controls which were necessary, they will generally respond well to a similarly reasoned approach in school. On the other hand, if discipline at home has been dictatorial, the school may find itself with pupils whose reactions vary from apathetically submissive to openly rebellious or destructive. The primary school teacher must know, as far as she can, the influences that are at work on the child in his home environment, and the education she provides must have regard for the differences in facilities and opportunities afforded by the homes and families from which her pupils come.

Equally she must take account of the types of locality in which her pupils spend their leisure, and of the kind of world in which they are growing up. The child who attends a large school in an industrial city has a view of life quite different from that of the pupil in a small rural school. The pupil from a highland glen has a different outlook from that of the child attending school in an East Coast fishing village. Their sense of values, their social awareness, their speech, their interests, their choice of leisure activities, all reflect in large measure the richness or the limitations of the background against which they live their early lives.

For most of them life and the conditions in which it is lived have changed markedly since the childhood of their parents and grand-parents. The primary school child of today lives in a world of wider horizons than his parents did, a world whose dominating feature is the phenomenal advance in the sciences, a world where mass media of communication provide powerful means of disseminating information, purveying entertainment, arousing interests, forming desires and influencing judgments and opinions. The child's environment no longer consists only of his home, his neighbourhood and the people he meets every day. Radio, television and the printed word daily bring him into contact with a much wider range of experience and ideas which arouse his interest and curiosity, add to his sum of knowledge, and influence his way of looking at things. The school has to accept that it may no longer be the principal source of information for the child, and that if its education is to be relevant it must recognise the wide range of interests which come to him through the mass media. The wise teacher does not disparage these agencies or discourage their use; instead, she helps the child to discriminate between what is worthwhile and what is worthless, to refuse to accept unquestioningly what he hears, or sees, or reads, and to think for himself in the face of ingenious attempts to sway his feelings and his judgment.

Scientific progress reveals itself in other aspects of his environment too. In his home he is surrounded and served by the products of comparatively recent invention and discovery—electric light, heating and cooking appliances, the refrigerator, the washing machine, mechanical toys and tools. Outside, highly developed forms of machinery such as cars, ships and aeroplanes are familiar features of his everyday life, and rockets, space capsules and nuclear bombs are an accepted part of the world as he sees it. Marvels of modern engineering in the form of bridges, hydro-electric schemes and towering blocks of flats change the landscape before his eyes. The opportunities for travel opened up by improvements in transport take him to places outside his own community which were once inaccessible to his parents. Consequently his knowledge and interests are more extensive than his parents' were, and not only is he concerned in his leisure pursuits with things scientific and mechanical, but he is often surprisingly knowledgeable about their nature and operation. The schools must be prepared to take cognisance of this knowledge and these interests, and to make appropriate modifications both in the content of the curriculum and in teaching method.

At the same time the aims of education must have regard for the needs and aspirations of the society for which it is preparing the child. The school, besides being a place in which the child finds security and the means of developing intellectually and emotionally, must concern itself with fostering in him the qualities, skills and attitudes which will make him useful to society and adaptable to the kind of environment in which he will live as an adult. In the past the achievement of these aims presented little difficulty to the schools, since conditions were comparatively stable, and the requirements of society varied little over the years. Consequently it was possible to predict with reasonable confidence what the needs of particular pupils would be on leaving school, and to develop in them such basic skills as would enable them to earn a living and to partake, at least in a modest degree, of the life of their community. Now, however, the rapid rate of change in all aspects of life demands a reassessment of aims and practices in education, if the citizens of the future are to be able to fit themselves into an increasingly complex and shifting social environment.

The scientific and technical revolution is causing the most striking changes in the working lives of modern men and women. New inventions and techniques are revolutionising most branches of industry and commerce; the operations required of individual workers are becoming simpler as machinery grows more complex; machinery is more and more replacing manpower; the demand for one particular kind of manufacture in one particular area may cease, as another elsewhere supersedes it; the need for a knowledge of a particular trade and for the special manual and physical skills of the past is declining. Changes such as these, and the virtual certainty of more drastic ones to come, place an obligation even on the primary schools to develop in their pupils the attitudes which will enable them to cope with changing conditions. In other words, the schools have to resolve the problem of how to help their pupils to become the kind of persons who, while being happy and well-adjusted in their private life, can effectively meet the demands of the modern world.

To an increasing extent the need of our present-day society is for men and women who are capable of adapting themselves to changing tasks and problems. The acquisition of knowledge and skills, once the main aim of education, is no longer as important as it was, though the need for exactness of knowledge in certain fields and for competence in certain skills may well be greater, not less, than before. Much more vital today, however, are the fostering of intellectual curiosity, and the development of the capacity to acquire knowledge independently. Factual knowledge in itself is of less importance than the urge to ask questions, and the will and ability to find the answers.

A further feature of modern living which presents a challenge to education is the increasing amount of leisure in the lives of most adults. More and more the schools will have to concern themselves with influencing the child's attitude to his leisure time and with helping him to make the best use of it. Radio, television, the cinema and commercialised sport exercise a powerful attraction, by providing opportunities for relaxation. Much of this type of entertainment, however, requires no physical or mental effort. The task of the schools in these circumstances is to help their pupils to see that leisure can offer much more than this. If in the primary school the pupils are encouraged to develop interests in, for example, reading, making and listening to music, art and craft activities, dramatic work, or physical recreation, they will be more likely to use them to enrich their leisure in later years.

The School Environment

More and more in recent years it has come to be realised that the environment which the school itself is able to provide for the child is of the utmost importance in his education, and that he develops and prospers best where physical conditions are comfortable and aesthetically pleasing, where he is surrounded by stimuli and facilities for learning, and where there is an atmosphere of security and emotional stability.

Education authorities have already done a great deal to provide new school buildings which are bright, spacious and well designed, and teachers everywhere have spoken of the difference which good material facilities can make. Even in older schools where conditions are far from ideal, much has been achieved by modernisation, by introducing attractive colour schemes, and by providing pictures, plants and flowers. If, however, the space and facilities required for modern developments in primary education are to be provided, further consideration will have to be given to the design and furnishing of schools. Excellent work is done by many teachers in unfavourable conditions, but if a progressive outlook is to be encouraged and full value secured from teachers' efforts, the best possible setting compatible with reasonable economy must be provided for their work.

The classroom, where the pupils spend by far the greatest proportion of their time, is the most important place in the school. Its size, lay-out and furnishing must be considered in relation to modern developments in curriculum and methods. Pupils at all stages are now expected to take an active part in their own learning, and free movement within the classroom is essential. It is no longer sufficient to provide an area to accommodate the pupils in serried rows, with a single teaching point. For activity methods, for learning, whether on a class, group, or individual basis, for assignments, projects and centres of interest, new demands are made on floor space, and these demands inevitably increase as the pupils grow in stature. Ideally the areas of classrooms should increase from class P I to class P VII to take account of the growth of the pupils and the larger furniture they require. Whatever floor space is provided should be used to best advantage. Everything on it should be easily movable, to allow flexibility of organisation. It should be possible to use desks and chairs separately, and the desks should be of a type which can be used individually or grouped as occasion demands to provide a larger, flat, continuous working surface. It has been estimated—and detailed sketches showing the working spaces desired and various arrangements of furniture have confirmed the estimate—that for a class of the maximum size permitted by the Code an area of some 850 square feet is required for the classroom.

Within each classroom there should be a number of blackboards, fixed or portable, to offer a variety of teaching points. The display of illustrative material and of pupils' work requires not only a suitable kind of wall-boarding of adequate depth but also shelving, tables or work-tops for three-dimensional exhibits. For the effective use of other visual and aural equipment—filmstrips, sound and television broadcasts, tape-recordings, record-players—the appropriate fitments should be installed within each classroom. Since, however, there are technical difficulties connected with the operation of a film projector, special provision should be made in one room, possibly in a general purposes area, to ensure good black-out, adequate ventilation and easy use of the apparatus.

In giving pupils the opportunity to acquire the right attitude to learning, one of the most significant provisions is the class library. With books for immediate use and reference the pupils have the opportunity not only of finding information for themselves as and when it is required in connection with the classroom activities, but also of developing their reading skills in meaningful situations. Consequently a classroom cannot be considered complete without a library area in which an appropriate range of books can be on view and readily accessible. Th area should also contain a few tables and chairs to enable pupils to pursue their library studies without returning to the main body of the class.

From the point of view of desirable educational practice much of the provision for the practical subjects should be made within the classroom, since they have a great deal to contribute to the development of other subjects and themselves derive meaning and relevance from being associated with them. Art will require appropriate desks and easels, a water trough and ample storage space. For crafts there should be a clearly defined area equipped with a craft sink, work-tops with a hard washable surface, and appropriate storage facilities. In science, which includes nature study, use can be made of the sinks available for art and crafts, but special provision for storage and display will be required. Piped gas and special electrical points are not necessary.

Some subjects and activities are most suitably taken partly within and partly outwith the classroom. For the full development of art and craft activities in the senior classes, another area, possibly part of a general purposes space, is desirable. Needlework in the traditional sense also requires a well-lit area equipped with suitable tables and chairs. The case for this kind of provision is strengthened where specialist teachers are available. Similarly, though most of the teaching of music and drama should be undertaken within the classroom, a larger area is required for the full development of dramatic activities and music with movement.

Storage should be ample for all the needs of the teacher and her class. It should not all be in fitments with working tops. A walk-in store opening from the classroom is also necessary. This should have open shelving in addition to enclosed space for the storing of work which must be kept clean, and its height should allow large maps to be hung by their ends in the rolled position.

Since it is not possible to conduct all activities within the classroom, additional areas are required, There should be a space for assembly large enough to provide seating accommodation for the whole school meeting as a unit. A stage should also be available when needed, but not necessarily of the traditional type, unless it can serve another purpose. A stage made up of portable units has much to commend it, since it can be built up anywhere and to any size, and can lend itself to a variety of uses. A space for physical education is also required. This need not be a gymnasium with fixed apparatus such as wall-bars, beams, and ropes, since movable apparatus is adequate for the primary school. Provision for dining must also be made.

It would be inconsistent with reasonable economy to expect a space to be set apart for each of these purposes. Communal areas can be designed to serve more than one function. Much depends on the size and organisation of the school. Some combinations of subjects or activities are more suitable for one size of school than another, and not all possible combinations are educationally sound. The amount of time allotted to the activities each week and the availability of visiting teachers are also determining factors. The use of the assembly space, for example, for both physical education and dining is not unreasonable, provided the dining area does not encroach upon the area set aside for physical education and each area is still large enough for its proper purpose. Nor is it unreasonable that in smaller schools one area should be shared by both physical education and dining, provided the arrangements for physical education leave an adequate gap, say of one hour, before and after the service of dinner. On the same principle another school might use the assembly area for dining, physical education, and activities connected with music and drama.

The sharing of areas in this way for different purposes can create awkward problems. It is suggested, however, that in a large school extra-classroom activities and subjects can reasonably be organised within two multi-purpose spaces, one perhaps for assembly, physical education and dining, and one to cope with the other requirements. How these spaces should be planned for different purposes is a matter for further experimentation.

A playground can also serve a variety of educational purposes. In addition to providing opportunities for free play and organised games, it may have slabs of various shapes and sizes and measured lengths, simple apparatus to record weather conditions, a bird-table, a gardening plot, facilities for keeping pets, and a play-corner with sand and appropriate constructional materials.

Another aspect of planning which deserves thought is the disposition of exits and of cloakroom and toilet facilities. Care has to be taken to provide enough exits, suitably situated, to prevent congestion at times of entry and departure. It is advisable also to disperse cloakrooms and toilets throughout the school and to provide appropriate sanitary arrangements for girls who have already reached the stage of puberty.

The design of the building itself and its decor should be such that the pupils find the school an attractive place to be in, providing an environment which not only gives them pleasure but also contributes to the development of their aesthetic awareness. To encourage this awareness, provision should also be made in the communal spaces of the school, such as the assembly, dining and circulation areas, for the mounting of displays and exhibitions.

The teacher's task is to use to the best advantage the physical facilities which education authorities and architects are able to give her. Many teachers have gone a long way in making the school environment rich and varied in material and apparatus which stimulate the child's interest and provide him with opportunities for learning. It is by working in situations which call for intelligent responses that intellectual potential develops, and the resources of the classroom at every stage should be such that cultural deficiencies can be made good and independent development can be encouraged through sensory experience, observation, enquiry and activity.

The school environment, however, is not to be thought of only in terms of material facilities. In children all aspects of growth are closely inter-related, and to ensure their all-round development there has to be provision for emotional and social, as well as physical and intellectual factors. Indeed, the emotional climate of the classroom and the school is of great importance, for if the atmosphere is such that the child's emotional needs are satisfied, almost everything he does is favourably affected. The way the teacher organises the class and the work, her treatment of and her attitude towards individual children, the opportunities she creates for the exercise of self-reliance, responsibility, honesty and perseverance, the extent to which she encourages co-operation and tolerance, the example she herself sets of the qualities she wishes to foster in her pupils, all contribute to the emotional and social development of her charges. In these various ways the good teacher can help her pupils to feel that they are members of a community which exists for their benefit, and in which they can play an acceptable part.

In favourable circumstances this feeling and the code of behaviour to which it gives rise extend outwards from each classroom to include finally the whole school. And because the good school does not confine its concern for the pupils to what are called "school hours", its influence may extend far beyond its immediate precincts to the wider community outside.

Just as the individual teacher does all she can to make the world of the classroom as rich and stimulating as possible, and to encourage every pupil to take full advantage of its opportunities, similarly all teachers—and also other members of the school staff—should co-operate to make the school as a whole community in which the child learns to extend his range of participation and with whose purposes and ideals he learns to identify himself. He should learn to belong to his school, to take pride in its beauty, its equipment, its surroundings and its achievements. There are many ways of fostering a desirable school spirit. Opportunities of meeting regularly as a unit, and of taking part in school activities such as concerts, religious services, parties, excursions, clubs and inter-school sport enlarge the child's understanding of what a school is and encourage his urge to share in its larger identity. A school badge, or song, or dance can also contribute to this end. A house system may be another useful way of providing the child with a cause towards which he can make his own effort individually and in co-operation with others. Care should be exercised not to encourage exaggerated attitudes of group rivalry, which too easily may become arrogance, and might tend to develop a class or sectarian bias; but school loyalty is a valuable step in the development of wider loyalties.

In the achievement of these aims the size of the school is an important factor. It should be of a size which makes it manageable as an administrative unit, and which allows the head teacher to know and be known by teachers, pupils and parents, and to guide the work of the school in all its aspects. If the head teacher is to have a chance of exercising adequately his educational responsibilities as they are described in the next chapter, the roll of the primary school should not exceed 600.

c

The Transition from the Home to the School Environment

The teacher who has the best interests of her pupils at heart not only knows what influences have been at work on the child in his pre-school days; she also knows that no matter how enthusiastic and well-intentioned she may be, her efforts on his behalf will not achieve the maximum effect unless the co-operation of the home is secured. In this the infant mistress has both a particular responsibility and a wonderful opportunity; for the interest of the parents, especially the mothers, is perhaps at its maximum when their children first go to school. Where time can be found, therefore, the good infant mistress makes a point of meeting and talking with the mothers before the actual enrolment. In quite a short conversation she can often learn much of value about the extent of the parents' interest in the child, his general background and experiences, his personality, his health, his rate of development and his interests.

Because much of the success of these talks depends on the informal atmosphere in which they are held, and on the degree of personal interest which the mothers feel is being taken in their children, it is usually best to invite them to attend one at a time rather than in large groups. It is appreciated that in a city school this may entail spreading the interviews over several weeks, but unless organisational difficulties are particularly acute, teachers may consider that the resulting benefit to the pupils is great enough to justify the temporary interruption to routine.

The parents of pupils in the youngest classes are usually very willing to co-operate with the school, but sometimes, remembering how they themselves were taught as young children, they do not appreciate the aims and methods of the modern primary school. It is helpful, therefore, if the head teacher and infant mistress meet the parents, to explain current educational thought and practice and to show them examples of pupils' work at different stages. An approach of this kind induces parents to have faith in the school's intentions in regard to their children, and makes them less prone to show concern if the school produces no immediately measurable "results".

As important as the approach to the parents, however, is the first contact between the school and the child. Generally, it has been found useful to give the new pupil a brief glimpse of the school before he begins his attendance there. If, for example, he can see something of the premises—the classroom which will be his base, the cloakrooms and toilets, the playground—and if he can perhaps sit at one of the little tables or desks, he feels that he already "belongs". This feeling of security is still more easily won if the child is already no stranger to part of the school precincts, as happens in areas where at least part of the play area is open after school hours to the children of the neighbourhood. Above all it is helpful if on a preliminary visit the child can meet the teacher in whose charge he will be, so that he feels she welcomes him as an individual. Some schools arrange in advance for the new pupils, in groups, to join the children in the existing lowest class for play activities, games and singing. This ensures that their first association with school is an entirely carefree one.

On the child's first day at school the attitude of the teacher is all-important. There is no need for her to over-sentimentalise her approach to the children, but by her manner she must make it clear that she is glad to see them. Some children may not be prepared to respond immediately to her friendliness, but they must be left in no doubt that her feeling towards them is sympathetic. It also helps children to settle happily if they see immediately some objects of a kind familiar to them—toys, books, blocks—and also interesting and attractive pieces of equipment which they can use without any need for explanation. Many are thrilled to be given at once something of their very own—a particular desk and chair, a cloakroom peg, and perhaps a tiny picture book which they can keep. Each of these can be labelled with a personal identifying emblem which the child can easily recognise; if each of them also bears his name, the teacher will be able quickly to call each pupil by name—another action which helps him to feel secure. By such means the teacher can make the child's first introduction to his new environment reassuring and exciting, and can help him to regard the school as an interesting and stimulating place to come to and as a happy community in which he is eager to play his part.

Chapter 3
The Staff

The Head Teacher

THE head teacher must regard himself, above all, as a teacher, and must see his main functions as educational rather than administrative. The amount of routine administrative work which is involved in the running of a school has increased in recent years, and the ultimate responsibility for its efficient execution rests with the head teacher. It should never, however, be allowed to assume such importance that it occupies the major part of his time. Much of it can and should be delegated to others, so that he may be enabled to concern himself, first and foremost, with providing for his pupils the most appropriate education that is possible with the means at his disposal—the task for which he is best equipped, by professional training and experience.

If he is to succeed in this task, he must know his pupils. This he can do only by regularly visiting the classrooms, talking to the children and observing them at work, conferring with the teachers, and occasionally taking over from them and teaching their classes himself. In this way he can acquire the knowledge that enables him to follow the progress of the pupils through the school, to give advice in cases of individual difficulty, and to ensure that at every level the education provided is appropriate. His concern must be not only with scholastic progress, but with every aspect of the child's development. The knowledge which he accumulates will also be of considerable value to the secondary schools to which his pupils go, and he must see to it that when his pupils leave him all the useful information at his disposal is passed on.

An adequate understanding of the child is not possible without some knowledge of the conditions of the home from which he comes. The head teacher must therefore gain the goodwill and co-operation of the parents of his pupils, and be ready, as circumstances require, to meet them collectively and to consult them individually about their children. Such contacts serve a variety of purposes: not only can he learn more about his pupils, and so be better equipped to treat them according to their needs; he can also explain the policy and practices of his school, which are likely to be very different from those of the schools where the parents were taught; and the interchange of information can be particularly helpful when the school has to assess the potentialities of the pupils for secondary courses.

The head teacher should also be as knowledgeable as possible about the abilities and interests of his staff, so that he may be able to use their resources to the full. Through his visits to their classrooms and his conversations with them, he must try to assess their talents, and decide where each can best be employed, what guidance each requires, and in what respects each should be given scope for her particular skills and enthusiasms. He has a special responsibility towards the young and inexperienced members of his staff. It is part of his duty to judge their potentialities and note their difficulties, and to give them the example, the encouragement and the help which may influence their future development as teachers.

In addition, he must know the physical conditions of his school building, assess its possibilities, and see that it is used to the best advantage. He must concern himself with the adequacy of the building's heating, lighting and ventilation, the suitability of its furnishings, and the cleanliness and tidiness of the school and its surroundings. In supervising these material matters he is largely dependent on the interest and co-operation of the janitor, the cleaners and the meals staff, and it is part of his responsibility to see that they are aware of the educational purpose behind the uses which are made of materials, equipment and furnishings, so as to enlist their sympathetic help.

It is only when he is equipped with this knowledge of his pupils, his staff, and his facilities that the head teacher can run his school as a well co-ordinated whole with all its members pursuing a progressive and consistent policy. By reason of the overall view which he has of the whole establishment, and through his contact with parents, officials, and the secondary schools to which his pupils will go, he is in a position to see, more clearly than his teachers or the parents of his pupils, the part that the primary school has to play in the whole educational process and to ensure the continuity that the pupils need. It is essential, therefore, that his should be the last word on organisation and planning, the content of the curriculum, the utilisation of time, teaching methods, and rules of behaviour.

On the other hand, the head teacher's knowledge and experience, vision and vitality may well be less than his staff can muster as a whole, and he is wise to give scope to the talents of his team so that their combined thinking may have weight in determining the policy of the school. Out of such professional collaboration come the morale and character which place a school high in the esteem of its community. Opportunities for full and free discussion, therefore, whether in staff meetings or by less formal means, are essential, not only on matters of administrative detail but on all aspects of the school's policy and activities.

In addition to his function as organiser of the resources at his disposal, the head teacher has a further responsibility—perhaps his most important in an age of exciting educational development— to stimulate the inflow and outflow of ideas which keep his school educationally alive. He must see to it that his teachers are not isolated in their own classrooms and unaware of the practices of others, that they are given opportunities to exchange ideas with their colleagues, in other schools as well as in their own, that they are given encouragement to follow up their own enthusiasms and make their own experiments, even though their methods may not be his own. He must ensure, too, that his staff are given facilities and equipment which are as varied and up-to-date as possible. It is essential that he himself should keep abreast of current theory and practice, so that he can discuss knowledgeably with his staff all aspects of their work, and can recognise the value of developments in their teaching which may be in advance of his own experience. It is no longer possible to master the skills of headship only through day-to-day experience of school, indispensable though this is. The findings of modern research and the changes that are taking place in educational thought and practice demand consideration, and require of the head teacher a willingness to learn through determined study, attendance at courses, visits to other schools, and talks with other teachers.

The Class Teacher

The education of children in their formative years is a difficult and vitally important trust, which places a considerable burden of responsibility on the teacher, and makes great demands on her resources. The qualities that have enabled teachers to carry this responsibility so well over the years are not easy to define. Yet these qualities exist in abundance in our primary schools, and it may be useful to try to enumerate some of those that characterise the good teacher in the primary school of today.

Qualities of heart and head go together in the making of a good teacher. Her whole attitude is optimistic and cheerful. She has the reserves to cope with the great physical and mental vitality of the class and the tenacity to press on with the job at all times. She does not pretend to be omniscient, but is lively, keen and receptive, enjoying her work and sharing with her pupils their zest for new discovery. The fact that her interests are far wider than the school curriculum helps to make her a more interesting teacher. She can explain a difficult point clearly, knows many ways of presenting information, and is resourceful in creating situations in which the pupils make discoveries for themselves.

Out of her daily contacts with children comes the understanding on which the mature teacher relies and from which she gains her greatest satisfaction. She is sympathetic, patient, especially with slow pupils, and is fair to all, avoiding any appearance of favouritism. Her sympathy is genuine but unsentimental; she can be firm when the situation demands it. Her pupils like the sense of security created by her quiet authority and by an organisation which establishes a consistent routine but allows them to use their own initiative and to exercise responsibility.

It is the responsibility for diagnosing educational needs that lifts the teacher's work out of the category of routine instruction into that of a highly responsible profession. When making demands on her pupils, the good teacher considers what is appropriate to each, so that all may be given the opportunity to reach their full capacity. She respects the power and determination within the child to further his own development along lines of his own choice, and knows that he learns best through participation, bringing his natural curiosity and imagination to bear on the evidence of his senses. Knowing what to expect in general from pupils of different age and ability, she is also on the look-out for special aptitudes— an original imagination, a gift of leadership, a power of expression, a love of nature—and finds ways of giving them scope, for the common good as well as for that of the individual.

Above all, the good teacher is alive to the possibility of improving the content and method of her teaching, and therefore keeps abreast of new developments, gives them adequate trial, and absorbs whatever elements are suited to her own situation. Conversely, she herself is able, through the discoveries which she makes in her own classroom, to contribute to the body of knowledge upon which educational progress depends. In accepting these responsibilities she ceases to be a teacher in isolation and becomes a member of a body professionally equipped to lead in educational development.

The influence of the successful teacher extends beyond her own classroom in yet another way—through the help which she is able to give to inexperienced colleagues who may at first find difficulty in translating educational theory into classroom practice. In return she is quick to appreciate the value of contacts with younger minds, trained in methods which have advanced with educational research.

The Promoted Staff

The function of the promoted staff in the primary school—deputy head teacher, senior assistant, infant mistress—is to assist the head teacher in the running of the school and in the formulation of its educational policy. All of them should have specific areas of responsibility, delegated by the head teacher, and a measure of relief from teaching to allow them to overtake their special duties.

The post of deputy head teacher should be regarded as a training-ground for headship. It is important, therefore, that the responsibilities of the deputy head should not be confined to routine administrative work, and that he should be able to share in all aspects of the head teacher's activities. Thus, in addition to specific tasks such as the supervision of registration, stock and supplies, he should be involved at times in the normal supervision of class work, diagnostic and remedial work, the treatment of exceptional pupils of all kinds, the guiding of new developments in curriculum and methods, educational aids, arrangements for specialist teaching and for the use of common areas, social activities and social training, transfer within the school and from primary to secondary education, the furtherance of cordial staff relationships, and liaison with parents.

The practice of appointing senior women assistants in large primary schools has much to commend it. The senior woman has a distinct contribution to make, especially when the head teacher and the deputy are both men. She should have special responsibility for girls, and for arrangements in connection with visits by the school doctor and nurse, and she can play a useful part in maintaining liaison with mothers in matters affecting the welfare of their children.

The infant mistress, with her concern for the child's first two or three years of schooling, has a particular responsibility for encouraging understanding and co-operation between home and school, and for providing a rich and interesting environment in which the child, as he develops, finds pleasure, satisfaction and security. As the head teacher's adviser on the education of younger children, she must be familiar with current developments in this field, and be prepared to adopt those which suit the circumstances of the school. Her skill in diagnosis and remedial work and her knowledge of the beginnings of reading and number enable her to give valuable help in the treatment of backward pupils, not only in her own department but throughout the school.

The Specialist Teacher

Visiting specialist teachers of music, speech and drama, art, and physical education are a valuable addition to the staff of a primary school, particularly if some of the class teachers have little or no aptitude for any of these subjects. The value of the specialist to the primary school lies principally in her knowledge and skill in her special field, and in her ability not only to teach her subject but also to impart some of her expertise to the class teacher. Competence in her own subject, however, is not enough. She must also be interested and skilled in the teaching of young children, and must understand what part her subject plays in the whole education of the child. She must remember, too, that each of the schools she visits has a tone and character of its own, and must be prepared to learn, by consultation with head teacher and class teacher, what approach is best suited to the characteristics and needs of the pupils and to the programme of work in other aspects of the curriculum. A more detailed consideration of the uses which can be made of specialist staff is contained in the chapter on "The Deployment of Teaching Resources".

It is to be hoped that more education authorities will follow the example of those that have appointed organisers, in, for example, infant methods, primary school methods, and various branches of the curriculum. Organisers perform a valuable function in advising schools and specialist teachers, and in supervising and co-ordinating the work in their own specialist field. In the present era perhaps their most useful contribution is to initiate and guide development and experimentation, and to arrange courses and conferences for teachers. Apart from the technical proficiency which organisers must have in their own field, they should be familiar with current thinking about primary education, and their personality should be such that they readily enlist the sympathy and co-operation of head teachers and teachers.

The Ancillary Staff

Ancillary staff—janitors, cleaners, meals staff, clerical assistants and auxiliaries—are indispensable members of the head teacher's team, with their own contributions to make to the smooth running of the school and the physical conditions in which teachers and pupils work. Since good relations with the teaching staff are essential, the head teacher must ensure that the ancillary staff appreciate the aims of the school and the need for co-operating with the teachers. In particular they must respect the wishes of the teachers with regard to the disposition of furniture and equipment and the use of working and display areas, realising that the educational needs of the pupils come before the appearance and polish of the classrooms.

The auxiliary is an innovation of recent date in some primary schools. For some time clerical assistants have been appointed in many areas to carry out the routine clerical work involved in the running of a primary school, and they have been of considerable help to head teachers in typing and duplicating, making inventories, filing records and dealing with other administrative details. However, the increased demands made on the professional skill of the class teacher may now require a reassessment of her duties, and a reallocation whereby some of her non-teaching tasks can be undertaken by non-professional helpers. At present some of her tasks are less than professional, and others, particularly where educational diagnosis and new techniques are concerned, are more onerous than before. The increased emphasis on practical work and activity methods, with their mounting array of materials to be repeatedly sorted, stored and distributed, also points to the need for auxiliaries of the kind that have already been appointed in a few places.

Auxiliaries can supervise the movement of pupils in and around the school, in the playground during intervals, and in the dining area at lunch-time. They can assist the teacher in the preparation and the organisation of classroom material and in the arrangement of class and school libraries, furniture and wall displays. Other duties may include help in the case of sickness and accidents, and with expeditions and outings, the maintenance and operation of mechanical aids, the care of pets and plants, the marking of objective tests, and the routine associated with registration, dinner money and dinner tickets. By accepting these tasks unaided, in a working week which leaves no time for preparation or correction, the class teacher is prevented from using her professional skill to full advantage. Moreover, the increasing rate of educational change makes additional demands upon her energies, and merely to be with forty or more children, without respite, for six hours every day, consumes nervous energy which is not quickly restored. The appointment of auxiliaries could give her much-needed relief from non-professional duties.

Part 2

Chapter 4

The Curriculum

THE pattern of primary education has changed considerably since the days when many teachers were content to confine their instruction to the "three Rs". Developments of great significance have taken place even since 1956, when the schools (Scotland) Code outlined the scope of the curriculum as follows:

"In each year of attendance at a primary department, pupils shall be given instruction in reading, writing and arithmetic; in the use and understanding of spoken and written English; in music; in art and handwork; in nature study; and in physical education. They shall also, from such stage as is appropriate having regard to their age, ability and aptitude, be given instruction in geography, history, written composition and in the case of girls, needlework."

This memorandum makes its appearance at a time when much thought is being given to the aims and content of primary education, and when quite drastic revision of the curriculum is already taking place in many schools.

The skills and subjects laid down by the Code still figure in the curriculum of all primary schools in Scotland, but others have been added, and the emphasis within many of the subjects has changed. The skills involved in reading, writing and arithmetic, and in the use and understanding of spoken and written English remain basic elements of the primary school course, but increased importance is attached to the practical application of these skills in realistic and meaningful contexts. Arithmetic is regarded only as one aspect—though a very important one—of the many mathematical activities in which the primary school pupil should be involved. In music, creative work is being given a more important place. Art and craft activities embrace both handwork and needlework from an early stage, for both boys and girls, and have moved in their emphasis from imitation to self-expression. Natural and physical science have replaced the traditional nature study and now provide opportunities for the pupils to explore the scientific aspects of their environment through observation and experiment. The scope of physical education has been extended to include a much freer use of movement as a means of expression and personal development. History and geography take their place along with science less as subjects in their own right than as aspects of environmental studies, through which the pupils can investigate and understand the past and the world around them. Dramatic activities are increasingly recognised as playing an important part in the personal and social development of the pupils. More recently, the claims of modern languages for a place in the curriculum have been pressed, and the teaching of a foreign language has been introduced experimentally in a number of areas.

More than ever before, too, the primary school has to concern itself with the emotional and social development of its pupils: in the words of the Code, "to train the pupils in habits of personal hygiene and cleanliness, of correct speech and of good manners; to cultivate the qualities of truthfulness, honesty, self-control and consideration for man and beast; to foster a love of beauty; to encourage industry, self-reliance and forethought; and to develop a sense of responsibility to the community and an attitude of good-will towards other peoples". The cultivation of desirable habits, attitudes, qualities of character and modes of behaviour cannot be reduced to the level of items on a time-table; it is nevertheless an essential part of education, which is achieved not through explicit instruction but as a result of the general tone and atmosphere of the school, the organisation and methods it employs, the standards it sets, and the opportunities the pupils are given to participate actively in its work and life.

In addition, in an age of increasing leisure the primary school has the task of training its pupils to make the best possible use of their spare time, by stimulating interest in a variety of worthwhile pursuits, and by helping the pupils to develop, in school hours, the interests and activities which they have already taken up of their own accord.

Changes such as those outlined above are to be welcomed; for education must constantly adapt itself to the needs of the age. If it is to be relevant, it must keep pace with fresh discoveries about the nature and needs of the child, changes in the world in which he lives, and the demands of society. Recent curricular developments, however, have been so numerous, so rapid and, in some cases, so radical that many people now feel that the curriculum is becoming overloaded, and the teacher's task unduly difficult. It is hoped that the recommendations contained in the succeeding chapters of this memorandum will dispel such fears; it may be useful, however, to deal briefly with a number of important general principles at this point.

It is true that the aims and content of primary education are much more comprehensive than ever before. It must be emphasised, however, that as innovations are introduced such aspects of the traditional content as are now seen to be unnecessary or irrelevant for the pupils must be pruned. Many of the activities now being recommended in language arts, for example, should occupy time hitherto given to the class reading lesson and to lessons and exercises on the technicalities of written English. In arithmetic, lengthy and repetitive mechanical computations should give way to the practical activities and the other aspects of mathematics now being suggested. The creative approaches advocated in music, physical education and art and craft activities should replace a great deal of the formal and repetitive work that once characterized these subjects. In environmental studies, time will be available for selected "patch" studies, sample studies, scientific investigations and the development of centres of interest if teachers abandon much of the exhaustive factual information which formerly was taught in the name of history, geography and nature study. If the schools are to make room for newer and more worthwhile activities, they must constantly keep the content of their teaching under review and be prepared to jettison what they cannot justify.

Furthermore, the curriculum is not to be thought of as a number of discrete subjects, each requiring a specific allocation of time each week or each month. Indeed, it is quite impossible to treat the subjects of the curriculum in isolation from one another if education is to be meaningful to the child. The chapters that follow describe many ways in which the curriculum can be organised so as to effect a linkage between subjects. Many of the activities which are recommended involve elements of more than one "subject", and serve to advance the pupils' knowledge and skill in more than one field. Thus linguistic and mathematical skills find application in environmental studies; art and craft activities, drama and music play a part in history and geography; projects and centres of interest embrace many different branches of the curriculum. "Integration" of this kind should be a feature of primary education at all stages.

It cannot be too strongly stressed that education is concerned as much with the personal development of the child as with the teaching of subjects. How the child learns is educationally no less important than what he learns. Certainly skills must be mastered, and knowledge must be acquired, and the curriculum must be carefully planned to ensure that basic skills and essential knowledge are adequately covered. Primary education, however, will have failed the age and the society it serves if children leave the primary school without the right attitude to learning or the resource and will to continue and further their own education.

The curricular chapters of this memorandum suggest many things that might be included in the primary school course. It is not to be expected that all of them will be attempted by every teacher; nor do they make any pretence to be exhaustive. In none of the subjects is there a predetermined and unchanging amount of content that must be covered. Much of the content of the curriculum will vary from school to school, from class to class within the same school, in certain instances from pupil to pupil within the same class, and from one time to another as circumstances change. It is for each head teacher and his staff to determine, in their own situation and with their own special knowledge of their pupils, precisely what is to be included and what part it is to play in their pupils' educational development.

Chapter 5
Schemes of Work

THE purpose of a scheme of work is to indicate in broad outline the scope of the work at each stage in the school. It should be drawn up by the head teacher in consultation with the members of his staff, each of whom should have a copy, not only of that part of it that most concerns her class, but of the entire scheme, so that she may see her own work in relation to what is being done at other stages, particularly those which immediately precede and follow her own. It should not attempt to lay down in detail the work to be covered, but should rather take the form of a policy document, embodying the general aims and objectives of the school, while allowing freedom to individual teachers to experiment, to adapt the scheme to the needs of individual pupils or groups, to develop their own special enthusiasms or those of the class, or to follow up current events and topics which arouse the pupils' interest.

The scheme should be kept under review, but if it is written in general terms, as has been suggested, it will not in normal circumstances require frequent revision. The class teacher's job is to prepare within the framework of the scheme, and in co-operation with the head teacher, a more detailed programme of work for her class for perhaps a month ahead, setting out the topics that are to be covered, the skills that are to be learned, and the activities that are to be undertaken, and allowing for the differing needs and abilities of the pupils. Even this programme, however, must be capable of adaptation to meet unexpected eventualities, and it may occasionally have to be modified in practice. Regular assessment is therefore necessary, to take stock of what has been achieved and what omitted, and to plan future programmes accordingly. The head teacher must exercise general supervision over the work of each class, satisfying himself that adequate ground is covered and appropriate progress is made, and guiding his teachers in their planning where necessary.

Schemes of work which education authorities draw up, through panels of teachers, for the primary schools under their management can be useful guides to head teachers in the framing of their educational policy. It is important, however, that schemes prepared at area level should be concerned only with broad matters of policy, and that the detailed application of the principles they contain

D

should be left to individual head teachers. If more specific guidance is given on content and methods, there should be no suggestion that it is to be followed rigidly by all schools. Since schools may differ so much in size and type even within one authority area, head teachers must be given freedom and encouragement to think out for themselves the type of education that is best suited to the needs of their own pupils, the resources of their own staff, and the nature of the environment in which their own particular school is situated.

Chapter 6
Classification

CLASSIFICATION by age is by far the most common arrangement in Scottish primary schools, and experience has shown that it is usually in the best interests of the pupils to move up the school along with their contemporaries, who share with them common interests and recreations, and who are on a broadly similar level of physical, emotional and social development. This means that each class covers a wide range of intellectual ability, and that the teacher must cater for this diversity through group and individual methods. There may also be a need for some kind of special tutorial instruction for the least able, for the ablest, and for those who have temporarily lost ground through absence.

Occasionally situations arise which make it inexpedient to carry out completely the principle of classification by age. The rise and fall in the size of the school population, for example, changes in the accommodation available, and fluctuations in the staffing situation may necessitate adjustments in the composition of classes in order to ensure that class rolls are reasonably balanced. From time to time, too, there may be sound educational reasons for promoting some of the abler pupils and retarding some of the less able. Repetition of a stage may be justifiable if a pupil is so far behind his contemporaries that his needs cannot be met by group or individual teaching within his normal class, and if, through shortage of teachers, tutorial facilities are not available. It is desirable, however, that the total time gained or lost through such departures from normal progress by any one pupil should rarely exceed twelve months. Care should be taken that able pupils whose promotion within the primary school has been accelerated are not transferred to the secondary school while they are still socially and emotionally immature. It should be appreciated too that slower pupils who are retained in a lower class may suffer from the lack of the stimulus provided by their abler contemporaries and from a loss of personal prestige, and may develop attitudes which are bad for themselves and affect their younger classmates.

In some larger schools, where the number of children at each stage is great enough to form two or more classes, head teachers have adopted a form of classification by ability and attainment within each age group. This type of organisation has come to be known as "streaming". Numerous arguments have been put forward for and against streaming, and as yet the final word cannot be said, but in spite of its obvious merits as a logical and administratively tidy system, an increasing number of educationists have doubts about its desirability and its effectiveness.

The main claim that is made for streaming is that the teacher's task of adapting the nature and speed of the work to the pupils is made easier when the class contains pupils of comparable ability. This kind of classification, however, is most often based merely on ability and attainment in easily examinable aspects of English and arithmetic, and ignores other facets of the pupils' intellectual development as well as other important social, emotional and physical considerations. Further, it proceeds on the assumption that it is possible to classify pupils by ability as early as age seven, for example, although increasingly doubt is being cast on the validity of attempts to do this even much later at the age of "transfer". There is also evidence that when pupils are segregated according to ability, those in the lower streams—and their teachers— become conditioned to low standards of attainment. Other undesirable effects may be feelings of resentment among parents, invidious comparisons in the local community, and unhappiness and anxiety for the pupils. There seems to be little doubt, therefore, that the disadvantages of streaming far outweigh its apparent advantages, and that it is out of place in an educational system which concerns itself with the development of the whole child, and not merely with his intellectual capacity.

In some places, experiments with other forms of classification have been undertaken in recent years. Some areas in England have adopted as their normal pattern of organisation in infant departments—even in those with a roll of several hundred children—a system which closely resembles that of the small school. The essential feature of this arrangement is the "composite" class, containing pupils who come to school at different entry dates. As is to be expected, there is variety from one part of the country to another in the way this system is operated, some areas preferring to limit the age range in each class to about one year, and others extending it to two years or more. It is claimed that the social or family atmosphere which results from the grouping together of children of different ages can play an important part in the emotional and social development of the pupils.

A few schools in Scotland have recently initiated experiments which are designed to cater for the wide range of interests and aptitudes among the older pupils. At certain times classes P V,

P VI and P VII, for example, are regrouped to enable the pupils to pursue special interests, under the guidance of teachers with appropriate skills. Thus pupils from different classes may come together for music, or drama, or science, or mathematics, or art, or some form of craftwork, or hobbies of one kind or another. In this way both pupils and teachers are given scope for their enthusiasms. It is to be hoped that experimentation of this kind will continue, and that further efforts will be made to try different groupings to suit the needs of the pupils and the requirements of the various branches of the curriculum. At the top of the school particularly, the "one-teacher-one-class" system may no longer be the most efficient for modern requirements, and a more flexible organisation would perhaps be more beneficial. In this connection the system of "team teaching", referred to in the following chapter, may have important implications.

Chapter 7

The Deployment of Teaching Resources

TRADITIONALLY, primary schools have been organised on the principle that each class should be in the charge of a teacher who is responsible for instruction in all branches of the curriculum. Basically this is a sound system, particularly if each teacher has her class for a year or longer. Such an arrangement enables the teacher to establish with her pupils a relationship in which they feel secure, and to acquire an intimate knowledge of them which makes it possible for her to utilise her time and adapt the curriculum in ways appropriate to their abilities and aptitudes. For several reasons, however, it may now be necessary to consider whether this type of organisation enables the resources of the teaching staff to be used to the full and whether more benefit would accrue to the pupils if some modification were made in the conventional system.

It is open to question whether it is reasonable to expect all teachers to have a high degree of skill over the whole range of the curriculum, especially in view of the developments that are taking place in, for example, mathematics, science, modern languages and physical education. Furthermore, it is being increasingly recognised that by the time children reach the upper classes of the primary school they exhibit a range of interests and a variety of needs with which the class teacher may be unable to cope adequately. At the same time it is apparent that in most schools there are teachers with special skills, interests and enthusiasms which, if given wider scope, would be beneficial both to their colleagues and to the pupils of classes other than their own, particularly at a time when a decreasing number of visiting specialists is available.

It is part of the head teacher's function to assess the resources of his staff, and to deploy to the best advantage the special abilities and interests which they possess. A teacher who is specially gifted or interested in the teaching of science, for example, or music, or physical education, or drama, may act as the school's adviser in that subject, and give help and guidance to other teachers. Or a teacher of class P VII who is an enthusiast for one particular subject may teach it also to class P VI, being relieved of another activity in which a colleague may have a deeper interest. Obviously it is not possible to provide for each school a team of teachers whose talents balance one another in different directions. It is to

44

be expected, however, that each head teacher will make the best use of the resources of his staff, and that he will encourage them through attendance at courses or by other means to take up or develop interests which will help him to effect the subject balance that he wants.

In the United States of America some schools have developed "team teaching", a system which has been evolved in order to make the most effective use of the skills of individual teachers and to achieve forms of grouping in keeping with the abilities and interests of the pupils. In these schools a group of teachers, balanced for age, experience and knowledge and assisted by an auxiliary, plans and carries through the programme of work under the leadership of a senior teacher. The whole team is involved in the teaching of a number of children much larger than the conventional class. Flexibility is obtained as the pupils form into groups of varying size, composition and interests under the charge of suitable teachers. It is considered that the mingling of groups of pupils who would not otherwise have much contact with one another leads to improved social adjustments. Head teachers might well examine critically the type of organisation that is traditional in their schools in the light of such developments, and consider if there are any implications which might be to the advantage of Scottish education.

It may be that in the older classes at least the case for the security afforded by the "one-teacher-one-class" system has been overstated, and that at these stages the pupils should be spending part of their day with other adult minds in other situations. There would seem to be sound educational reason for experimenting with a more flexible organisation at least in classes P VI and P VII, not only to develop the pupils' gifts and interests and improve their attitudes and skills, but also to create the conditions which would make the transition to secondary education much easier than it is at present.

Changes of this kind demand special efforts to ensure that the interchange of teachers does not result in unsettling variations in method and routine for the pupils, or in the limitation of opportunities for the linkage of the various branches of the curriculum. Nor must it mean that a pupil will lose the kind of close personal association with a teacher which often follows easily from the one-teacher-one-class system. The security which such an association can bring to him must be preserved and he still must feel that among the different members of staff with whom he comes in contact there is one special person to whom he can turn for help and advice. Equally it must be the responsibility of certain teachers to collect and record the kind of information about pupils which is essential for planning their work in future years. The problem is how best to secure for the pupils the advantages of skilled instruction in the different branches of the curriculum without incurring the disadvantages that may arise from changes of teacher. The solution lies in consultation among teachers, co-operation in the planning of programmes, and the keeping of records, under the supervision of the head teacher.

Similar steps have to be taken in schools which are visited by specialist teachers. Here also it is essential that head teacher, class teacher and specialist should work closely together. The specialist's value to the school lies in her knowledge and skill in her own subject, but she and the head teacher and class teacher together must ensure that her special skills are applied in ways which are appropriate to the children and to the school's educational policy, and that the content of her instruction is relevant to the work of the pupils in other branches of the curriculum.

It is for the head teacher to decide how the services of specialists should be employed, and his decision will depend on the circumstances of the school. He may feel, for example, that a visiting music specialist should devote most of her time to those classes where the teachers are least able to provide adequate instruction in music themselves. On the other hand, he may arrange for an art specialist to visit a teacher who is gifted in this direction or a class which is undertaking a particular project in art or craft, in order to stimulate further developments. He may on occasion regroup a number of classes in order to allow the specialists to teach groups of pupils who have particular interests or aptitudes in, for example, physical education or drama. He may decide that specialists should have opportunities to see all his classes and their teachers so that all may benefit from their advice. It is unlikely, however, that the visits of a specialist will be frequent enough or of sufficient duration to enable her to see every class on every occasion, and even if this were possible, it is probable that she will do more good by visiting only a selection of classes, and spending a correspondingly longer time with each of them.

In devising a time-table for visiting specialists, the head teacher has particularly to bear in mind the needs of his oldest pupils, who have reached a stage in their development when they are most likely to benefit from specialist teaching, and when it is most difficult for the class teacher to cope satisfactorily with every aspect of their education.

Up till now, part-time teachers have as a rule been employed only in cases of emergency, when no full-time members of staff could be obtained. Because of changing social patterns, however, it may well be that in future the services of many women teachers, at least for part of their professional lives, will be available only on a part-time basis, and in schools the appointment of part-time teachers may become normal rather than exceptional practice. It is the responsibility of the head teacher to use the services of part-time teachers to the pupils' best advantage. This task is seldom easy, being complicated by the fact that for domestic or other personal reasons the teachers concerned may have to keep rather rigidly to certain specified hours and may not be available at the times which would be most convenient for the school. At present, a common arrangement is for two teachers to share the work of a class, one perhaps coming in the mornings and the other in the afternoons. Alternatively, one may teach for, say, two full days and her opposite number for the remainder of the week. No matter which system of sharing is followed, it is important that as much information as possible about the pupils should be passed from one teacher to the other, if possible by discussion as well as in writing, so that there may be full agreement on methods and content, and an opportunity of assessing progress. It is also important that part-time teachers should regard themselves, and be regarded by their colleagues, as "part-time" only in regard to the number of hours they spend with the pupils. In other respects they are full members of staff, with the same aims, loyalties and responsibilities as the others.

Chapter 8
Assessment

AT every stage of education, assessment is an important part of teaching and an essential element in the provision for each child of an education suited to his age, aptitude and ability. Assessments must constantly be made by the teacher to ascertain the progress a child has made, to diagnose his difficulties, and to discover his capabilities, so that she may plan for him a programme which is appropriate to his needs. They are essential, too, in enabling the teacher to evaluate the efficiency of her own teaching. Assessments are also necessary in order to give parents information about their children's performance in school. In addition, a duty is laid upon primary schools to assess their pupils' gifts and potentialities with a view to selection for secondary education, and on the school's estimate depends to a large extent the effectiveness of an education authority's transfer procedures. Assessment, therefore, serves a variety of purposes, and it can be carried out in a number of ways.

Assessment begins in an informal way very early in the child's school career, when the teacher first observes him at play, and notices how he reacts to his new surroundings, his degree of confidence or inhibition, his attitude to others, his speech, his manual ability and so on. By observation the teacher can learn a great deal that is of use to her in deciding how to treat each child and how to allow for the differences among her pupils in the planning and organisation of her work. Throughout the primary school the teacher's day-to-day observation of her pupils remains one of her most valuable methods of assessing not only individual qualities of character and aspects of social behaviour, but also strengths and weaknesses in various branches of the curriculum. She will see, for example, the success or failure of her teaching in the everyday work of the pupils in written English or in mathematics; creative ability will emerge in the art and craft activities or in the dramatic work which the pupils undertake; the progress which pupils have made in the application of the skills they have learned will come to light in their work on projects and centres of interest. Without the aid of tests or examinations, therefore, the teacher can form fairly accurate assessments of her pupils, simply through her contact with them and her observation of them over a period of time.

At times other means of assessment require to be employed.

The teacher may, for example, wish to set a test for a group of pupils in order to ascertain how well certain facts or a particular process have been learned. She may use a diagnostic test to help her decide how to proceed with a particular pupil. She may set her pupils a standardised test in English or arithmetic to check that her own standards are reliable. At the stage of transfer to secondary education, attainment tests and verbal reasoning tests frequently play a part in selection procedure.

Care must be taken to ensure that tests and examinations do not take up an inordinate amount of time, assume undue importance in the work of the school, or impose an undesirable rigidity on curriculum and methods. In the early stages particularly, it is pointless and unnecessary to test and label children merely in order to provide a set of marks for the parents or for the head teacher; and the use of such assessments to seat the pupils in a class in order of merit cannot be too strongly condemned. Moreover, at this stage the results of objective tests reflect the quality of the child's home environment rather than his innate ability, and are therefore of little prognostic value. Even at the later stages, much time can be misspent in the holding of weekly or monthly tests in the various school subjects. Very often they provide no more information than the teacher has already acquired from her daily observation of her pupils' work. Further they tend to be confined to aspects of the curriculum which can be readily examined, and therefore give undue importance to such things as grammar, spelling, mechanical computation and the acquisition of facts, disregarding creative ability, imagination, initiative and original thinking. Worse still, the existence of tests of this kind in a school may cause some teachers to limit the content of their teaching to those aspects of the curriculum which are known to figure regularly in the examinations. In these circumstances some subjects—music, physical education, art and craft, for example—suffer neglect, and the teaching of others becomes restricted to certain examinable aspects. The teaching and assessment of written English come to be preoccupied with mechanical accuracy, to the neglect of the more creative aspects of writing; practical activities in mathematics give way to mechanical "sums", frequently long and repetitive; history, geography and science become unduly concerned with facts, to the exclusion of independent investigation, research, discussion and recording; text-books become all-important, library activities sporadic and peripheral; instruction takes precedence over learning through activity.

Formal tests and examinations, therefore, are of limited value, and if badly constructed or unwisely used, can be harmful. Some subjects should certainly never be examined in the traditional way —music, for example, art and craft, and poetry. It is doubtful too if environmental subjects such as history, geography and science should be formally examined, if, as it is hoped, the emphasis in these activities is placed on enquiry and discovery rather than on the acquisition of examinable facts. If, for internal reasons or for selection for secondary education, attainment tests are considered to be necessary in English and mathematics, they must be designed to take account of creative and inventive ability as well as mechanical accuracy, and they should allow for differences in the ability and the profession of work among different groups and individual pupils.

Certain tests are specially devised to assist the teacher in diagnosing the difficulties of individual pupils in, for example, reading, language usage and arithmetic, and they could be used more frequently than they normally are in schools. Sometimes, however, full diagnosis requires psychological skill which the teacher does not possess. In such cases a psychologist should be asked to help in diagnosing the difficulties and suggesting appropriate remedial measures. Referral of this kind need not be restricted to backward pupils: the gifted as well as the less able very often present problems which call for specialist advice and guidance.

Assessment, however, is not to be thought of only in terms of intellectual progress. If primary education is to be concerned with all aspects of the child's personality, the school must regularly turn its attention also to the character, attitudes, conduct, health, and emotional and social development of its pupils. Some of these are not easy to assess in any precise way, but a great deal of educational value can emerge if careful records are kept, and if there is consultation among teachers about individual pupils.

It is important that the school should keep, for each child, a record of any information that may have a bearing, direct or indirect, on his educational development. A profile of this kind should contain as complete an account as possible of the child, compiled from information that comes to light from time to time within the school or from other sources. It should include assessments of mental age and reading age as determined by objective tests, as well as broad assessments of attainment in the basic language and mathematical skills, a note of interests or hobbies, and comment on special attributes such as ability in music or art, manual dexterity, or mechanical skill. Some assessment should also be attempted of general aspects of personality and behaviour, such as attitude to work, application, initiative, leadership, sense of responsibility, and ability to get on with others. It may also be useful in some cases to have information about the child's social background, his parents and his place in the family. Where necessary, there should be a note of exceptional matters such as serious illness, behaviour problems or extraordinary home conditions. Such a comprehensive record is a valuable guide to head teachers and teachers in the treatment of individual children, and can be useful when assessments have to be made at the stage of transfer, When a pupil passes into a secondary school, the profile should go to the receiving head teacher. At all times the information it contains must be regarded as confidential to the schools concerned. Information of the kind suggested might be incorporated in the Pupil's Progress Record, which in its present form allows for several of the items listed above.

There is also an onus on the school to communicate to the parents the assessments which it makes of each child's progress. There is, however, little merit in report cards of the kind to be found in most schools. Most of those in use at present cover certain aspects of the curriculum in an over-precise way, and exaggerate the importance of achievement in, for example, spelling, grammar, and mechanical arithmetic, so that the prominence given to them is out of all proportion to their place in the curriculum. Moreover, the common practice of merely entering numerical marks for each of the subjects is not at all helpful to parents. In many cases, indeed, parents are given a false impression of their child's potentialities, since an aggregate of marks for the easily examinable aspects of the curriculum may place a pupil high in the class order of merit, taking no account of other qualities—for example, creative ability in language or the capacity to apply skills in practical situations—which have a greater predictive value. Much more thought should be given to the kind of information to be passed on to parents. Broad assessments of the child's progress in the acquisition and application of the main mathematical and language skills are obviously necessary, along with comments on special abilities, interests and weaknesses in other branches of the curriculum, and on qualities of temperament, character and conduct revealed in school. In the older classes an estimate of the type of secondary education for which the child appears to be fitted might save some parents disappointment at a later stage.

Selection procedures for transfer to secondary education, and the part that the teacher's assessments should play in them, are fully dealt with in the Department's Circular 501 of 20th June, 1962. The recommendations made in that Circular are based to a large extent on those contained in the Report of the Advisory Council on

"Transfer from Primary to Secondary Education" (Cmnd. 1538, 1961), and it is not considered necessary to add anything to what is said in these two documents. It is the task of the schools to implement, to the best advantage of their pupils and in consultation with the parents, whatever transfer scheme is laid down by the education authority. Perhaps the most important consideration is that both teachers and parents should understand the purpose of the procedures and the provisional nature of the allocations that are made. Schools must help to enlighten parents in this matter and take steps to give them a realistic view of their children's potentialities. At the sane time, teachers of the older classes must resist the temptation to concentrate their efforts on the examinable aspects of the curriculum. Concentration of this kind does not serve the best interests of the pupils.

Chapter 9
Backward, Able and Gifted Pupils

Backward Pupils

PUPILS in the primary school who are unable to progress as quickly as their contemporaries and whose attainment falls markedly below the level for their age group may be classified as backward. Backwardness cannot be cured. It is wrong, however, to regard backward pupils as hopeless; to describe them so in their hearing is unpardonable. To condemn them to continual failure by attempting to bring them up to an arbitrary standard called "normal", and to blame them for errors they cannot avoid can only create emotional attitudes which may result in anti-social behaviour and even delinquency. Like other children, they will grow up to be citizens of the future; like other children, they have to be educated in accordance with their age, ability and aptitude.

Ths proportion of backward pupils varies from school to school, but it can be assumed that a national age group contains some 15 to 20 per cent of such pupils. It is the school's duty to identify its backward pupils and the degree of their backwardness as early as possible, and to make for them the kind of provision which will develop their maximum potential, at the same time giving them a sense of success and making them feel worthwhile in the class community.

While there are emotional, physical and environmental as well as intellectual factors associated with backwardness, and their influence and interaction have to be considered, the major criterion for identifying backwardness is limitation of attainment. In the infant classes, because of the difficulty in making objective assessments at this early stage, the greatest care must be taken to avoid any premature judgment which would label a pupil as backward. Nevertheless, by observation of the pupils, information can be gathered which can be helpful later. Circumstances of educational significance should be noted—absence, physical and sensory defects, the extent of the pupils' vigour and liveliness, their emotional and social characteristics, the nature of their home environment and the opportunities it offers or lacks for. talk and play—and an estimate attempted of their intellectual potential, particularly whether they have an aptitude for symbolic learning—a prerequisite of success in learning to read. At the end of class P II the lowest 20 per cent of the pupils in attainment may be noted, and a decision taken on whether any of these should be retained in an infant class for perhaps a further six months. A decision of this kind should take into account not only attainment in the basic subjects but also the pupil's physical development, his level of maturity and the attitude of his parents. It should be emphasized that retention is justified only as an exceptional measure, where it is clearly in the child's interest.

In classes P III and P IV the general assessments formed on the basis of the information collected in the infant classes can be supplemented by the use of standardised tests to ascertain more precisely each pupil's relative level of intelligence and attainment. By means of intelligence and attainment tests, judiciously used, the teacher will discover how each pupil fits into the general pattern of his age group, and will be able to identify those whose attainment falls a year or more behind the average, and who may therefore be regarded as backward. It is at this stage that the school must begin its major effort in the education of these backward pupils.

When the backward pupils have been noted, their education has to be organised. A great deal will depend on the size of the school, the number of backward pupils and the degree of their backwardness, and on the staff and accommodation available. The pupils may remain in their class with their own age group, and the teacher will deal with the problem by group and individual methods. They may form part of a tutorial group at set periods for instruction in the basic subjects, but rejoin their own class for other activities. The aim should be to avoid complete segregation of the backward pupils from their contemporaries. For social and emotional reasons a permanent backward class cannot be justified.

On the whole, it is better for a backward pupil to remain in his own classroom environment along with his age peers, especially if his teacher is experienced and gifted in the teaching of the basic reading and mathematical skills, and if she is able to organise her work so that the backward pupils receive adequate attention in the basic subjects, individually or in small groups. On the other hand, if the range of ability in the class is wide, the teacher may be unable

---

FACING PAGE:

Above: Seriously and deliberately pursuing his own edcuation on lines of his own choice (page 12).

Below: Desks used individually or grouped as occasion demands to provide a larger, flat, continuous working surface (page 19).

to devote sufficient attention to her backward pupils, and if a separate room and a suitable teacher are available these pupils may be taken from their class at set periods for tutorial work in the basic subjects. The infant mistress, with her knowledge of the teaching of reading and number, may be able to give valuable advice and help. Careful organisation is required to ensure that there is co-operation and exchange of information between the class teacher and the tutorial teacher, and that no stigma is attached to membership of a tutorial group.

The progress of the pupils in a tutorial group should be kept under review by the head teacher, so that he can decide whether a pupil has improved sufficiently to rejoin his own class for instruction in the basic subjects. In this review the school should co-operate wherever possible with the Child Guidance Service, so that pupils who present particularly serious problems of backwardness may be referred as early as possible for ascertainment and, if necessary, transferred to a special school.

Whether the backward pupils remain in their own class or receive part-time tutorial teaching separately, both the content of the curriculum and the teacher's methods must be carefully considered in relation to the pupils' needs. So far as the basic skills are concerned, the teacher must have a clear idea of her aims, based on the limited ability of the pupils and the limited time at her disposal. There should be no suggestion that the backward pupils should follow at a slower pace the same programmes of work as the rest of the class. Much of the written work, for example, in language and mathematics which her average and above-average pupils undertake will be inappropriate, and it will be necessary for her to draw up a programme of minimum essentials. The development of reading skill to a functional level must take first place in the list of priorities. In mathematics the aim will be competence at a practical level in handling money, weights and measures. In written English there will be opportunities for free writing, but the demands made in directed writing will be modest, and the teaching of formal skills limited to the simplest sentence patterns. In other branches of the curriculum, however—other environmental studies, art and

---

FACING PAGE:

Above: Easels at which the pupils can paint standing up and using the full movement of the arm (page 163).

Below: An area set aside as a weighing and measuring corner (page 127).

E

craft activities, music, physical education—the backward pupils must have opportunities to make their contribution to the work of the class or the group, sharing in the investigations, the aesthetic experiences, the practical activities and the corporate enterprises as far as their ability and aptitude will allow.

The methods which are appropriate for backward pupils make particular demands on the teacher's skill. Such pupils need short spells of work and frequent changes of activity. Since their powers of retention are limited and they are less capable than others of incidental learning, they need a great deal of direct teaching, much repetition and "over-learning". They learn best when an appeal is made to as many senses as possible. Their confidence is easily destroyed by failure, their attitude to learning often coloured by the memory of lack of success in the past. They need, therefore, objectives which are within their reach and the security which comes from frequent success, even at a low level. The teacher must be quick to notice when they have ceased to make progress, to diagnose the cause and to adjust her methods accordingly. Even such simple physical features as a clean book, a new sheet of paper, a fresh jotter on which to work may help to stimulate them to renewed effort. In reading and mathematics in particular several different methods and media may have to be tried before an effective one is found. Above all, a happy and stimulating environment and a varied and enjoyable range of activities are no less important for the backward pupils than for others. It is vital, therefore, that in her anxiety to teach the basic skills the teacher should not deprive the backward pupils of those many other experiences which the primary school should provide, and which may be necessary to compensate for deficiencies in the home and to assist their personal and social development.

The handicapped child who requires to be educated in a special school does not come within the scope of this memorandum. Problems arise, however, in some areas—sparsely populated rural areas, for example—where special educational provision is not available and where in consequence physically or mentally handicapped children have to be catered for in the primary school. In such circumstances there is all the more need for co-operation between the school and the specialised ancillary services. In primary schools where there are pupils suffering from physical disabilities or sensory defects the teachers should be given guidance on the functioning of equipment such as the hearing aid and the reading lens, and on the day-to-day care of epileptics, diabetics, and cardiac cases. Specialist advice and help should also if possible be given on the education of mentally handicapped pupils. The principles which should underlie their education differ little from those outlined above for backward pupils, but mentally handicapped pupils can make particularly great demands on the patience and resourcefulness of the teacher, and she should be given as much assistance as possible through visits from psychologists, a generous supply of material, and constructive guidance on appropriate approaches and activities.

Occasionally there are pupils who cannot be described as backward but who for one reason or another—a change of school or absence because of illness, for example—are temporarily unable to maintain progress in keeping with their capacity. Normally provision should be made for them within the class organisation. Group and individual methods will enable them to make good the ground they have lost or to adjust themselves to the change of approach in their new school. Exceptionally, tutorial instruction of the kind provided for backward pupils may be necessary.

Able and Gifted Pupils

At the opposite end of the spectrum of ability from the backward pupils is a section of the primary school population—some 15 to 20 per cent of an age group—which presents the school with its own particular challenge. The able pupils—and included in this number will be a small proportion of specially gifted children—are among the country's principal assets, and it is essential that for their own sake and for the sake of the nation their talents should be developed to the full. It is important, therefore, that as early as possible in the primary school they should be identified and provided with appropriate opportunities.

One of the difficulties in the identification of able pupils is that they are not a homogeneous group, but display considerable diversity and variability in their talents. In addition to those who have obvious intellectual gifts which reveal themselves generally over the whole curriculum, there are those whose ability expresses itself in only one branch—for example art, or music, or drama. It is now accepted that some facets of ability can be measured objectively and with reasonable accuracy by verbal reasoning and attainment tests. There are other facets, however, no less important —variety and depths of interests, degree of maturity, aptitude for creative as opposed to reproductive thinking and for creative expression—for which as yet objective tests are not in common use. Even so, the teacher must recognise the various ways in which ability manifests itself, so that she may provide the course and conditions and employ the methods essential for the maximum development of the able pupils' powers. If they are held back by an organisation which forces them to the pace of the average, if they can perform the work of the class without effort, if they are deprived of opportunities for pursuing their own interests, they are unlikely to develop the qualities of character and the attitudes which will be necessary if they are to make the most of their talents at a later stage.

One way of providing for the very able pupils within the school organisation is to accelerate their progress through the school, so that they complete class P VII a year ahead of their contemporaries and are transferred to the secondary school a year earlier than normal. A second method, which itself does not exclude the possibility of acceleration, is to provide for them an enriched curriculum which is interesting, challenging, purposeful and meaningful and which offers them opportunities, through assignments undertaken individually or in groups, for the pursuit of topics and activities to the fullest extent of which they are capable. A third method which has been tried is the centralisation in an appropriate centre of the very able pupils at stage P VII from a number of schools. A further possibility is that pupils with particular kinds of ability may be for part of the time taken from their class and given special tutorial instruction by teachers with appropriate skills. By this means valuable opportunities for development may be given to pupils gifted in, for example, language, or mathematics, or science, or art, or music. The practical implications of this arrangement are more fully discussed in Chapter 7 on "The Deployment of Teaching Resources".

The curricular chapters of this memorandum offer **many** suggestions which allow scope for individual gifts in language, mathematics, history, geography, science, art and craft activities, music and physical education. All of them make considerable calls on the resources of the teacher. It is vital, however, that they should not be rejected on this account. One of the most important things for the teacher to realise is that learning rather than teaching is the most essential element in the education of the able pupil. Her function, therefore, is not to teach him all that he wants to know—she may not have the knowledge to do so—but to create situations in which he will learn for himself. She must give him freedom and encouragement to read widely, to experiment with language, to conduct his own investigations in environmental studies, to discover mathematical relationships for himself, to express himself in two or three dimensions, guiding his efforts when guidance is needed, indicating sources when information is sought. When an able pupil goes further in his study than she herself has gone, she must resist the temptation to hold him back, and be prepared to learn along with him, sharing his enthusiasm for new discoveries.

A curriculum and methods of this kind demand adequate facilities for their implementation. A liberal supply of books in the class library and access to a more comprehensive central stock are obvious needs. A wide variety of material suitable for improvised experiments in science and for art and craft activities should be available. School museum services can be exploited with advantage. A tape-recorder can be valuable for individual use. It may be also that one of the most effective uses of teaching machines in the primary school will be for individual learning by the able and the gifted.

It has been suggested that it would be in the national interest to centralise a small proportion of the most gifted pupils—some 2 per cent of an age group—on an area or on a regional basis and to provide for them a stimulating environment with specially designed curricula and specialist teaching to develop their interests and talents to the full. Whether this is a feasible proposition for pupils of primary school age, and whether it is desirable on educational grounds to segregate such pupils from their less able and less gifted contemporaries with whom they have much in common and with whom they will later have to live, are matters which might be the subject of research. It is beyond question that much more requires to be done by the schools to identify able and gifted pupils and give them the facilities and the education that their capacity merits.

Chapter 10

Activity Methods

"ACTIVITY methods" is a general term which has come into currency in recent years to denote the newer and freer methods which progressive teachers are now employing as a result of their increased knowledge of children's mental development and their wider conception of education. It is now recognised that learning occurs most effectively when the learner is personally involved in purposeful activity which captures his interest or arises from it. Consequently the emphasis in primary education is now more on learning by the pupil than on instruction by the teacher. "Activity", however, should not be taken to imply that the child should always be physically active, always bustling about, always "doing", always manipulating; thought itself is activity, and in this sense the child may be most active at times when he is perfectly still and quiet. Nor does this newer conception of education mean that the teacher's role is diminished. Her function is still to teach; but if she accepts the principle of "activity" in education, she will, to a greater extent than hitherto, encourage the child to do as much as possible for himself, in the knowledge that the more he learns through his own experiences and discoveries, the more meaningful and the more lasting his learning is likely to be.

The teacher's role is changing as teacher-dominated methods and subject-centred curricula give way to methods and curricula based on the needs and interests of the child. Increasingly she teaches indirectly through the environment, organising the variety of materials supplied by the authorities, or brought by the pupils or by herself, and creating opportunities for activity arising from the interesting and thought-provoking environment which she has thus provided. She also must ensure that the pupils attend to the job in hand with real concentration, guide them in what they attempt so that the difficulties they meet are appropriately graded, and provide sufficient practice for them to master essential processes, skills, and facts. Thus they are led, while their interests last, to observe and experiment, to read and write, to talk and act—in a word, to learn. In this way the child's natural curiosity is harnessed, and through constructive activity he learns how things work, where they come from, and how they grow and develop, and extends his understanding and skill in mathematics and language. His creative urge finds expression in painting, modelling, writing, speech and drama, and when he is ready for certain information, he is motivated to acquire it for himself. His independence and self-reliance are fostered, he learns how to use available information, and he develops the capacity to work without constant reference to the teacher. The academically minded as well as the practical find satisfaction and enrichment in such whole-hearted participation in their own education.

For some time now activity methods have been employed to good effect by many teachers of infant classes, but too often from stage P III activity has been replaced by formal methods of instruction which demand little more from the children than compliance with instructions and the memorisation of facts. It is vital that teachers should appreciate the need for learning through activity, as it has been defined above, in all branches of the curriculum and at all stages. The curricular section of this memorandum contains a great many suggestions which illustrate the application of activity methods in various fields. A few examples may be useful at this point, however, to exemplify what has so far been expressed in general terms.

In arithmetic it is only too easy for a child to go through the motions of computation, obtaining the correct answers, and for him to have little idea of what he is really doing. Mathematics, of which arithmetic is a part, is essentially a study of relationships, the recognition of which is essential to the child if he is to understand even the basic concepts involved in simple everyday calculations. His understanding will be more secure if he discovers these relationships for himself. At all stages, therefore, he needs a stimulating environment with a wide variety of activities involving experience of number, quantity and space, freedom to explore this environment, and time to draw his own conclusions. For example, practical work with any material to hand (children, beads, milk bottles, books) should be used to give the child a grasp of the significance of what he is doing when he combines groups into one larger group before he meets this operation as addition or multiplication. Similarly, experience of weighing and measuring in practical situations should help the child to appreciate that comparison with an arbitrarily determined unit is the basis of all measurement, before he is asked to perform calculations of length, weight, capacity or time. As concepts are formed, and techniques are learned, every opportunity should be taken to enable the child to apply his knowledge in real life situations, in order not only to develop his skill but also to deepen his understanding.

Other environmental subjects such as history and geography have in the past been too much associated merely with the acquisition of facts, and too little with the development of the child's powers of investigation, criticism and expression, and with his attitude to learning. The study of these subjects should involve the pupil in finding information for himself, evaluating the information which he obtains from books or from other sources, discussing, writing, drawing and painting, modelling, miming and acting. All this implies that the teacher has to make available as great a variety of appropriate books, encyclopedias, atlases, maps, pictures, documents and materials as she can muster, and that the child should have easy access to all these things.

It follows that where activity methods are used the curriculum cannot be divided rigidly into watertight compartments. This approach demands that the child should apply the skills and the knowledge that he has gained in one subject to the study of others. Language will, of course, pervade all his activities, since whatever he does will involve him from time to time in reading, in discussion or oral reporting, and in writing. Art and craft, as well as having a place in the time-table in their own right, will play a part in other subjects. Environmental studies will throw up opportunities for the application of the processes which have been acquired in mathematics. Further examples of this kind of linkage are contained in the curricular chapters.

A further implication of activity methods, based as they are on the principle that the child should actively participate in his own learning, is that the teacher, while retaining overall control of the work of her class, should be ready to encourage investigations and projects which arise spontaneously out of the interests of her pupils. She should, furthermore, be prepared to allow such activities to develop along lines of the children's own choice, and to continue just as long as their interest in them is maintained. Especially in younger children, enthusiasm can be killed, and valuable opportunities for self-education can be lost, if the teacher tries too insistently to direct the progress of a project in which children are engaged or to carry further the study of a topic once interest in it has died.

The importance in all this of the richness and variety of the classroom environment cannot be over-stressed. The teacher must try to make her classroom a place in which her pupils find their imagination fired and their curiosity whetted, where there is a host of things they can look at and handle and read and study, where materials abound for painting, constructing, modelling and acting. She must also recognise the importance of stimulating, first-hand experience, and be willing in her search for it to look outside the classroom. The teaching of measurement, for example, might take her pupils into the playground; small scale local studies in geography, or field work in natural science, might take them into the environs of the school. History and geography should also include fairly frequent excursions beyond the immediate locality. Visits to places of special interest—stations, harbours, farms, factories, museums, art galleries —will provide interest and information for individual and group activities, and include many different subjects of the curriculum in their scope. Town children will benefit from excursions to the country, country children from visits to the town. Purposeful ventures of this kind are a valuable means of enlarging the child's experience, and should figure as prominently as possible in his life in the primary school.

Chapter 11

Class Organisation

THE ways in which the teacher organises her class must vary according to the nature and needs of her pupils and the kinds of activity in which they are engaged. At times she may take the class as a unit—for singing, for example, or a branch of environmental studies, or physical education, or poetry. At others she may be teaching some aspect of language arts or mathematics to only one pupil, or to a small group, while the remainder of the class are working independently on assignments, or co-operating in groups on a project. Class, group and individual methods, therefore, all have a place in the primary school classroom. The good teacher evolves a pattern of organisation which enables her to suit the content and methods of her instruction to the range of ability in her class, and to provide opportunities for the sharing of experience and for both independent and co-operative activity.

During a child's first year at school the teacher must provide an environment which will offer him opportunities for individual learning and social adjustment, satisfy his play needs, and encourage him to look, experiment, discover and talk. There should be a large number of interesting things for him to do and speak about; he should as far as possible have free choice among the activities available; and he should be able to move from one to another. For such a child the school day will consist of fairly long periods of self-chosen activity varied with "get together" times for stories, rhymes, singing, informal talks, class conversation, or periods for class or group observations. The material available should provide opportunities for all kinds of play—constructive, manipulative, creative and imaginative. Because of the self-centred nature of young children much of the play will probably tend to be individual at first, but will gradually acquire social and co-operative elements as the children play together or share a common interest. The first grouping within a class, therefore, is "social" or "interest" grouping, and it arises spontaneously among the pupils without direction from the teacher.

As the teacher watches and records the reactions of the children, she soon discovers the first group—perhaps six, eight or ten pupils—who appear to show reading or number readiness. Thereafter the class begins to form into a collection of small ability groups at varying stages of maturity, intelligence and attainment. For lessons in reading and number these groups will usually remain fairly constant. Although individuals may move from one group to another, no extensive changes are likely. Within the social or interest groupings, however, quite radical changes of personnel may take place.

Even when the different groups have emerged, the general organisation of the day should not greatly alter. The child should still have plenty of opportunity for free choice of activities, but the content of at least some of these activities will gradually change, as elements of the basic subjects are introduced. The library corner, for example, the weighing and measuring corner, and the shop begin to assume new roles. Play groups will gradually develop into project groups, formed according to voluntary choice, interest or aptitude. Such groupings will last while interest in a particular enterprise is maintained. This may be for as short a time as a day, or part of a day—if the children are very young—or, in the case of older pupils, for several weeks. Groups may evolve and the personnel change according to the needs of the project and the ability or personal wishes of individual pupils. The class unit may sometimes be appropriate for instruction by radio, television and films, and for lessons which gain from the sharing of experience by the class as a whole—for example, in music and games, some forms of art and craft, poetry or story-telling.

One of the greatest problems for the teacher of young children is how to keep all her pupils purposefully employed, so that she may be free to teach reading or number to one ability group, or even to one individual. In class P I it is essential to have a wide variety of material which to some extent is self-teaching and self-corrective and which is graded to meet the needs of different levels of ability. The teacher's task is to encourage able pupils to tackle more difficult apparatus and to ensure that a slow child is working at something which will afford him a considerable measure of success. Gradually, too, she will train them to undertake a number of different activities in succession, explaining what is required in each and then expecting the pupils to proceed without further direction from her. By stage P II they should be able to work their way through a short programme of assignments listed on the blackboard or on cards, moving from one activity to the next and seeking the teacher's guidance only when they find themselves in difficulty.

Beyond the infant stages the development of the children's powers of concentration enables them to work for longer periods on their own, and the widening of the curriculum and of their range of interests makes possible an increasing variety of assignments which they can tackle individually or in groups. Assignments may be set daily for the younger pupils or for the less able, and weekly for the older pupils. In the upper classes the children can help to plan their own individual and group assignments, with the teacher's guidance. They thus become accustomed to considering a piece of work in relation to the time available and are able to take pride in completing tasks that require a certain amount of endeavour. They begin to realise that a group is a "team", a number of children working together with a common purpose. As a rule they will be free to help one another and to consult members of other groups if they wish. When, however, the teacher wishes to assess individual proficiency, they will be expected to work unaided.

The success of an assignment system depends on a few basic principles. The work provided must be graded according to the levels of ability and attainment in the class, so that each pupil or each group is set tasks of appropriate length and difficulty. All the material required to complete the assignment should be accessible to the pupils. The teacher must be clear about the purpose of the exercises which she sets, in order to ensure that they really give practice in those elements of the subject which she wishes to emphasise. Any new apparatus or new types of exercise which she introduces should be very carefully explained to the pupils concerned before they are asked to work on their own. Methods of supervision and correction should be made clear to each child, so that he knows when to expect help, when to proceed to a fresh task, and where to put finished work. In the older classes, at least some of the correction, particularly in mathematics, can be done by the pupils themselves. The teacher herself must be constantly vigilant in assessing the progress of individual children, and in keeping the type of record which will enable her to plan for their future needs.

What is said in the following chapter about flexibility in time-tabling is of particular relevance in connection with a system of assignments. The teacher has to exercise general supervision over the allotment of time to the different aspects of the curriculum— tool, environmental, aesthetic and recreational subjects alike—but within certain limits considerable latitude may be allowed to the individual pupil, especially in the older classes. Even where a teacher prefers to retain the outline of a daily time-table, some freedom is still possible where subjects are grouped in general terms, as, for example, "environmental studies" instead of history, geography, mathematics and science, or as "language arts" instead of reading, composition, and so on.

Within such a broad framework, a variety of activities involving groups of different size and composition can be carried on. While, for example, the pupils are occupied with assignments in language arts and mathematics, the teacher can take individual pupils or ability groups for instruction in some aspect of these two fields. The composition of these ability groups may vary: for example, a pupil who is in the ablest group for reading may not be in the same group for mathematics, and pupils may move from one group to another within the same subject, if they show marked improvement, or if they temporarily fall behind. At other times social or interest groups may be formed which are not based on ability but allow able, average and slow pupils to work together on some aspect of environmental studies, art and craft, music, or drama. These groupings may result from an interest which several pupils have in common, or they may be deliberately chosen by the teacher, and they are likely to change as the pupils pass from one activity to another. In addition, as has already been indicated, there will be occasions when the class group is the most appropriate unit, for example, when the children are brought together for singing or listening to music, for radio and television programmes or films, for physical or religious education, for poetry, or for a lesson and discussion on history or geography.

The older the pupils become, the more desirable it is that interest grouping should be extended beyond the confines of their classroom, and that there should be arrangements whereby pupils from different classes but with a similar interest—music, drama, crafts, stamp-collecting, sports, for example—can join together. Children with special aptitudes should also have their opportunities: groups such as the school choir and orchestra encourage the musically gifted, and clubs in and out of school hours can cater for those whose gifts lie in other directions.

Children who are fully employed in work which interests them and who feel they are capable of overtaking it successfully usually behave well, and seldom abuse the freedom they are given by this kind of organisation. They must, however, show consideration both to their classmates and to their teacher. They must learn to go about their work in the classroom quietly, with the minimum of disturbance to others, and not to interrupt the teacher while she is busy with another group. They must learn also to look after books and materials carefully, and see that everything is returned to its proper place.

A further important consideration in a classroom where the organisation is flexible is the arrangement of furniture. The immovable rows of desks which once formed the pattern of seating in primary schools are no longer appropriate. The arrangement should be simple and should change according to the requirements of the activities in which the pupils are engaged. Some teachers find it expedient to seat the members of each ability group together; others prefer a more informal "social" or "vertical" grouping. No matter how the pupils are seated, if the teacher wishes to see the members of any particular group, she merely has to ask them to come to her, and if she wishes them to work together, it should be easy for them to put their desks together. If the furniture is easily movable, it can quickly be re-arranged, as required, to allow for individual work, group projects requiring a large, flat working surface, class lessons, and drama or movement. Under this system, therefore, each pupil may find himself in different parts of the room at different times of the day. It is nevertheless desirable that he should have a place to keep the books and materials which he uses from day to day. The desks themselves can, of course, be used for this purpose without any restriction on their mobility. Some teachers have also found it helpful to provide each pupil with a "tote" tray which holds at least some of his belongings and which he can carry with him from place to place in the classroom.

It is appreciated that some teachers are diffident about the adoption of group and assignment methods, partly perhaps because they feel that these methods may cause a lowering of standards of attainment and that pupils may not work to full capacity when they are allowed the greater degree of latitude involved in this type of organisation. Perhaps also some teachers are doubtful of their ability to retain adequate control when freedom of activity and movement is allowed. It is undoubtedly true that teachers and pupils take some time to adjust themselves to this new approach. Nevertheless, the evidence is overwhelming that once the adjustment has been made the benefits that derive from group methods entirely justify the effort. Many teachers have proved that in the permissive yet controlled atmosphere of the classroom where there is a flexible organisation and group methods are skilfully employed, the able pupils can realise their potential, and all can achieve success at appropriate levels. In addition, self-reliance and initiative are developed, and the pupils have opportunities of pursuing individual enthusiasms, and of learning to share in co-operative enterprises.

Chapter 12
Time-Tabling

IT is no longer considered desirable to give in a memorandum of this kind the detailed guidance on time-tabling that was offered in "The Primary School in Scotland". In that publication suggestions were made about the amount of time that should be devoted each week to each branch of the curriculum, the times of day at which certain activities should be undertaken, and the length of time pupils should remain at one type of task. These suggestions have tended to be interpreted rather narrowly, and so to perpetuate a subject-based time-table which varied little from day to day or week to week. Under such a system the day tended to be divided into short periods during which all the pupils worked on a particular aspect of the curriculum, and time was found every week for every subject. Each day had its arithmetic period, its reading period, its spelling period; each week had its history periods, its art periods, its music periods, and so on.

Such an inflexible organisation is increasingly inappropriate in the modern primary school, where the emphasis has passed from the subjects of the curriculum to the needs of the child, and where the attitude to work is considered no less important than the acquisition of skills and knowledge. Differences among children and the consequent need for group and individual methods mean that not all the pupils will spend the same amount of time on each subject or be engaged on the same tasks at the same time. A curriculum which has meaning and purpose for the pupils will inevitably include centres of interest and projects of various kinds which cut across subject barriers. Moreover, if pupils are to follow up topics in which they are interested, some parts of the curriculum may for them temporarily disappear from the time-table. It is unrealistic, therefore, to think of the time-table as an unchanging daily or weekly pattern, applying equally to all the pupils in the class, or even to expect all branches to have an unalterable allocation of time each week. If the policies advocated throughout this memorandum are to be carried out, the time-table must be regarded as flexible, and may change from day to day, from week to week, from term to term to suit circumstances.

There are certain aspects of the work which must be strictly time-tabled by the head teacher in consultation with his staff.

Arrangements must be made for the use of common areas for assembly, physical education and general purposes; radio and television programmes must be fitted in; the use of certain aural and visual equipment by different teachers may have to be co-ordinated; programmes must be drawn up for visits by specialist teachers; times may have to be set aside for special activities involving the regrouping or the interchange of classes. Apart from these considerations, however, each school has a good deal of freedom in the disposal of time, and each teacher, under the supervision of the head teacher, should develop a practice which suits the needs of her pupils and her own particular skills and interests.

Although a flexible organisation is being recommended, the teacher must still have a framework within which she can organise the activities of her pupils, and which will enable her over a period of time to ensure that she covers a reasonably balanced programme of work. It is part of her function to plan ahead. Each teacher should, in consultation with her head teacher, draw up in general terms a plan for perhaps a month ahead in language arts, environmental studies, art and craft activities, music, physical education, projects, outdoor activities and so on. Such a plan should take into account not only activities in which the whole class will be involved, but also the varying needs in certain subjects of different groups and individuals. The programme will be under continual review, as regular assessments must be made of the amount of work covered, so as to ensure that over a term or a session the curriculum has been well balanced and there are no serious omissions.

Within this broad framework the teacher must plan a programme for each week or each day, covering all the activities which she wishes to include, and allowing for group and individual work by the pupils, group and individual teaching, and occasions when the whole class will be taken together. For this purpose it is best to portion out the school day in large blocks of time within which the teacher can achieve as much flexibility of organisation as she desires.

In the first two or three years the day may be arranged roughly in three broad time divisions, during one of which, not necessarily the first, the pupils should have the opportunity to choose amongst the various activities afforded by the material and apparatus available

---

FACING PAGE:

The pupils are organised informally in small groups and the accent is on varied activity and individual effort (page 188.)

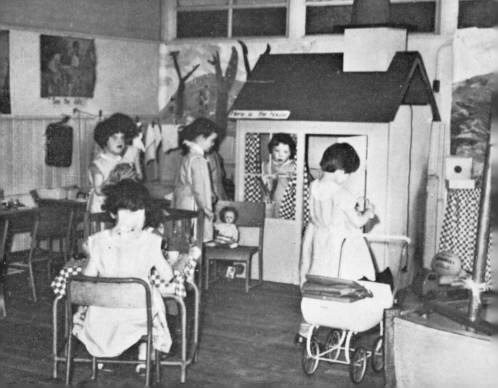

in the classroom. A second block of time may be set aside for activities involving the acquisition of skills. During most of this period the pupils may be engaged in individual assignments in reading, writing and number, while the teacher takes individuals or groups for instruction in reading and number. Occasion may also be taken during this time to bring the class together for a discussion on topics of interest to the children, for a "news" period, or for a demonstration by the teacher. During the third block other parts of the curriculum—music, poetry, dramatic work, story-telling, creative activities in art and craft, and observation out of doors— can be undertaken, by groups or by the class as a whole, whichever is appropriate.

The contents of these three time divisions are not mutually exclusive, and the order in which the activities occur may not always be the same. In class P I, indeed, the children should not feel that activities in number, reading, or drama differ very much from their play activities. At stages P II and P III, as skills in reading, writing and number are acquired, there is a marked change in the nature of the children's play, and they begin of their own accord to follow up group and individual interests which have emerged from their classwork, engaging in art and craft activities, making up their own "plays", weighing and measuring, handling money and change in the shop, browsing in the library corner, or writing their own stories. The framework which has been suggested, therefore, cannot be regarded as rigidly controlling the day's activities. The age and interests of the children and the teacher's objectives will determine the activities undertaken in any one day or week, the time of day at which they are undertaken, and the length of time they occupy. Over a number of weeks, however, the teacher must ensure that a sufficient range of activities is covered and that appropriate progress has been made in the basic skills.

Beyond the first three years the widening of the curriculum may make it appropriate to allocate blocks of time of varying lengths to broad curricular sub-divisions—language arts, environmental studies, art and craft activities, music, and so on. On one day, for example, the period up to the morning interval may be given over

---

FACING PAGE:

Above: Objects can be classified as sinking or floating (page 127).

Below: Play will acquire social and co-operative elements as the children play together or share a common interest (page 64).

F

to language arts, and while the pupils are occupied in free writing or in assignments of various kinds involving reading, writing or library work, the teacher may be engaged with groups or individuals for reading or for training in some aspect of written English. A similar length of time may normally be allocated to assignments and group and individual teaching in mathematics. Other aspects of environmental studies may on occasion require a complete afternoon. During this time, for example, the pupils may go out of doors to conduct observations or investigations and then return to discuss and record their findings; or they may be engaged in scientific experiments or in patch or sample studies in history or geography. Art and craft activities may occupy at different times half the morning, of half the afternoon, or even the whole afternoon if large-scale projects are being undertaken. Large blocks of time may also occasionally be set aside for "interest" groups to work on activities of their own choice, or for individual pupils to pursue their particular enthusiasms. At other times, quite short periods may be devoted to music, for example, or poetry, or dramatic work, or physical education.

As in the younger classes, the pattern will change from day to day and from week to week according to circumstances, and only the teacher herself in her own situation and with her own special knowledge of her pupils can determine the content of her programmes of work and plan her time in ways that will enable her to overtake it efficiently. If her pupils are provided with a suitable variety of material and occupations, and are gradually trained to work through a number of individual and group assignments without direction, she should be able to achieve considerable flexibility and to ensure that all aspects of the curriculum are adequately covered and are treated at times when they are most appropriate.

In view of the principles that have been set out in this section, it will be apparent that it is scarcely possible to give any recommendation about the proportions of time that should be allotted to the various parts of the curriculum. What can be suggested is that, in general, of the time available approximately one third should be devoted to language arts, approximately one third to environmental studies and approximately one third to the remainder of the curriculum. It must be stressed, however, that the time which is spent on any activity is educationally of less significance than the amount of work that is effectively covered, and that the assessments which teacher and head teacher make at regular intervals should be in terms of achievement rather than time.

Chapter 13

Audio-Visual Methods

THE value of visual and aural aids has long been recognised, and an ever-increasing amount of apparatus and material is available. The word "aids" itself, however, has tended to convey a wrong impression about the proper use of films, filmstrips, tapes, broadcasts and so on, and has caused teachers to think of these, not as an integral part of the education they provide, but merely as helpful additions to their teaching. At the same time, some teachers profess themselves incompetent to operate mechanical equipment. These two factors have combined to produce a reluctance on the part of many teachers to make regular use of visual and aural apparatus, with the result that audio-visual methods have not been given their proper place in many primary schools.

Much remains to be learned about the use of audio-visual material, but there is ample evidence to put its value beyond doubt, especially in an age when visual presentation on film and television is becoming one of the principal means of disseminating information and providing entertainment. Recent developments in the production of material and in the refinement and simplification of procedures for operating equipment have opened up exciting new possibilities for the teacher. Advances in the fields of film and television, in particular, have shown that these can be important media of education in their own right, providing not only illustrations to illuminate the teacher's instruction, but also direct teaching of a kind and on a scale that is outwith the resources of the class teacher. Moreover, the latest types of equipment present no greater problems, even to the least technically minded, than the domestic radio or the electric cooker. It is vital for teachers to realise that visual and aural material should be, and can be, central to primary education, and thought must be given to the provision of up-to-date apparatus in schools and to the most efficient ways of integrating its use into the programme of work at every stage.

If audio-visual material is to be used effectively, a number of principles have to be borne in mind. In the first place, the material and the apparatus must be of high quality. Primary school pupils of today are maturing earlier and are more sophisticated than ever before. They expect to see and hear in school products that stand comparison with the best that they experience daily from their own radios, television sets and record-players. There can be no place for antiquated or badly maintained equipment or for inexpert handling which results in breakdowns or inferior sound or vision. In the design of schools, therefore, account must be taken of facilities for the efficient use of audo-visual equipment. Within each classroom there should be power points, placed conveniently so that apparatus can quickly be brought into use, as it is required, by the teacher or by an auxiliary. If there is a separate room or multi-purpose space where films can be shown, adequate blackout, together with efficient ventilation, is essential, and the room should be designed to provide optimum conditions for sound and for the setting up and storing of the apparatus.

The material must also be available when it is wanted. This places on the head teacher the responsibility of organising the use of equipment in such a way as to reconcile the conflicting claims of his teachers. It also means that each teacher, in her planning ahead, must consider what use she wishes to make of equipment and material, and when she is likely to require them.

Every piece of equipment and material brought into use should have a definite purpose. There should be no suggestion that each class should have, for example, a routine weekly allocation of films from a central library. Films must be more than merely a means of filling in time. Entertainment films have a place in the primary school, but even these should be selected and introduced for the purpose of creating standards or fostering aesthetic appreciation. The films, broadcasts and recordings which the teacher uses should be chosen for their relevance to her programme of work and for the contribution they can make to particular learning situations. For this reason she should know beforehand what the material contains, so that she can decide how well it suits her purpose and how she can best make use of it.

The use of audio-visual methods should not lead to passive listening or watching on the part of the pupils. It is part of the teacher's task to use the material in such a way as to encourage active participation in the learning process, and to ensure that the pupils derive the greatest benefit from it through preparatory and follow-up activities.

Two further general points may be made. Some of the older boys in the primary school are experienced and adept in the handling of apparatus, and might well be encouraged to operate electrical equipment as long as proper safeguards are taken and adequate instruction is given in its use. At the same time, since proper maintenance and operation are vital, it is advisable for one member of staff—perhaps an auxiliary—to have responsibility for the availability, condition and servicing of equipment.

Radio Broadcasts

Radio broadcasts are a well-established feature of education, and in recent years developments in their scope and technique have made a wide range of excellent material available to schools. Most branches of the curriculum are now catered for, and the possibility of recording programmes for future use has removed the difficulties that occasionally arose from the timing of broadcasts. More than ever, therefore, the radio is a medium of great value to the teacher, especially in fields in which she lacks knowledge and skill, or in which she cannot match the resources and the means of presentation available to the broadcaster.

Reception should be of the highest quality; in particular the tuning of the master set should be very precise, when this system is in use. The pamphlet, "Hints on Improving School Broadcast Reception", by the School Broadcasting Council for Scotland, is helpful in this connection; but if reception is very poor, technical advice should be sought.

Since schools have now had considerable experience of broadcast lessons, it is no longer necessary to give detailed advice about their use. A number of points, however, require emphasis. Whether a broadcast series is used as a syllabus in itself or as a means of enriching the teacher's programme of work, the associated activities are just as important as the broadcast lessons themselves. A series loses much of its value unless there is adequate preparation and follow-up. For this reason the teacher should make herself thoroughly familiar with the nature and aims of the series, and every child should have a copy of the pamphlet relating to the broadcasts. Teachers must also have regard to the age-range for which a series is produced, and should not be using broadcast lessons which in content and presentation are inappropriate for their pupils.

Tape Recorders and Records

The value of the tape recorder in education has gradually become more widely recognised in recent years, and it is probable that all its possible uses have not yet been explored. The recording of radio broadcasts, which has already been mentioned, is only one of the ways in which it has been employed in schools. Another obvious use for it as a means of letting children hear and listen critically to their own speech, so that they can detect their faults and try to eliminate them. A further possibility, if earphones are available, is that it may be used by absentees so that they may hear a broadcast they have missed or overtake the work of their group, or by able pupils, to work independently on material of a more advanced nature. Pre-recorded music or song accompaniments may be helpful to teachers who are not instrumentalists. The tape-recorder is also likely to play an important part in the teaching of modern languages in the primary school; it is now possible, by the use of simple attachments, to convert many makes of tape recorder into language laboratories for individual work.

Probably, however, the tape recorder can make its most important contribution as a creative rather than as a receptive instrument. It can, for example, help to overcome shyness in an individual or a group in dramatic activities. It can provide the sound-effects which add realism to a play, or the pre-recorded sound background for a puppet show. Portable recorders can be used for interviewing personalities, for conducting investigations in the local area, or for recording the sounds that can be heard in the countryside, the street, the factory, the zoo, and so on. Projects, class magazines and inter-school correspondence may be recorded rather than written. Many of the techniques evolved over the years in sound radio for the presentation of information and entertainment may be imitated by the pupils in programmes which they devise and record themselves.

Most of the purposes which the tape recorder can serve will be defeated if it is not properly operated and adjusted. Faithful reproduction is all-important, especially when it is used with the object of improving the pupils' speech.

Gramophone records offer a plentiful source of material, though they are more easily damaged than tape and require good storage facilities. An ever-increasing range of records is now available which covers music for listening and appreciation, melodies and rhythms for free movement and dancing, spoken prose and verse, and drama. These can be used in a variety of ways by all teachers, but are particularly valuable to those who lack skill or confidence in music or in the speaking of poetry.

Non-Projected Visual Material

Even without the use of mechanical or electronic apparatus, there is a great deal of visual material which the teacher can use to make learning more effective. The blackboard, for example, has a time-honoured place in the classroom, and its uses are too well-known to need enumeration. One point, however, deserves to be made: in the modern classroom, with its emphasis on individual and group activity and flexibility of organisation, the single fixed blackboard is no longer appropriate. If different groups within the same classroom are to be working on different tasks simultaneously, there is an obvious need for blackboards at various points in the room, or preferably for light movable boards which can be placed according to the teacher's requirements.

Other items of equipment that can be used for visual presentation of material during a lesson, without the disadvantage of chalk dust, are the flannelgraph and the plastigraph. Both can be useful to build up a story or a lesson, and can afterwards be stored for subsequent use. With the first, a little experimentation is all that is needed to find the materials—multi-hooked gauze, for example—that adhere most successfully. The second depends on air pressure for adhesion, and can be used effectively so long as it is kept free from dust, and provided that the view of the pupils is not made difficult by reflected light from the highly polished surface.

A wealth of visual material is now available in the form of pictures, charts, maps and diagrams, produced by educational firms and various commercial and industrial concerns, and these can provide interesting illustrations for the teacher's lessons as well as material for projects, undertaken by the children. The teacher must be careful in her selection, however, whether her choice is based on educational or on aesthetic grounds. For example, the content of many pictures published for schools is either too childish or too advanced, and many have too much depth and perspective or too much elaboration for young children. The resourceful teacher can very often produce her own pictorial and diagrammatic material, or cull it from newspapers, magazines and other publications. The children themselves should be encouraged to bring suitable illustrations to school, and their own creative efforts should have a conspicuous place in their note-books and diaries and on the walls of the classroom.

Three-dimensional material—specimens, models, collections of various kinds—is specially valuable because it can be examined and handled by the pupils. Much of it will be brought or made by the pupils themselves or by the teacher, but advantage should also be taken of school museum services, which offer a plentiful and widely varying supply of interesting material. Developments in the teaching of physical science in primary schools underline the possibilities in working models, especially those made by the pupils for their own use.

The increase in the use of visual material of the kinds described above makes it essential that schools should have adequate facilities for display and storage. Generous areas of pinning surfaces in classrooms, corridors and multi-purpose spaces are needed, as are also cupboards, table-tops and shelves of the right height for working and for display, and peg-boarding or metal surfaces with magnets for three-dimensional items. Storage, particularly of large sheets, presents problems which must be catered for in the design of schools. It would be unreasonable, however, to expect every classroom to have sufficient accommodation to house a large accumulation of such material. Much that is used will be of only temporary value, and can be discarded once it has served its purpose. Material which is to be preserved for future use by the same pupils or by another class is best kept centrally, and each school should consider the organisation of a central collection of illustrative material, efficiently filed and indexed so that teachers can quickly obtain what they require.

The use of non-projected visual material is one of the ways in which the teacher can make the classroom environment interesting and stimulating. Not all classrooms are suitably designed for this, but the teacher must use to the best advantage whatever wall space and horizontal surfaces are available to her. The purpose will be defeated, however, unless the material is of immediate interest to the pupils or of relevance to activities in which they are engaged. There is no place for the tired frieze left over from a long-forgotten project.

Projected Visual Material

The last two decades have seen remarkable developments in the design of projectors and in the scope of projected material for use in schools. The following paragraphs cannot hope to do more than merely mention a few of the main possibilities open to teachers.

The still projector is light, portable and easily operated, and can be used to show filmstrips or slide transparencies. The filmstrip is more easily stored and carried, and more easily used, but it wears out much more quickly in use than slides, and the order of the frames cannot be varied. Improvements in colour film and in 35-millimetre cameras have also enabled teachers to produce good coloured slides of their own. A more recent and very valuable development is the magazine-loaded automatic projector which can be operated by remote control and used in conjunction with a tape-recorder.

Opaque projectors such as the episcope and the epidiascope are bulky and of limited usefulness. The episcope can project two-dimensional and three-dimensional material, but almost always requires a full blackout. The epidiascope has largely been superseded by modern portable projectors capable of adequately showing 35-millimetre transparencies.

The overhead projector allows the teacher to face the group she is teaching while the material is displayed behind her or over her head. It can be used in daylight, is easy to store, and has a very long working life. Material can be prepared beforehand, or built up during the lesson, as on a blackboard. A further advantage is that better contrast is obtained than on the blackboard.

In the field of film projection the standard equipment is currently the 16-millimetre projector with an optical sound system or, more recently, a magnetic sound system which enables the teacher to provide her own commentary on the film, if necessary adapting it to a particular group of pupils. 8-millimetre projectors have also developed greatly in quality and reliability, and can be used in conjunction with tape-recorders by means of couplers and synchronisers. The 8-millimetre cassette-loaded loop film which takes three or four minutes to show can be an excellent teaching device, and may be used by groups of pupils when they are working on their own.

Films bring into the classroom the great wealth of visual experience which lies outside and is not available to the pupils at first-hand. In this way, for example, pupils can enter vicariously into life in other countries or in other times, and processes can be accelerated or slowed down so that they may be comprehended in their entirety or seen in a way that is not possible with the naked eye. Sound films in colour, in particular, make an impact and exercise an attraction which lead to greater retention of what is learned. Films vary considerably, of course, in quality and suitability, and before making her selection the teacher would do well to consult the reports of an authoritative reviewing group. She should also have a prior view of the films she intends to show, so that she may know their contents and be able to plan appropriate related activities for her pupils.

Consideration must also be given to the type of screen which is used for projection, and to keeping it in good condition. A matt-white surface is the most suitable, especially in the classroom, where some of the pupils almost inevitably have an angled view. A screen deteriorates quickly if it is allowed to become creased and dirty, and it should always be packed in such a way that it is protected. Rear-projection, which can be used for daylight viewing, allows the teacher to face the class while she operates the projector, but it has the disadvantage of providing a comparatively small picture, if optimum contrast and brightness are to be achieved. Television, however, has probably already conditioned children to the smaller screen.

Television

In schools, as in our society as a whole, television is a new and important medium with which we have not yet fully come to terms. There can be no doubt that it exerts a strong influence on children of school age. Some of them, indeed, may spend more time watching television than they spend in formal education: at any rate, reliable surveys appear to demonstrate that in very many homes sets are switched on throughout the evening viewing hours. For this reason, if for no other, television deserves to be explored as a potentially powerful educational instrument.

Since television was first introduced into schools, great strides have been made both in technique and in the range of programmes available. Initially, the medium was used for "enrichment" programmes, but there has been a gradual acceptance of the idea that direct instruction can be given by television. As recently as 1959 there was no television series addressed to primary school audiences, but since then there has been a gradual development of programmes appropriate to primary school children. Recently, too, experiments have begun with closed circuit television, which has the advantage of being organised at a local level, and thus of bringing teachers into the planning and assessment of programmes. These experiments are still in their infancy, but it is clear that closed circuit television has considerable possibilities, particularly since it can adapt its material and adjust its timing to suit local circumstances in a way which is impossible in "network" television. Future developments of importance to education will undoubtedly include colour television and cheap video-tape recording.

It is to be hoped that in time all schools, irrespective of their size, will have television sets, and that experiments in the use of television will be undertaken by more education authorities. Some authorities have been understandably reluctant to lay out expenditure on equipment until they could be sure of its value in schools. For this reason it is essential that as experiments proceed they should be carefully evaluated and that knowledge and experience should be shared by teachers, education authorities and the producers of programmes.

The teacher has an important part to play in this field in experimenting, assessing, and advising on ways in which television can be integrated into the curriculum. Although television has some of the characteristics of older media such as films and radio, it has greater educational potentialities, which require the teacher to evolve new and appropriate ways of using it. She has to consider, for example, the optimum size of the audience, ways of treating programmes to allow for individual differences among pupils, ways of ensuring pupil participation, and the role she herself has to play in helping the pupils to interpret, grasp and follow up the instruction given on television. Rapid advances are being made in the technology of the medium, and teachers must ensure that their own methods keep pace with them.

Chapter 14

Library Facilities

IN the primary school, class libraries are a basic need, since it is essential that books should be on the spot for immediate consultation as need arises during the school day. Library books should be regarded, not as something extraneous to and separate from ordinary classroom work, but as a normal source of information in most activities.

Space is needed in the classroom, not only for housing library books, but also to enable pupils to read or work individually or in groups. The most convenient arrangement is for each classroom to have a special library corner or alcove, suitably furnished, where four or five children can read in semi-privacy.

The class library should contain all that the class requires for its immediate use. There is some advantage in also having a central stock from which class collections can be changed from time to time. As new books are acquired, they may be added to the central stock before issue to individual classrooms is made.

Although often pupils will merely go to the central collection and bring back a book to the classroom for consultation there is obvious advantage in having sufficient space to enable individuals or groups to browse or to carry out a little research on their own before returning to the classroom. If a separate library room can be made available, the housing of the central collection of books presents no problem, and display space is available to a far greater extent than is possible in the classroom. Moreover, a central library may provide incidental opportunities for the use of a simple form of catalogue or index.

A separate library room almost inevitably presupposes some form of time-tabling in order to avoid the conflicting claims of different classes. It is undesirable, however, that the library room should merely be a place to which a class is taken at a prescribed time. The books should be available for consultation by individuals or groups at all times. The atmosphere of the library room should be as natural and free as that of the classroom; it is a mistake, for example, to insist on silence.

In schools which have no separate library room, it may be possible to use the general purposes room to house the central collection, provided that access to it can be gained at any time without interference with the normal activities of the room. Space may also be found in entrance halls, dining rooms or corridors. In small schools, where separate space cannot easily be provided, the central stock may perhaps be kept on moveable trolleys. Wherever the central collection is kept, it is important that it should be reasonably accessible to the classrooms, particularly those of classes P V, P VI and P VII.

Where there is a primary department attached to a secondary school, there is no reason why primary pupils should not make use of the main library. In such a library the stock should include an adequate range of books suited to the needs and interests of pupils of primary school age.

Expensive equipment is not essential either in the class library or in the central collection. Shelving should preferably be of the open access type, so that books are instantly available; it may, however, be necessary to provide some means of keeping books protected and free from dust outside school hours.

Careful consideration should be given to means of attractive and effective display both in the classroom and at strategic points throughout the school. It is important, particularly with younger children, that arrangements for display should allow the front of a book sometimes to be seen rather than its spine. Attractive books are now the rule, and the use of drab protective covers should be avoided; transparent plastic wrappers both protect the jackets and allow a colourful display. Worn-out and out-of-date books should be discarded and replaced at the earliest opportunity.

In the choice of books, account has to be taken of differences in ability, the range of the children's interests, and the topics which will be investigated in the various branches of the curriculum. Reference books—not necessarily of an expensive type—a suitable variety of fiction and non-fiction, and an appropriate selection of books for use in work on environmental studies, art and craft and so on should be provided in each classroom; the central stock, in addition to these categories, might also, with advantage, contain some reference books for teachers. Every effort should be made to ensure that books which are in use for reference contain up-to-date and accurate information. The ratio of fiction to non-fiction will vary from class to class. There should be a considerable number of books which are easy to read, but also some which will extend pupils and tempt them beyond their normal reading range. The needs of the less able pupils must be borne in mind; and in the choice of books for general reading, the differences in the interests of boys and girls should not be overlooked. In many areas schools have been able to use the resources of the County Library Service to supplement their own book stock. This is an excellent arrangement provided that teachers and librarians co-operate in ensuring that the books supplied are appropriate to the needs of the pupils. It is especially useful in helping small schools to maintain adequate class libraries. Children's librarians in particular, with the knowledge they possess of the reading matter available for children, can offer advice and help in the selection of suitable books and in the introduction of simple library procedures.

Liaison with public libraries should be developed as far as possible. Apart from availing herself of the skilled advice of trained librarians, the teacher may be able to increase children's interest in and willingness to use the public library. Visits to local libraries are already quite common in many areas. Encouragement can be given to pupils to use the public library as a source of reference outside school hours.

Chapter 15

Programmed Learning

THE expression "programmed learning"—often used in association with another comparatively new term, "teaching machines"—is one which is being heard more and more frequently, and though the special techniques involved have so far been most fully developed with older students, there has also been some experimentation at the primary school level.

Essentially, "programming" consists of taking a certain amount of subject-content and breaking it down into small steps, each of which has to be mastered before the next can be attempted. To a large extent the good teacher always does this when she plans a lesson, going progressively from the familiar or the easy to the more difficult and making sure that her pupils consolidate each step before proceeding to the next. What is new in programmed learning as it is understood today is that once a programme has been prepared it is presented not directly by a teacher but by one of the devices collectively referred to as "teaching machines". This is a very comprehensive term denoting any device which will display information in an organised and pre-arranged way, and the "machines" may range in cost, size and complexity from cards or text-books to mechanical or electronic apparatus. A simple type of machine, for example, with which some primary school teachers have been experimenting, consists of a box with a transparent "window" in the lid for showing information and presenting a question, a place for the pupil to record his answers, and a winder which allows the correct answer to be brought into view for comparison. Some machines incorporate a device to prevent the pupil from changing his response once he has seen the correct one.

Great as is the variety of these machines the programmes they utilise are alike in several respects. The instruction they provide is on an individual basis, and allows the pupil to proceed at his own rate; they directly involve each pupil in his own learning processes by demanding from him some kind of active response, perhaps an answer to a question or a choice from among a number of possible solutions; and they help him to achieve success by carefully subdividing the work into small units of increasing difficulty and by making the sequence sufficiently gradual to ensure that he has the satisfaction of being correct most of the time. It is a feature of all the programmes that a pupil is made aware immediately whether his answer is right or wrong, and in some programmes—the "branching" type—the pupil who has made a mistake is directed to a further sequence which explains his error and brings him back to answer the question again or takes him on by another route to the next question.

The fact, already mentioned above, that programmed learning has been less developed in the primary school than with older students is by no means accidental. Because programmes have to be constructed in advance and must move in predictable fashion from one point to the next, they are most appropriate for those subjects or parts of subjects which develop on clearly defined, logical lines. Where, however, a subject cannot readily be analysed into small constituent units or where the essence of learning by a young child calls for his own personal observations, experiments, tentative deductions or judgments, the place for pre-arranged programmes seems doubtful. It is for these reasons that much of the investigation into programmed learning in the primary school has been done in mathematics, for example in such aspects as the number bonds and the multiplication tables. Experimentation is, however, proceeding in other primary fields, and the results are being awaited with much interest.

In some quarters the term "teaching machines" has been unfavourably received, the argument against it being that only a human being can teach. This is to misunderstand the intention of programmed learning. Teachers will always retain in their hands the general control of the work in their classrooms, since much of the material to be fed into the machines will have been prepared and organised by their own profession and all of it evaluated by them. When programmes become available in sufficient quantity the teacher may well find that at the very least they can relieve her of some routine tasks, for example by providing material for consolidation and revision, thus allowing her to devote more time to those pupils who require her personal attention.

The success of programmed learning in the primary school, as indeed at all levels, depends essentially on two factors, namely the wise choice of the subject matter to be programmed, and the degree of expertise possessed by those who do the writing. Programme writing is a technical and difficult skill, requiring much time and patience as well as knowledge of the way children learn and of the difficulties that tend to arise. Eventually, perhaps, it may be found that the best programmes can be written by teams consisting of both teacher-practitioners and persons skilled in programme techniques, the experience and knowledge of the one complementing those of the other. Even, however, if the majority of teachers do not aspire to writing their own programmes, they can play a valuable part in testing and evaluating those produced by others, and they may find it useful, in appropriate subjects, to examine some of their present methods in the light of the techniques used in programming. Such a scrutiny, by focusing their attention on details of presentation, may lead them to make minor or even major changes in their normal procedures which could add significantly to the effectiveness of their work.

Chapter 16
Homework and Leisure

SCHOOLS differ considerably in the emphasis which they place on homework, and in the amount and nature of the work which they set. Some continue the tradition which began many years ago of prescribing a definite amount of work each night, for example a passage for reading, an allocation of spelling words, a number of "sums". Compulsory homework of this kind, however, set as a matter of routine to all the pupils in a class without regard for individual ability and attainment or home circumstances, can have little justification. Any homework that is given should be geared to the needs and circumstances of individual pupils. If the teacher considers that a pupil in his own interests should have additional practice at home in some routine operation in mathematics or language, she must be careful to select tasks which can be overtaken in a very short time and which are within the pupil's powers. Moreover, she should make sure that he appreciates the need for these assignments and understands their purpose. When practice of this kind is required, however, it is better if time is given for it in school, where conditions are likely to be conducive to independent study. Many children come from homes where they have neither the space nor the quietness to enable them to concentrate and work well.

Experience has shown that if the right attitudes to learning are fostered in school, and if the pupils are encouraged to play an active part in their own education, the interests which they develop in the classroom spill over into their leisure at home. Of their own accord they will follow up some of the activities in which they have been involved at school. Thus individual pupils, according to their particular inclinations, may quite voluntarily occupy their leisure with mathematical problems, creative writing, the making of scrap books, the keeping of illustrated diaries, some form of art or craft, scientific experiments and observations, various kinds of field studies, music-making, reading or independent research connected with a class or group project or with some interest arising from it. "Homework" of this kind, undertaken spontaneously or indirectly inspired by the teacher, can take many forms, and may help to develop a lasting interest in worthwhile leisure pursuits.

The children's own hobbies can also be used to advantage by the school. For example, models, pieces of embroidery, collections of coins and stamps can be shown to the class and discussed. Short talks can be given by the pupils on birds, railways, aircraft, cooking, gardening, sports, or any other topics about which they are particularly knowledgeable. In the library there should be a hobbies section, which may from time to time be augmented by hobbies books brought from home by pupils with particular enthusiasms. The pupils may mount their own exhibitions of specimens, models or books in the classroom or in a place where other classes can also see them. Time may occasionally be set aside for pupils to pursue their hobbies in schools, individually or in groups. By thus exploiting and co-operating in their spare time occupations, and by using them as appropriate to develop the pupils' powers of self-expression, both orally and in writing, the school can make an important contribution to their all-round education and at the same time forge a valuable link with the home and the parents.

The school should also take an interest in what the children read and hear and see in their home environment. In these days of comics, records, radio, television, and films, the teacher must try—with tact and sympathetic understanding—to sharpen her pupils' powers of evaluation and help them to discriminate between the worthwhile and the meretricious. She may, for example, discuss with them the comics they read, the records and radio and television programmes they enjoy, the films they have seen. Without imposing her own preferences, she may suggest other publications they might try, other music or broadcasts they might listen to or watch, other films they might go to see. Older pupils may be encouraged to think of the issues and problems that are raised by particular magazine stories or television plays or films, the extent to which they mirror real life, the motives and actions of the characters. In such ways the teacher can help her pupils to form standards of comparison and criteria which will enable them to think for themselves and choose the best ways of occupying their leisure hours.

Chapter 17

Conduct and Discipline

THE primary school is to an increasing extent concerned with the moral and social education of its pupils. The school routine, the organisation of the classroom, the teachers' methods, the content of the programme of work, the conduct of school meals and other social occasions, and particularly the outlook and example of the head teacher and the teachers, all help to condition the attitudes and behaviour of the pupils. Where children have an active part in their own learning, where they feel secure in the knowledge that they can achieve success and have a particular place in class and school activities, where they understand the routine and rules which order their lives, where the school is an interesting place to come to and they can accept the teachers as their friends, they readily develop not only the qualities of character which they need as individuals but also the qualities of conduct which living with others demands.

Even in the best ordered community, however, there may be occasions when a pupil is careless, or lacking in industry, or guilty of some misdemeanour. The teacher, with her knowledge of individual pupils, will readily recognise the cause, and will have little difficulty in deciding the most appropriate form of correction, should indeed correction be required. Often a mere word or a look may suffice. Whatever she does must be seen to be just. In particular, she should take care that relations with her pupils and respect for her authority are not impaired by the exaggeration of minor aberrations. Censure or disparaging comment for lack of native ability is less than professional and cannot be too strongly condemned.

Corporal punishment remains a controversial issue. It is clear that the use of corporal punishment has diminished in recent years, especially in those schools which have adopted up-to-date methods and progressive attitudes towards the education of their pupils. Some schools and many teachers have already learned to do without it, but even these would wish to retain the right to use it as an ultimate sanction. Many others resort to corporal punishment only for serious breaches of discipline and grave misdemeanours, in order to protect the school and class community and enable the work to go on. Whatever the justification for this kind of punishment, it must be recognised that major and repeated offences may be

90

symptoms of deep-seated maladjustment which it is beyond the resources of the school to remedy. The teacher should not be expected to cope with a pupil who constantly refuses to co-operate with her or who is persistently guilty of anti-social behaviour. In such cases the exclusion of the pupils—or even merely the threat of exclusion—may bring home to the parents the gravity of the situation and may be sufficient to secure their co-operation. It is nevertheless the school's responsibility to refer the problem to the Child Guidance Service so that specialist help may be obtained.

Corporal punishment should not be necessary in the modern primary school. The use of this sanction, however, is a matter essentially for the professional judgment of teachers within their general responsibility to their education authorities, and teachers themselves, through their professional bodies and in consultation with education authorities, should review the use of corporal punishment in primary schools.

Chapter 18

Links with Ancillary Services

IN its task of securing the all-round development of its pupils, the primary school is able to call on the support and help of a number of ancillary services, the value of which in turn depends largely on the degree of co-operation that exists between them and the schools.

All education authorities, through their School Health Service, provide for the medical examination and supervision of children in schools under their management, and make available facilities for free medical and dental treatment. For all pupils routine medical inspection is carried out at certain stages of school life, and in addition head teachers may refer individual children to the school doctor at any time. After each examination, a note is made of the doctor's findings, thus enabling a reliable medical history of each child to be built up. It is particularly important that any feature of a child's health which has educational implications—a defect of vision or hearing, for example—should be immediately communicated to the head teacher and through him to the teacher concerned. Only in this way can the teacher adjust her methods and her demands to suit the pupils concerned. The responsibility for liaison with the School Health Service rests, of course, with the head teacher, who must see to it that there is adequate interchange of information between the school, the parents and the Health Service, and that appropriate action is taken when it is necessary. Some of the work involved may usefully be delegated to a member of staff who is specially interested in health education.

An increasing number of education authorities have established a Child Guidance Service, to which schools can refer cases of special scholastic disability or abnormal behaviour. Throughout the country, however, there is considerable variation in the extent of the provision, and it is hoped that those areas which have as yet not adequately developed this aspect of educational service will take steps to do so. Properly used, the Child Guidance Service can be of invaluable assistance to schools in the treatment of children who present special problems. Its functions are both educational and social; its aims, broadly speaking, are to help the child to adjust himself intellectually and emotionally to cope with his environment, and to rearrange or change his environment to make it possible for him to make the adjustment. Sometimes this demands more than the obvious co-operation between psychologist and teacher: it may well involve the parents and perhaps also the medical officer and the social worker. All must collaborate in the collection and evaluation of information about the child and his environmental background. It is the special responsibility of psychologist and teacher to plan the child's education accordingly. The schools have a vital part to play, not only in referring cases to the Child Guidance Service, but also in indicating the kind of help they would most welcome —assessment, advice, details of suggested treatment—and in co-operating in whatever course of action is deemed appropriate. It is important that psychologists should not be too heavily committed to handicapped pupils only, or unduly involved in, for example, the routine work of selection for secondary education. Their concern should be with exceptional pupils of all kinds, in the treatment of whom their expert knowledge and experience can be of great value.

Facilities for speech therapy are now available in most areas. The number of speech therapists, however, is often not equal to the demand, and education authorities should in their own interests formulate a policy which will allow the most efficient use to be made of this specialist help. It is unproductive, for example, where there is a shortage of speech therapists, to use them in the lengthy treatment of difficult cases when the probability of any improvement is remote. It may also be wise in such circumstances to ask head teachers to be as selective as possible in the cases they refer; otherwise the inevitable delay in assessment and treatment may give rise to frustration in both teachers and pupils. It is better, when a shortage exists, to use therapists to advise teachers in cases where the super-vision by a teacher of prescribed remedial work will be sufficient to effect a measurable improvement. Whatever the policy, one of the most important considerations is that the school should be kept informed of the findings and decisions of the speech therapist and of the progress of its pupils under treatment. Only in this way can the support and co-operation of teachers be assured, and the maximum benefit be obtained by the pupils.

The provision of meals in schools for those who require them is a duty which all education authorities discharge through their School Meals Service. This service, as well as giving pupils an appetising and well-balanced meal, offers opportunities for social training, and in this respect the co-operation and goodwill of school staffs have in the past been of considerable value. The whole question of the supervision of meals by teachers has, however, been the subject of some controversy, and there is much that could be said on both sides. For educational reasons it may be very desirable for teachers to dine at table with the pupils, but they should not be compelled to do so. Such an arrangement is appropriate in the small school, where there is an atmosphere of family intimacy which makes ordinary conversation natural and easy. A large dining room, however, where control and organisation are necessary, cannot have the relaxed conditions which teachers must have during their mid-day break. The expedient of allowing teachers who are on a rota for supervision to have time off before or after the lunch interval to compensate for their supervisory duties is educationally unsound, since an arrangement of this kind interrupts the teacher's normal and more important educational duties. The solution may lie in the use of suitable auxiliaries for the supervision of meals, and in the adoption of a system of "family service" which gives the pupils themselves opportunities for responsibility and self-discipline.

Part 3

Chapter 19

Language Arts

THE term "Language Arts" embraces all those aspects of language development traditionally regarded as essential for literacy, as well as others which are now seen to be of no less importance. In the past, reading, oral composition, written composition, spelling, grammar and poetry have often been thought of as separate branches of the curriculum, and indeed have usually been taught as separate time-table subjects. This fragmentation has disadvantages. In the first place, there tends to be little overlap between the "subjects", and transfer of skills from one to another is seldom effective unless deliberate efforts are made to ensure that it takes place. In some classes, for example, spelling is almost entirely treated as a subject in its own right, and it is not uncommon to find that pupils who spell words correctly in a spelling test may misspell the same words in their continuous writing. Again, the "subjects", being treated separately and having special time allotted to them, are not felt to be essentially involved in other classroom activities. It is convenient and perhaps inevitable that in any attempt at systematic description of language development different aspects should be treated under particular headings. The use of a single comprehensive term will, however, emphasise the "seamless robe" of learning; and "Language Arts", however imperfect as a description of activities which include a number of "skills", is readily intelligible and has within recent years acquired some currency.

The growing child needs an incentive for using speech or writing to express himself; he must also develop the capacity to express himself clearly so that he may be understood; and he must be enabled to understand and interpret the experience and ideas of others. From this it follows that the aims of teaching in the language arts are:

(*a*) to encourage fluent self-expression in speech and in writing;
(*b*) to develop the child's power to express himself in an intelligible and acceptable form;
(*c*) to cultivate the habit of intelligent listening;
(*d*) to train the child to read thoughtfully and critically, acquiring the basic ability to read with understanding, forming lasting reading habits, and extending his experience by the exploration of factual and imaginative writing.

97

Spoken English

Spoken English is the most common form of communication and expression, and it is the only form which some people will continue to use after their school life is over. If children are to acquire the precision and fluency necessary for effective communication, spoken English must occupy a central place in any curriculum. Because speech is personal, pupils must learn in accordance with personal interests, habits and environmental traits; because it is subject to a continuous process of change, modern usage must not be rejected out of hand or criticised by some arbitrary standard of correctness.

When children first come to school, although there may be wide differences in the extent of their vocabulary and the fluency of their speech, it is significant that the majority usually have plenty to say, to each other if not to the teacher. Outside school there have usually been opportunities to talk and ask questions, and it is vitally important that this freedom should not end upon entry to school. Opportunities must be afforded to pupils to converse with one another and with the teacher, the only qualification being that talk should not disturb concentration and that precocious and excessively voluble children should not be allowed to monopolise the conversation to the detriment of others who are shy or reticent and therefore all the more in need of encouragement to speak.

In the early stages the teacher must ensure that the child has abundant opportunity for the type of experience which will stimulate the desire to communicate. A classroom which is well equipped with interesting and colourful material will encourage readiness to talk. Elaborate material is not necessary: an improvised house or shop or hospital will provide ample incentive for talk and discussion. So too will play with water, sand and clay. It is during such periods of free play that a teacher can observe her children closely, notice those who are already fluent in speech, and detect those who have little to say and require special encouragement.

Most children, once they begin to feel a sense of security at school, will be willing and eager to volunteer items of personal news. In many schools the "news" period forms a regular part of the activities of the classroom, and it is of undoubted value in developing pupils' confidence and fluency. Care needs to be exercised, however, so that children do not become anxious through feeling that they all must have items of news to contribute every day. On the other hand, as many children as possible should have the opportunity to speak, if they so wish.

Many classroom activities can give rise to spontaneous talk. For example, most children like to talk about what they draw or paint or make, and some weave imaginative stories about their own creations. Stimulus to discussion can also be provided by the use of pictures, photographs and newspaper cuttings, and children are often eager to bring to school material which interests them or which is connected with some activity or topic in which they are involved in the classroom. The use of such material, though it can provide a useful starting-point, has its dangers. Unless the teacher's questions are carefully chosen and carefully framed, pupils' answers can easily assume a stereotyped form; and, if only a single picture is used, the possibilities it affords may be exhausted very quickly.

Speaking and writing are essentially different, and the teacher, in seeking to develop her pupils' powers of self-expression in speech, must take account of this. In writing, the sentence—in the conventional sense—is the common unit of expression. Speech, on the other hand, is more flexible and varied, a word, a phrase or a sentence being all appropriate in different contexts. It is wrong, therefore, to insist that pupils should always speak in complete sentences.

As children grow older, they will inevitably be writing much more than at the earlier stages. It is then all the more important to maintain a satisfactory balance between oral and written work, to avoid any suggestion that spoken English is only a preparation for written English, and to ensure that opportunities for oral expression exist. From time to time children will still feel the urge to speak about themselves and their own experiences outside school, and if what they want to say is likely to be of general interest, they should be given every encouragement to tell it to the class. To an increasing extent, however, communication will be about the work and activities of the classroom. Topics and projects in history, geography and science will afford natural opportunities for pupils to ask questions, to pass on information and to interchange ideas. So too will the interest aroused by current affairs and people in the news. Films, filmstrips, transparencies, and sound and television broadcasts will provide an obvious stimulus for class or group discussion. There is also plenty of scope for individual contribution in accounts of hobbies or particular interests and in the expression of personal opinions, for example about books read. An occasional demand for an impromptu speech or talk may help to develop resourcefulness. Abler pupils can be encouraged to describe how to do or make something, a difficult exercise involving precision and lucidity.

The teacher's part is primarily to ensure that the atmosphere and seating arrangements of the classroom are such that opportunities for discussion arise and are taken readily. She may seek to guide the course of a particular discussion by interposing skilful questions.

She will try to encourage the diffident and reticent to take their full share. She will tactfully suggest ways in which statements and opinions can be expressed more clearly, more succinctly, and more appropriately to the requirements of the situation. She will herself, without obtrusive attempts to criticise or correct, set an example in the accepted conventions of educated speech.

Speech training, or speech education as it may be more appropriately called, has sometimes in the past proceeded on the mistaken assumption that there is one absolute standard of pronunciation, and that all divergences from it are to be proscribed and corrected. This leads to much loose talk about "bilingualism", as if it were a bad thing. It is not. On the contrary, a child who has mastered two different kinds of speech has taken an important step forward in his language development. The purpose of speech education ought, in fact, to be to extend the range of children's speech, to make them aware that different kinds of speech are appropriate in different contexts and to help them as far as possible to speak in ways that are generally acceptable. Dramatic work is very helpful in developing the ability to do this.

This does not mean that faulty articulation should not be corrected. Faulty articulation is a barrier to intelligibility, and it is essential that speech should be intelligible in whatever situation it is used. Courtesy is also involved: slovenly articulation and inaudibility—faults by no means confined to the "uneducated"—show an insensitive disregard for the listener, as well as being a hindrance to effective communication. Talk of "bad" or "unpleasant" accents, on the other hand, is simply a subjective judgment about different accents which one does not happen to like. Nevertheless, there are many forms of local speech which may not be readily understood outside the areas in which they are current. Since it is desirable that every individual should be able to communicate with others outside his own environment, it is expedient that pupils should gradually be acquainted with a form of speech which will be intelligible and accepted in all parts of the country. This, however, should not be taken to imply that there is one ideal standard towards which all pupils should strive.

Since the principal that learning should start from experience is valid here as elsewhere, it is desirable that teachers should be as familiar as possible with their pupils' natural ways of speaking. If the teacher shows that she understands and accepts her pupils' speech, an immediate bond of contact exists, which, particularly at the early stages, helps the growth of the self-confidence needed for language development.

The improvement of articulation requires tact and sympathy, and can only be brought about gradually. Formal exercises designed specifically to this end may be necessary, and can be beneficial if they are appropriately used by a teacher who understands their purpose. Repeated and pointed correction, however, will simply make a child self-conscious and curb his spontaneity. Clearly the example of the teacher herself will play a decisive part; and it is desirable that her speech should provide a model that is clear, intelligible and free from artificiality and exaggeration. In a class-room where clear speech is being constantly heard and where the child himself has ample opportunity to speak, there will be much unconscious imitation, and a strong impulse to speak well. The use of the tape-recorder to enable pupils to hear their own speech can be helpful.

Pupils with particular speech defects may require treatment from specialists in speech therapy. The head teacher should ensure that notification of serious cases is passed on to them as soon as possible. The class teacher should co-operate in the remedial measures prescribed by the specialist and should see that the child is not exposed to embarrassment in the classroom as the result of his handicap.

Drama

Dramatic work of the kind envisaged in this memorandum has as its basis the child's own play, and takes its place alongside art and craft, spoken and written English as one of the means by which the child may be encouraged to express himself. It is not to be thought of in terms of finished, polished performances to be acted on a stage before an audience. Such a conception of drama may have a place for some of the older children in the primary school, but at all stages the real value of dramatic activities derives from participation by the pupils in a pleasurable experience, not from presentation to an audience. It is the making of drama that has most to contribute to the development of children, and its importance is such that it should have a regular place at all stages. By being provided with opportunities for self-expression, the child is given an outlet for his feelings and helped to gain some control over his emotions. By identifying himself with other people, real or imagined, by acting out situations within his experience or his imaginative range, by expressing in movement and speech the feelings of himself and of others, he is enlarging his experience, and learning in ways that are natural to him. His imagination is stimulated, and his powers of discrimination, observation and awareness are increased. Furthermore, the freedom which such activities allow for the sharing of ideas and for spontaneous discussion enables children to learn to work well with others, and increases their confidence and their willingness to speak.

Dramatic activities may arise in a variety of ways—through spontaneous play with material in the classroom, out of a story heard or read, or from a situation which children have experienced (in a railway station, a department store, a hospital), or an abstract idea (the seasons), or an activity (spring-cleaning, harvesting, gardening), or an object (a key, a letter, a purse), or an incident in history or literature. The role of the teacher, with her knowledge and understanding of her children's needs and stage of development, is to supply appropriate situations, and to guide, in an unobtrusive way, the ideas which the children suggest.

Direction should be kept to a minimum, and the teacher should resist the temptation to put words into the children's mouths or to impose adult ideas on them. She should recognise that the value of this kind of work lies in self-expression, and allow the children freedom to develop their own ideas and to vary their actions and their words as their ideas change. Her main function is to stimulate, and though she will at all times observe and assess the progress of the children, and occasionally may offer suggestions, there is no place for explicit criticism or direct instruction.

The beginnings of drama are already present in children's play before they come to school, and may be seen in the youngest classes when children choose material which lies to hand in the classroom and act out a situation with which they are familiar. The child who picks up, for example, a hat and a bag from the "dressing-up" box and plays at "going shopping" is already dramatising, and every encouragement should be given to this kind of spontaneous activity. Much of this play will at first be individual but gradually children will begin to co-operate with one another and to play in groups. A group of children, for instance, may decide to "build" a railway station, a hospital or a shop, and act the characters they have met there.

Quite soon the child can be led from the dramatisation of his own everyday experiences to the interpretation of the experiences of others. Nursery rhymes and simple stories provide satisfactory starting-points at this level. Since the children's vocabulary will still be very restricted, the main emphasis will be on action, and the teacher may start with simple occupational mime such as sweeping, chopping, marching, or galloping, with all the pupils participating.

Inevitably some children will be capable of greater concentration and will become more completely absorbed in the activity than others, but the teacher will find that enthusiasm will spread and that the less imaginative children will learn from those of their classmates whose fertile imaginations suggest to them a wide range of gestures and movements. At this stage there is a place for telling the story, discussing it, and acting it out immediately, so as to give a sense of completeness which is so important to young children.

No dialogue is to be expected of children at this level, but speech which arises spontaneously should be encouraged. Several children, indeed, may speak simultaneously, or make sounds appropriate to the character or the action they are trying to portray. A certain amount of noise is, therefore, often to be expected as a necessary part of the activity.

When the child has worked through nursery rhymes and simple stories and has had experience of miming and moving freely, he is usually eager to participate and willing to speak. When he reaches the stage of speaking easily and with some fluency, it is possible to move on to stories which have a greater content, and, though the emphasis will still be on self-expression, the child will now be capable to a greater degree of organising his material and giving it form.

The choice of story for dramatisation is important. The teacher should try to find short stories in which the development of character is simple, the action plentiful, and the climax clear. She may tell the story, or read it—if the language in which it is written is appropriate and particularly effective—or she may make use of stories presented on radio or television.

After the telling of the story the children may discuss with the teacher which scenes should be acted, which characters appear in the story, what they are like, how they act, how they feel. This may be followed by the acting of parts of the story by groups of children, each group developing their "play" in their own way, with the others as an audience. The children may now be encouraged to observe the efforts of their fellows, and to offer suggestions and criticisms. In this way further opportunities can be offered for observation and discussion.

Dramatisation and discussion of this kind help to develop the children's initiative and their appreciation of the purpose of gesture, movement and speech. At this point it is possible to introduce them to improvisation based on ideas and incidents suggested by the children themselves, on words or phrases given by the teacher, or on material drawn from other branches of the curriculum.

H

A group of children may decide to improvise on an event which has taken place locally, such as a fire, a rescue, or a ceremony. Another group may be given words such as "fish", "rope", "castle", and asked to develop a scene around these. In each case the children will discuss the possible development of their assignment among themselves, and work their ideas into a "play" to be presented informally to the other groups. Some may wish to use actions alone, but many older children will wish to add dialogue, and this should certainly be encouraged. Many branches of the curriculum will suggest ideas for improvisation; history perhaps presents the most obvious and the most numerous possibilities.

Children who have done a good deal of improvisation may want to give a more permanent form to the plays which they have created, and they should be encouraged to record them in writing or on tape if they wish. This allows for further discussion, and may lead to improvements and refinements. Individuals and groups can thus gain an added satisfaction from their dramatic activities, and the written versions of their plays may provide useful scripted material for other groups or other classes.

Up to this point the emphasis has been placed on the creation of character, scene, plot and dialogue. Most children, however, having gained some mastery over speech and movement, are ready, before they leave the primary school, to interpret the ideas and words of others, and will gain a great deal in speech and in thought from the interpretation of suitable scripted material, provided that the teacher understands that the fundamental purpose of this work is the sharing of thought, feelings and ideas.

Some older primary school children, having had plentiful opportunities for dramatisation in the classroom, are ready and eager to present their work to a wider audience, and if they wish, they should be given occasional opportunities to do so. Presentation to an audience places a responsibility on the children to adapt their speaking, their gestures and their movements in such a way as to make their work audible and visually satisfying, and thus introduces them to the techniques involved in play production. Initially the audience should not be too large, and should be composed of children or adults who are aware of and sympathetic towards the aims and purposes of the activities presented. At first, other classes in which the pupils are of roughly the same level of maturity as the performers probably make the most suitable audience.

Ideally, children require a large space for dramatic activities, so that all may have freedom of movement. The space, however, should not be so big as to make them feel lost. Often only the classroom may be available, and space may be very restricted, but it is usually possible to remove or rearrange some of the desks to provide an acting area. Since most of the work which has been outlined above needs no audience, there is no need of a stage. Indeed, the artificiality of a stage may hinder the very self-expression which drama is intended to foster. When older children are in need of an audience, the centre of the school hall may prove satisfactory as an acting area, with the audience seated in a semi-circle. If a stage is used, it should be in the form of a low platform, and in a place where an intimate atmosphere can be established with an audience. Light, movable blocks and ramps can give varied levels in the acting area, and can help the children by giving prominence to the dominating area in a scene.

Elaborate properties are unnecessary. It is useful if each room has a simple "dressing-up" box and a collection of junk material for use as improvised properties. The children might be encouraged to exercise their resourcefulness by bringing to school articles which may be helpful to them in the creation of a scene. In the older classes there will be some pupils who have no wish to take part in the presentation of a play as actors, but who will be willing to be associated with the painting of scenery, the making of properties or the sewing of costumes, and they should be encouraged to make their contribution in this way.

At all stages puppetry is an excellent medium for dramatisation; stick or rod puppets, shadow puppets and glove puppets can all be used in the primary school. Often a self-conscious child who is reluctant to stand up and express himself in his own person will be more ready to do so through puppetry, particularly if by means of a simple screen he is enabled to perform without being seen. Initially, puppets which are quickly and simply made will suffice. Later, the pupils may become more ambitious, and may give more thought and care to the making and painting of the puppets, the making of costumes and properties, the writing of plays, the decoration of backcloths, the making of a simple theatre, and the manipulation of the puppets. In the older classes a puppet play can involve a large number of children, each contributing according to his talents. It must be stressed, however, that the value of puppetry lies in the use of the puppets for dramatisation, rather than in the making of them, and that puppets which satisfy the requirements of most children can be made without the outlay of a great deal of time and labour.

Listening

A child begins as a listener, hearing the sounds made by others. Gradually he comes to imitate and understand these sounds. Listening is, therefore, a very important element in the young child's growing knowledge and mastery of the outside world. In school his ability to listen and reproduce what he hears will have a considerable influence on his speech development.

The teacher has, therefore, to ensure that her own practices and the general atmosphere and organisation of the classroom are conducive to active and attentive listening. If she talks too much, she is likely to produce fatigue and lack of concentration in her pupils, and if she habitually repeats a question or answer, they will soon come to realise that it is unnecessary to listen the first time. Where groups are engaged in a number of different activities, the general level of noise in the classroom has to some extent to be controlled so that individual pupils can talk and listen without strain to others working with them. The development of intelligent listening, however, requires more than the mere absence of conditions which inhibit it. In the modern world more and more noise assails the ears, and through the media of radio and television people are subjected to a ceaseless barrage of words. The task of the teacher is made more difficult by the fact that many pupils are conditioned by their experience outside school to disregard to a considerable extent what they hear. Training in listening is, therefore, more vital than ever and more exacting. Positive encouragement is needed so that children will look for meaning in what they hear, ask for explanations when they fail to understand, be critical of what is vaguely expressed, and, so far as is possible in the primary school, come to distinguish what is significant from what is not.

Story-Telling

One important opportunity for listening, and one which children enjoy, is provided by the reading or the telling of a story. This is desirable for other reasons, not least because it appears to be much less common nowadays for parents to read to their children. In schools, too, partly because of the increased emphasis attached to individual and group reading activities, there may be some danger that the traditional practice of story-telling or reading by the teacher will decline. This would be unfortunate, because a good story well told may kindle the imagination in a way which few other experiences can match. In a story a child can see and come face to face with the problems of his environment without the complication of personal involvement. He may find in a story some compensation or relief from the strains of everyday life. In the early stages story-telling can play a vital part in stimulating an interest in books before pupils are ready to read for themselves. Later on it is often a means of introducing children to books which they might not find for themselves; the practice of reading specially chosen passages and then inviting those who are interested to finish the book for themselves can be particularly effective.

Simple folk tales involving a good deal of repetition, realistic stories about people and things closely corresponding to their own experience, and stories about animals are the most suitable for young children. It may be necessary at this stage to exercise some care so as to avoid stories which may disturb certain children. By the age of eight most children have passed from an exclusive pre-occupation with the here-and-now to a perception, however dim, of what is more remote in space and time. Stories about children and life in other lands become appropriate, and a beginning can be made with such stories as "Tales from the Arabian Nights" and the Gaelic, Norse or Greek myths. Later still, some children will demand true adventure stories about real-life heroes and explorers; but few will fail to respond to the appeal of such favourites as Alan Breck or Huckleberry Finn or Gulliver.

Much depends on the manner of telling. A pleasant, natural delivery, careful but not over-precise, is desirable, and an avoidance of whimsy or condescension. Over-dramatic presentation may at first excite and amuse, but children soon become weary of it. In passages of dialogue, however, it is useful to indicate changes of speaker by appropriate changes of voice. At the later stages the reading may sometimes be entrusted to pupils who have an assured fluency and some ability to vary the pace and pitch of their reading. Sound and television broadcasts and films of stories are valuable in allowing children to hear other voices and other ways of speech.

Reading

Reading has always enjoyed a central place in the curriculum, since it has been generally agreed that through reading man obtains necessary and useful information, extends his knowledge of other people, places and times, and finds food for relaxation and for the exercise of imagination. The rapid and continuing development of non-literary media within recent years, however, suggests the need for reappraisal and restatement of the function of reading in the modern world. Not that the mass media are necessarily hostile to the growth of reading habits. On the contrary, there is abundant evidence that many people have been led, through the agency of television and to a lesser extent of films, to read books which in previous times they would never have contemplated reading. Nevertheless, as a means of keeping men acquainted with current affairs, reading may lack the immediacy of radio and television; and knowledge of other places, people and things may be extended more rapidly and sometimes more effectively through these media than through reading. Granted all this, reading has, in relation to the needs of the individual, certain important and lasting advantages over the mass media. With the latter he has to take what is given as it is given; content and pace are alike beamed at some imaginary average person. Books, on the other hand, can be used at the reader's will; he can go as fast or as slow as he likes; he can find what he wants at the moment when he wants it.

Reading, therefore, will continue to be of crucial importance. The challenge of other media does, however, emphasise one point of which the schools must take account. If reading is to play any lasting part in the life of an individual, he must always see a purpose in reading, whether it is for personal satisfaction and pleasure, or to obtain information. Hence the importance of establishing interest in books and lasting reading habits as early as possible. What is called the "mechanics of reading" cannot be isolated and treated *in vacuo*. Reading matter must therefore always be meaningful, and if the pupil's techniques and interest in reading are to be fully developed, it must at all stages be stimulating and varied.

Effective reading involves:

(*a*) the ability to read silently and, if necessary, aloud, with ease and enjoyment;

(*b*) understanding of what is read;

(*c*) some capacity for reflecting on what has been read; (Obviously this cannot be carried very far at the primary school stage, but if a child is eventually to attain the power of balanced criticism and appraisal, he must be encouraged as early as possible to relate what he reads to his own background of knowledge and experience and to form and express his own opinions and judgments).

(*d*) taking action, if necessary, on what has been read. (Clearly it is of the greatest importance to be able to follow written or printed instructions carefully).

Reading should not be regarded as an isolated subject in the curriculum, since it is involved in most classroom activities at some time or other. When the child is learning to read, it is expedient and necessary to take reading practice separately; but even at this stage, the child should be realising that reading enters into many of the things he is doing both in the classroom and outside.

Getting Ready to Read

By the time they come to school, most children have already been used to seeing printed notices, advertisements and the like all round them outside school, and know that these have a significance for daily life. Thus the incentive to learn to read may be present; but most children are not ready to begin the process at once. In order to be able to read with understanding, a child needs a vocabulary of spoken words, based on his experience, with which printed words can be associated. The level of his intelligence and the nature of his environment are contributory factors in determining the spoken vocabulary which he has acquired before entering school. The child who comes from a home where speech is freely used or who has attended a nursery school will have a richer experience of language than one who has not had these opportunities; it is already clear, however, that as television penetrates into more and more homes the opportunities of the linguistically under-privileged are being progressively extended. At present it is still true to say that only a minority will be ready to begin reading immediately they come to school; for the great majority of children a preparatory period is necessary in which both their general experience and their range of language may be widened.

It is the school's first duty, therefore, to provide an environment fruitful in possibilities of varied experience and in opportunities for free and spontaneous talk. Stories told by the teacher and by the pupils help to enlarge vocabulary and give a valuable training in listening and concentration. Visual material of all kinds can interest and stimulate. Not least, if an interest in reading is to be fostered, it is most important to ensure that from the beginning the child is surrounded by books and by other printed material.

No attempt is made here to give an exhaustive list of the criteria which indicate that a particular child is ready to begin learning to read. The first essential is that he should seem to want to do so. Indications of this are an obvious interest in books, in pictures and in printed words. He should also be able to express himself fluently and intelligibly, and should have developed some degree of visual, oral and aural discrimination.

When the transition from informal pre-reading activities is being made, each child has to be considered individually. Some children, because of poor general ability, immaturity, emotional difficulties or adverse home circumstances, may not be fit for systematic learning until they have been at school a year or more. On the other hand, children who are ready to begin learning at once should not be held back, though this does not mean that they should omit altogether the activities associated with the pre-reading period, since these may benefit them in other ways.

Learning to Read

The various methods of teaching reading which have been fashionable at different periods of time are too well-known to bear further repetition. It will be sufficient to say, therefore, that methods which rely on a predominantly phonic approach are open to the objections that many words in common everyday use cannot be mastered by phonic analysis, and that reading matter which is based solely on a vocabulary of words which can be sounded is apt to be very dull and stilted. On the other hand, look-and-say methods can at the outset provide reading matter which is both meaningful and interesting but by themselves they give the child no means of coping with unfamiliar words. Standard practice, therefore, represents a compromise which gives the child the advantages of both approaches without their defects, a look-and-say beginning being supplemented at a later stage by training in phonics. Recent attacks on the compromise have made much of the fact that some children have failed to learn by mixed methods and, having failed, have been successfully taught by other, usually modified phonic methods; it does not, of course, follow from this that these children would have been any more successful if they had been taught by phonic methods from the beginning. It must be recognised, however, that not all pupils will necessarily respond to the same approach and that, if one procedure fails, it may be time to experiment with another. For this reason, some teachers utilise more than one series of reading books as material for basic practice.

Concern at the number of children who fail to learn to read or who find difficulty in reading even under enlightened modern teaching methods has resulted in experiments based on different approaches. One of these is based on the assumption that for many pupils traditional spelling is a major obstacle to progress in reading, since in English there are often numerous ways of writing one sound, and several different sounds which can be represented by the same letter. By adding to and modifying the letters of the traditional alphabet, a revised set of symbols (the Augmented Roman or Initial Teaching Alphabet) has been devised, which eliminates these variations in spelling and pronunciation and ensures consistency in the formation of words. Other systems are being tried in which colours are used to help the child over the difficulties which may be created by traditional spelling. Each of these new approaches has found enthusiastic supporters, but it would be premature to attempt any final assessment of them at this stage.

With the ablest pupils phonic instruction may be unnecessary or largely incidental, as these pupils soon demonstrate their ability to recognise in a new word phonic elements already learned in other words. For the great majority of pupils, however, phonic instruction, if given at the appropriate time, can be very beneficial. As a rule, phonic teaching should not be begun until pupils have acquired a reading vocabulary by look-and-say methods, and can appreciate that the various sounds of which words are composed are represented by letters, singly or in combination. The learning of even a small vocabulary of look-and-say words gives a pupil opportunities of making the desired association between sound and symbol, and therefore makes phonics meaningful to him. With slower learners it may be advisable to postpone the introduction of phonics for a considerable time, since such children are easily confused by phonic drill if it is introduced too early. Phonic instruction should be closely associated with the rest of the pupils' reading material, and the words chosen to illustrate phonic rules should as far as possible be within their own vocabulary.

A good way of ensuring that reading material is meaningful and related to pupils' interests and stages of development is by means of story sheets, or books made by the teacher, with illustrations and wording often suggested by the pupils. An experienced and skilful teacher can, in fact, provide in this way sufficient reading material until the child is ready to attempt simple story books. On the other hand, established reading series, which most teachers use, have the virtue of ensuring ordered progress. The important thing, however, is that there should be no cessation of other activities which involve reading. In particular, pupils should be introduced to as many varieties of reading material as possible, including notices, posters, street names, and so on. In order to encourage reading for pleasure, there should be a good supply of library books and supplementary reading books suitable for a fairly wide range of ability.

Because of differences in the rates at which pupils learn, individual and group teaching, as has already been emphasised, is necessary throughout the primary school. It is, of course, essential that the composition of groups should be kept continuously under review and should be adjusted in accordance with the progress made by each individual pupil. It is particularly important that account should be taken of temporary retardation resulting from absence. At the later stages, when the mechanics of reading are fully mastered and there is no need for oral reading as a check on accuracy, group organisation is less natural than individual reading, except in connection with an activity which involves a number of children.

Continuity and co-ordination are essential throughout, but they are specially important during the period when a pupil has still not completely mastered the mechanical skills. It should not be assumed that all pupils will learn to read without difficulty, even by the most enlightened methods. There will always be some whose progress will be slow. Each teacher should be thoroughly familiar with the individual needs of her pupils; and the importance of co-operation between teachers, particularly in the exchange of information about individual difficulties and the methods used in the effort to overcome them, cannot be over-stated.

The Development and Use of Reading

Once the mechanics of reading are mastered, reading can and should enter into all or most classroom activities. Except in the case of the least able pupils, there should be no occasion for periods to be set apart specifically for the teaching of the mechanics of reading. Since individual and group methods will be the rule, the common practice of providing large sets of class readers is pointless, and the cost of doing so hinders the building up of a wide variety of books to meet individual needs and different purposes. In order to provide ample material for all pupils and for various types of activity, a classroom should be plentifully supplied with reading matter which covers a fair range of difficulty and content.

Since the fundamental purpose of reading is to understand what is read, and since in everyday life silent reading is the normal practice, training a pupil to read aloud is little more than a means to an end. In the early stages, some practice in reading aloud is necessary so that the teacher can help the pupil, correct his errors and assess his progress; even then, however, once the learner begins to show progress, he should be given opportunities to read silently. When the mechanics of reading have been mastered, reading aloud, in so far as it takes place at all, should have a different function. Ability to read aloud fluently and confidently is useful for pupils who have to communicate to a group or to the class some items of information, the results of some piece of research, or reports on some group or individual activity. Poetry will normally be read aloud by teacher and pupils. Apart from these occasions, reading aloud has little or no place in the work of the later stages of the primary school. Indeed, within recent years some interesting experiments on speed in reading have shown that vocalisation in silent reading has a slowing effect and may arise from an excess of oral reading. The practical implications of this are that silent reading should be introduced at the earliest stage as an essential element in learning to read, and that oral reading should be discarded as soon as possible, except for some special purpose.

Nevertheless, since any pupil may be called on at some time to read aloud, it is important that some attention should be paid to good technique. Audibility is obviously important, and may require some conscious emphasis where individual and group methods of learning tend to make pupils speak quietly in order to avoid disturbing others. Correct phrasing is unlikely to be much of a difficulty if the initial training has been effectively directed towards reading for meaning and if good habits of silent reading, with a minimum of vocalisation, have been encouraged.

The teacher's main effort, however, must be directed to developing the pupils' skill in silent reading, and providing them with occasions and material for exercising it. The concept of learning as mainly activity in which the pupil finds out as much as possible for himself is likely to involve a great deal more reading than is often done at present and much more reading harnessed to specific purposes. To be suitably equipped to undertake this, the pupils need careful training in silent reading techniques. The aim is to enable them

(*a*) to read a passage rapidly in order to grasp its general gist;
(*b*) to read rapidly in order to find a particular piece of information;
(*c*) to read a passage carefully in order to understand as completely as possible the ideas it contains.

These aims can be achieved to a large extent by means of individua work, possibly through some such approach as that recently made familiar by reading laboratories, in which sets of reading cards carefully graded and interesting in content, provide ample self-corrective material for interpretation and also for various aspects of language study. Books of extracts for comprehension can also be useful for this purpose; but it is important, in the selection of such material, to ensure that the length and content of an extract are suited to the stage of development of the pupils, and that the questions asked are sufficiently searching. Suitable material may also be found in information books, books of instructions, novels newspapers, brochures, pamphlets, or magazines, and assignments of various kinds may be based on them; much of the material may require to be duplicated in school. In this way the pupils can be given experience of handling different kinds of reading material for a variety of purposes, and can develop a mastery of a progressively wider range of vocabulary and language usage.

At the same time there is a place for the group lesson in which the pupils, under skilful direction from the teacher, read a passage with a particular purpose in view, and perhaps go on to discuss some aspect of it. Here, as in individual work, it is important that the teacher should select material which is interesting, suitable for the stage of the pupils' development, and as varied as possible in content and style. The treatment will vary according to the nature of the passage and the teacher's purpose. The pupils may be asked to read a passage rapidly in order to find a few specific points, or to discuss its content in general. They may be required to read it with care in order to consider in detail the ideas it contains, and to express their opinions about the writer's arguments and conclusions. The teacher, by judicious questioning, can enable the pupils to read more and more into the passage, and to weigh words and sentences carefully, so that they appreciate not only what is said but also something of what is assumed or implied. Attention may be directed to the vocabulary of the passage, or to such features as punctuation or sentence or paragraph structure. There will also be opportunities for considering the effects that the writer has tried to create and the ways in which he has used language to achieve them. The emphasis should be on silent reading; there is no need for the passage to be read aloud before it is discussed.

As the pupil's skill in silent reading develops, he should be encouraged to an increasing extent to apply it to reading in connection with activities or work in any branch of the curriculum where it is appropriate, and he should learn how to use books of information in the class or school library. This type of reading requires much training and encouragement from the teacher, since the purposeful use of books of information involves the power to select what is relevant to the immediate need and also the ability to present it either orally or in writing in an acceptable form. Particularly in the early stages pupils may be bewildered or discouraged by vague injunctions to go and find out about something. Preparatory work will usually be needed, in the form of demonstration by the teacher, followed by oral discussion and closely supervised practice in the use of simple reference material. For development on group or individual lines some system of assignment or "discovery" cards may be useful. The cards will increase in difficulty as the pupils acquire greater facility and confidence. The earliest cards should ask simple factual questions, indicating precisely where the answer is to be found on the particular page of a particular book. Later cards might refer simply to the book, and later still to a variety of appropriate books. Such a system, however, is only a means to an end, and must be discontinued as soon as the pupil can apply his experience and knowledge of what is available in the class or school library to find out some piece of information which he needs.

As a child progresses in his ability to use books of reference competently, a good deal of his reading and of his writing can be done in this way in connection with the various branches of the curriculum. There is, for example, much scope for developing group activities connected with the study of topics and centres of interest; the various tasks of discovering, discussing, recording and reporting can be assigned to individuals or groups, each group concerning itself with a particular aspect of the topic under consideration. The sharing of information often helps to overcome the difficulty some pupils find in putting together information collected from a number of different sources. Pupils should become aware that books are not the only source of information, and for this purpose a plentiful supply of magazines, newspapers, pamphlets and illustrative material of all kinds is needed.

If the pupils' ability to make efficient use of reference material is to develop, it is essential that they should be familiarised as soon as possible with alphabetic order and with the use of an index and a table of contents. Preliminary training can be done with the simplest of all books of reference, a dictionary. Dictionary training might be, and indeed often is, informally begun in the infant classes. Dictionaries of appropriate difficulty and range should be available at all stages, and the pupils should be encouraged to use them freely to check the spelling of words they wish to use in their written work, to look up the meaning of unfamiliar words which they encounter in their reading, and to find out interesting things about words.

Since in the full development of the child the imagination as well as the intellect has to be catered for, reading for enjoyment is no less important than purposeful reading for information. If more than lip-service is to be paid to this idea, it is essential that the child should have time and opportunity within school hours for reading of his own choice, and that he should be allowed to take books home. There are risks, but a child who has not finished a book in school and shows the urge to finish it in his own spare time should receive every encouragement. In any case, it is an essential part of

children's education that they should be trained to respect and care
for books.

It has already been suggested that the reading of a story or part
of a book by the teacher will often help to encourage children to
read for themselves. Any interest which is aroused, however, may
be quenched if the teacher, uneasy because this kind of reading
cannot be assessed in the traditional way, tries to examine the child
on what he has read. The only test of value is whether he shows the
desire to read more. Sometimes, however, pupils will be quite ready
to engage in an informal discussion about books which they have
read and enjoyed, and this may help to encourage others. Sometimes
also they will wish to write about incidents or stories or characters
they have encountered in their private reading; this should not be
made a compulsory task.

Any attempt to influence children's choice of reading matter
requires great tact. The teacher should begin by showing an interest
in whatever pupils may happen to be reading. Almost all children
pass through a stage at which comic papers and the like bulk largely
in their reading. No good is done by attempting to apply adult
standards or by suggesting that this kind of material is worthless.
If, on the other hand, the teacher encourages her pupils to talk
freely about anything they may be reading, and if she appears
sympathetic, they will listen more readily to an occasional gentle
hint that the qualities which interest them can be found also in other
books of more permanent value.

Poetry

Poetry should provide an enjoyable experience. Young children,
indeed, make an immediate response to its sound and rhythm and
are excited by the vivid, colourful use of words. It is important to
ensure that this spontaneous delight is not replaced, as sometimes
happens at present, by a feeling of indifference, if not of repulsion.
Ideally, a teacher should enjoy poetry herself; if she does not, or if
she feels some diffidence about her ability to make the experience
an enjoyable one for her pupils, she might choose to take advantage
of wireless programmes and gramophone records of poetry readings
or even enlist the aid of some other member of staff who is enthusiastic about poetry and can fire pupils with her enthusiasm.

The first essential, then, is a recognition that poetry is something
valuable and pleasurable in its own right. It is not something to be
presented to the pupils merely because it has been traditionally
included in the curriculum. Nor is it a means of speech training or

a way of filling up odd moments between more "important" activities, or a quarry for exercises in comprehension.

It is vital that poetry should be read aloud or spoken, so that children can savour the sounds and the rhythms, and that there should be many occasions for hearing poems. Nothing, however, does more to kill the love of poetry than the time-honoured practice of insisting that children repeat over and over again the words of a poem as a prescribed task. Indeed, far too much emphasis has been placed on the memorisation of poems chosen by the teacher. If children are allowed to enjoy poetry and have access to a wide range of poems, they will, given a little encouragement, be willing to learn by heart anything which particularly appeals to them.

The selection of poems to meet children's interests requires considerable skill. At the early stages there is no difficulty, since the traditional nursery rhymes with their direct language and robust rhythms make an immediate appeal and provide obvious scope for a spontaneous response through movement. Many anthologies designed for children, however, are marred by sentimentality or insincerity and should be used with care. Ample material exists to satisfy the interests of children at this period—poems about animals, poems about familiar everyday things and people, poems which tell stories, both fanciful and realistic, humorous poems. Scots verse should find a place at all stages. There is no need to reject poems on the ground that they contain words or images which may not be immediately understood; often children respond intuitively to a poem because of its sound and rhythm when their intellectual comprehension of its content is imperfect. Nor should the choice be limited to poems with regular rhythms and rhyme schemes; many poems which are suitable for young children follow no recognisable pattern, but make their impact through a particularly vital and vivid use of words. Children should not leave the primary school with the idea that poetry has to rhyme, and that all the lines must be of the same length.

Verse-speaking in chorus, besides being an activity which children enjoy, can be a rewarding experience. In considering how different parts of a poem should be spoken, the pupils can come to appreciate the effects which the poet has tried to create. Not all poems are suitable for this treatment. It is best if the poem chosen has some variety of rhythm and mood, so that the pupils may see the need to vary the pace, volume and pitch of their speaking, and so that some lines may be spoken by the whole class, others by different sections of the class, others again by solo voices. The temptation always to polish choral verse-speaking so as to make it fit for performance

should be resisted. Occasionally, however, the pupils may want to
have the satisfaction of perfecting their own rendering of a poem
of which they are particularly fond, and they should be encouraged
to do so.

No one anthology, however good, is sufficient to satisfy the
needs of a teacher or her pupils. The class library should certainly
contain a good deal of poetry. A variety of books will encourage
pupils to read poetry in their spare time and to build up their own
anthologies of favourite poems.

If the pupils have enjoyed a poem, the experience in itself is
sufficient, and it is not necessary that they should be asked to talk
or write about it. On occasion, however, they will welcome the
opportunity to make a drawing or painting to illustrate a poem or
to dramatise its content. This is usually a much more satisfactory
way of discovering what impression the poem has made upon them,
if this is felt to be necessary, than asking them factual questions
about the content. They should also be invited, if they wish, to
write poems of their own on the same or similar themes. There is
in general much more room for the writing of poetry in class
than normally takes place. At present this activity is often only
encouraged for a particular purpose, such as a contribution to a
school magazine. No attempt should be made to restrict the children
to particular patterns of rhythm or rhyme; verse-writing should
rather be regarded as an opportunity to experiment with language
as an expression of feeling and experience.

Written English

Written English, like spoken English, is a means of communication
as well as self-expression. Like speech, it may be personal and
individualistic, but it is subject to more conventions and involves
more skills which must be learned. In teaching written English,
therefore, the aims are two-fold:

    (*a*) to encourage fluent expression in as spontaneous and varied a
         form as possible;

    (*b*) to train the pupils gradually to a mastery of the accepted
         conventions.

In the achievement of these aims timing is of great importance. If
excessive or premature emphasis is placed on formal elements,
spontaneity can easily be lost, and the pupils' work, though perhaps
mechanically flawless, becomes lifeless and lacking in originality;
on the other hand, complete disregard of spelling, punctuation and,
above all, sentence structure makes writing as communication
unintelligible and unacceptable.

Continuous Writing

The first crude impulse to write is already present in the scrawl which the child of pre-school age makes in imitation of his parents or older brothers or sisters. At the infant level in school, drawing, writing, reading and speaking are all closely linked. When a child has made a drawing, the teacher commonly writes what the child says about it below or on the opposite page of his book. The child will try to copy what the teacher has written, and eventually he will reach the stage at which he is ready to write his own "story", first with help from the teacher, finally by his own unaided effort. Often the child wishes to write about something he has made or done. Every encouragement should be given to these tentative attempts at composition, in which the children have a free choice to write as much as they like about anything they like. It is important, however, not to force the pace; if the teacher always seems to require a story or a caption, writing can easily become distasteful to the child. Children must also be allowed to progress in accordance with their abilities and individual interests. For example, not all children have something to write about every day. No attempt should be made at this stage to insist on the correct spelling of difficult words or on high standards of handwriting. The teacher should, however, take note of badly formed letters and ensure that the child receives guidance in writing them correctly in a handwriting lesson.

Too often at present the free writing which is common in many infant classrooms ceases abruptly in class P III or class P IV just at a time when more opportunities are presenting themselves. This break in the continuity of an important development cannot be justified. From class P III onwards, as the curriculum and the interests of the children widen, all their interests and activities, both inside and outside the classroom, can provide occasions for writing which is spontaneous and not restricted by considerations of form and accuracy, and which, above all, can be an enjoyable experience. Among the forms of writing which have already proved popular are diaries, books about personal interests, original stories, dramatic scenes and even whole plays. The teacher who is prepared to encourage her pupils to write will find no lack of opportunity or material in the curriculum itself—in topics studied in history and geography, in discussions of current events, in art and craft activities, in dramatic work, in natural and physical science, in aspects of health education and road safety, in observations made in field studies or in visits to places of interest, in library work and recreational reading, in projects and centres of interest.

If children were given more opportunity for free writing in the

I

later stages of the primary school, it is possible that a not inconsiderable number would reveal a talent for creative self-expression, in verse as well as in prose. Indeed, there is a definite place in the primary school for imaginative self-expression in writing, just as there is in art and craft, music and drama, as a means by which the pupils can express their feelings and exercise their imagination. If children are allowed to write freely, some will naturally "splash about with words". Others may be stimulated to do so as a result of experiences provided by the teacher—a piece of music, a picture, a poem or a piece of prose, a passage from the Bible, a film, a story, or a particularly strong sensory experience. They may also be encouraged to imagine how various other people would feel in particular situations, and to express themselves in appropriate ways. By such means the teacher may extend the range of written work beyond what the children might normally attempt in their free writing and may help them to see how language can be adapted to various purposes.

At the same time the pupils must have training and practice in the plain, clear, precise writing which is essential for the effective communication of information and ideas, and it will be necessary for the teacher to discuss with them how form and language are influenced by the subject-matter and the intention of the writer. She may take, for example, an area which they have studied in geography, and consider with them how a straightforward description of it might be written. An account of a simple experiment in science may provide an occasion for learning ways of setting down clearly and accurately the various steps in a process. Letters requesting background material for projects, letters to absent classmates, to other schools, or to children in other countries will involve discussion of appropriate forms of language and presentation. Various other ways in which the form of writing can be made to suit the writer's purpose can be demonstrated and practised through the writing of telegrams, post-cards, notices, instructions, lists, definitions, descriptions and so on. The ablest pupils may be able to tackle the difficult exercise of presenting a logically developed argument. In the older classes especially, the pupils can derive benefit from the study of models which illustrate effective writing in various styles, and the able pupils particularly should be helped to note features of form and language which they can use in their own writing.

Pupils are often eager to write when they know that their efforts will command a wider audience than the teacher, and in these circumstances are ready to examine their work with a critical eye.

The teacher, therefore, should make a point of displaying the pupils' work and of reading aloud interesting examples of their writing. Class books, wall newspapers, and class and school magazines also provide added incentives for both factual and imaginative writing; and the communal report which results from a project or from group research can be a most useful activity.

It will be evident from what has been said above that there is now much less need than hitherto for the traditional type of formal composition on a theme prescribed by the teacher. Occasionally, however, in class P VI or class P VII a subject may be set, provided the subject chosen is within the experience, actual or imaginative, of the pupils, in order that teacher and pupils together may discuss its possibilities and the different ways in which it might be developed. More useful, perhaps, than full-length compositions of this kind are frequent short pieces of writing, on some topic suggested by the teacher, perhaps as a result of class discussion or of some item of news.

The Development of Formal Skills

In written English, whether free or directed, fluency is at all times of cardinal importance. This quality is only too easily stifled by premature or excessive pre-occupation with formal accuracy. On the other hand, a child must eventually realise that effective communication involves intelligibility and conformity with certain accepted conventions. The appropriate time for the teacher to intervene can be determined only by a careful consideration of the circumstances of the individual child.

Course books may provide material for teaching the conventions of written English; but the practice of indiscriminately following the exercises in such books, regardless of the needs of individual pupils, results in disappointingly little transfer of what has been practised. The selection of exercises ought to be determined by the pupil's stage of development, the evidence of his written work, and the purpose of the lesson. Such exercises are, moreover, only useful supplements to and never substitutes for actual writing.

The teaching of the formal aspects of written English in the primary school should be closely linked with the fundamental aim of developing fluent and varied expression. For the majority of pupils, grammar in the traditional sense, with its system of prescriptive rules based on outmoded notions of "correctness", has contributed very little to this end. The more modern approach, on the other hand, should assist them to use words, phrases and sentences in as interesting and colourful a way as possible. It demonstrates that in English, as distinct from inflected languages such as Latin, meaning depends more on word order than upon any other grammatical principle. Moreover, it shows how the choice of words and constructions varies according to the situation and purpose of the speaker or the writer.

Some children absorb the patterns of normal written English unconsciously through imitation of what they hear and read, and reproduce them in their writing from quite an early stage. But the majority of pupils do not seem to make marked improvement in their ability to construct sentences unless some supplementary training is given. In the younger classes this may take the form of judicious suggestion and guidance given informally by the teacher to individual pupils while they are engaged in free writing. Later, however, it may also be necessary to provide systematic training and practice, in order to secure the writing of sentences that are acceptable in form and varied in type. Some success has recently been achieved in the realisation of this aim through the systematic treatment of basic sentence patterns, which pupils use as models and imitate; from the simple patterns used for statements, questions and commands pupils proceed, as their ability to imitate and repeat develops, to more advanced patterns involving co-ordination and subordination. This approach has much to recommend it, provided that pupils have ample opportunity at each stage to practise in their continuous writing the patterns they are learning. It is important also to diagnose and cater for the varying abilities of pupils; it is, for example, pointless to require pupils to work through examples of patterns with which their writing shows them to be already familiar.

The progressive understanding of the structure of sentence patterns involves, in the first place, the classification of words according to their function, and, in the second place, the examination of structure in terms of subject, predicate and so on. Thus a noun should be referred to first as a naming word that "patterns" like "boys", or has the same function as "boys", in the sentence pattern "Boys play football", then, for convenience, as a noun. The other parts of speech should be introduced in a similar way. The consideration of sentence structure, which is a more sophisticated process, should also be associated with pattern and function. The depth to which study of this kind should be taken depends on the ability and interest of the pupils. For the least able, it is sufficient that they should recognise the simpler sentence patterns. For the ablest pupils grammar may become an interesting and rewarding study in its own right.

Since punctuation is no more than a series of conventions designed to help the reader, and is subject, moreover, to changes of fashion, it should not be over-stressed or treated too elaborately. On the other hand, children have to become aware that in writing intelligibility can often be ensured only by means of punctuation. The use of the comma, period, question mark and quotation marks should, therefore, be taught as required by the pupils for their written work. Some, even from quite an early age, punctuate naturally through observation and imitation of what they find in the books they read. The need for punctuation can often be brought home to young children if they are asked to read their own work aloud and if attention is drawn to places where they instinctively pause in their reading, All should be encouraged, once awareness of the purpose of punctuation has begun to develop, to look carefully at the pointing of passages in their reading.

Writing in an acceptable form requires correct spelling. Spelling should not, however, be regarded as an end in itself and treated as a separate subject. The aim is to ensure that in their continuous writing children are able to spell correctly the words which they want or need to use.

From this it follows that to a considerable extent spelling should be treated as something personal to each child, and many teachers have found that one effective way of awakening the interest of individual pupils in the correct forms of words is to encourage them to make their own spelling dictionaries. These consist of words which the pupils tend to use frequently in their free writing, and to which, probably because of misspellings, the teacher has drawn their attention. Other words which arouse their interest, encountered perhaps in reading or in the preliminary discussion of a piece of writing, may also be entered for future reference. For convenience the pages of these individual lists should be in alphabetical order, but it is by no means necessary that this order should be known by heart. This would, for example, be quite inappropriate in class P II, a stage at which many infant pupils begin to enjoy compiling a simple, personal "dictionary". These lists provide a valuable first step in training the children to look closely at words, and to rely more and more on their own ability to verify spellings about which they are uncertain. This last point is particularly important. At all stages it is desirable that dictionaries appropriate to the needs of the pupils should be available for reference, and that every encouragement should be given to the pupils to use them whenever they are in doubt.

There is, of course, a certain basic vocabulary which it is desirable that all children should be able to spell, and in an attempt to guarantee that such words are learned some teachers make use of standard spelling lists, specifying units of various sizes, perhaps of four or five words, for each day's work. Some pupils, however, as a result of wide reading may not need such routine or systematic practice, which should be kept for those whose written work shows them to be in need of it. If lists are used, care must be taken to see that the words chosen for learning are related to the pupils' needs and that the words are learned in meaningful contexts and not in isolation.

Since correct spelling is largely a matter of visual recall, and since the only evidence of a pupil's mastery of spelling is his ability to reproduce words accurately on paper, practice in writing words is of fundamental importance. As, however, pupils sometimes wish to write words they have only heard and not seen, it is also important to try to guard against the type of errors which arise because of inaccurate pronunciation. Careful enunciation and articulation help to prevent such mistakes.

A short piece of dictation can be on occasion an effective revision test of words which the pupils have already learned. The value of dictation, however, should not be exaggerated. Dictation tests spelling; it does not teach it. Consequently, if used at all, it should be used sparingly. The most useful type of dictation exercise is one which the teacher has compiled herself using words which the pupils' written work has shown to require particular care and practice.

Assessment and Correction

In all the activities outlined above, the teacher has a vital part to play, not only in providing occasions and stimuli for writing, but also in evaluating the pupils' progress, diagnosing particular weaknesses, and deciding what kind of action is appropriate. She must at all times keep a watchful eye on the written work of her pupils, whether it is free or directed, so that she may give praise and encouragement where it is appropriate, and note aspects of their composition which require to be taken up with individual children, with a particular group, or if need be with the whole class. Any comments that she makes to a pupil about his work, either orally or in writing, should, as far as possible, be expressed in positive and encouraging terms, and should take into account his ability and the effort he has made.

The extent to which the teacher should correct written composition, or insist on correction by the pupils, is a matter for her to decide in the light of her own circumstances. It is probable, however, that teachers in the past have been too concerned with the correction of errors, and the more important aspects of good writing such as originality of thought and expression have been overlooked in the search for technical inaccuracies. Excessive correction, mechanically applied to pupils of all levels of ability, serves very little purpose, and may do more harm than good. It is particularly important to avoid premature application of adult standards, especially in spelling and punctuation. Indeed, it is debatable whether the free writing which the pupils undertake should be corrected at all. In directed writing, the object of correction by the teacher should be to draw the pupil's attention to errors which he might reasonably be expected at his stage of development to avoid, and to ways in which his writing might be improved. Correction, therefore, should be selective and confined to a few specific points which have been recently emphasised by the teacher or which the pupil, in view of his ability and attainment, should have mastered. Just as important, however, as the correction of errors is the recognition of positive merits—choice of words, variety of expression, development of ideas. As far as possible, it is better for the teacher to discuss errors with individual pupils while writing is in progress. In the early stages the teacher will normally have to specify the type of errors and suggest the correction herself, though even quite young pupils can be encouraged to check their own spelling by reference to an appropriate dictionary. Later she will be able, by the use of a code of symbols, to refer merely to the type of error and to ask the pupil to correct it for himself. At the upper stages the pupils should be encouraged to look for their own mistakes, by reading over their work from one point of view at a time. In classes P VI and P VII there is much to be said for allowing pupils, working perhaps in pairs, to exchange their writing and to scrutinise one another's efforts with a critical eye; this kind of practice may serve to make the pupil examine his own work more carefully.

Time should not be wasted in requiring pupils as a matter of routine to make a draft, and after correction, a fair copy of every piece of writing; nor is it necessary that they should write out corrected versions even of parts of their compositions. Nevertheless, the practice of roughing out a draft or plan before writing a final version is of value, and should be encouraged in the older pupils, especially when they are engaged in directed writing, or are writing something for display, or a contribution to a class magazine or newspaper, or a report on a group project.

Chapter 20

Environmental Studies

TRADITIONALLY arithmetic, history, geography, and science—at least in the form of nature study—have been pursued largely as separate studies from about stage P III. While it is still recognised that each of these subjects has a place in the primary school curriculum, they have been grouped together in this chapter under the general title of "Environmental Studies", since they all in some degree involve activities which are grounded in the child's observation and investigation of his surroundings. Furthermore, they have in common the two-fold aim of fostering in the child a desire to know more about the world around him and of training him in the skills he needs to interpret it. This is not intended to suggest that all the material to be studied can be found directly in the environment, or that none of these subjects is ever to be pursued as a separate discipline. Indeed, in the case of mathematics, especially that part of it which is concerned with number, there must be from the earliest stages training in specific skills that will enable the pupils to handle quickly and efficiently the mathematical situations which will arise in the course of their other activities. It is mainly for this reason that mathematics is treated in a separate section in this chapter. Nevertheless, even in mathematics the environment is the base from which the pupils will most frequently set out on their explorations further afield, and to which they will frequently return.

Classes P I to P IV

In the early school years the child's awareness of his surroundings is vivid but indiscriminating. It is the teacher's task to encourage him to look more closely at his environment, and to help him, through observation and exploration, to isolate, identify and understand the various aspects of his environmental experience and to develop the language he needs to describe them.

At these stages history, geography and science should not be treated as separate disciplines. The approach should rather be through "centres of interest"—aspects of the environment chosen by the teacher because of the opportunities they offer for observation, investigation, discussion and recording, and for the development

126

of the concepts of quantity, space and time. Centres of interest might arise from a specific event, from a topic in which the children show a spontaneous interest, or from a situation which the teacher has deliberately created to arouse their curiosity. Some of these will involve "geographical" work; some will involve "scientific" experimentation; some will lead to stories about past people and events; some will involve all these types of exploration. All will be concerned with using the child's interest in his environment in order to train him to observe it more closely and more accurately, and in order to introduce him to special kinds of study which, when he is ready to do so, he will distinguish as "history", "geography" and "science". In this chapter, therefore, no attempt is made to differentiate historical, geographical and scientific investigations until stage P V; for it is not until then that most children have progressed far enough in the organisation of their knowledge to appreciate the need for subject studies.

In the rich setting of the modern infant room with its clay, sandpit, Wendy House, junk box, nature table, and dressing-up chest, the teacher is constantly creating opportunities for that training of the senses which is the starting-point of environmental studies. By playing with such material and talking about it, the child comes to perceive similarities and differences of an elementary but significant kind, and at the same time acquires the vocabulary to describe what he sees or discovers. Objects can be classified, for example, as long or short, heavy or light, rough or smooth, hard or soft, hot or cold, sinking or floating; sounds as loud or soft, high or low; colours as light or dark, bright or dull. Playing with sand and water, pebbles and stones gives experience of the behaviour of these substances under various conditions and can develop notions of pouring, packing and weighing. An area set aside as a weighing and measuring corner can be useful for the development of the concepts of weight, length and capacity. The concept of time may be encouraged by reference to the times of events during the school day and also by reference to the broad divisions of the clock.

As children grow and develop, they more and more imitate the adult world and arrange their play material in recognisable patterns such as shops and farms. The patterns will vary according to the environment of the school. The shop can provide first-hand experience of number and money. The classification of the articles displayed for sale might be made in various ways and the children made aware that many of our common commodities come from other countries. A model of a farm is sure to delight and interest children; some may wish actually to model the farm and the animals; others who have small animal toys at home may wish to bring them to school and place them in position on the model; and through discussion the children will learn of farm produce, both animal and vegetable, and perhaps something of the cycle of activities on the farm. Wherever possible, the children should engage in simple practical tasks such as preparing soil, planting seeds in a classroom garden or outside, or making butter in a simple way.

At the infant stages the teacher should also draw the children's attention to the people, the places, the objects and the natural phenomena that make up their everyday environment. The functions of various people who work in or near the school—the janitor, the postman, the dustman, the policeman, the traffic warden, special visitors such as the doctor, the dentist, the nurse—may be considered. The children may be encouraged to make a simple three-dimensional representation of the neighbourhood by laying out on the classroom floor models, blocks or other materials to indicate the location of factories, churches, houses, traffic signs, farms, fields, streams, and other features. Later, they may be introduced to the idea of a plan by drawing round the various items in the model. They may also make simple weather observations, and record them first by drawings and later by symbols and words; they may learn about local weather lore. Every opportunity should be taken to foster an interest in the appearance and habits of plants, birds and other animals. If the children have pets, they might be encouraged to bring them to school, or even to keep them in school, provided that they can be adequately housed and cared for.

In all these enterprises the teacher is mainly concerned with creating situations which provide opportunities for activity and discovery. Much of this activity should stimulate conversation and self-expression through modelling, drawing, painting, dramatisation and simple statements in writing.

At stages P III and P IV the pupils are generally eager to enter into the lives and experiences of people whose background is different from their own. Stories of prehistoric children, of earlier civilisations, of man as hunter, farmer, and city dweller, of people in other countries provide in the first instance imaginative experiences worthwhile in themselves, and in addition can lead to questions and discussion, and may stimulate some children to follow up certain topics in their own reading. Moreover, they will suggest interesting opportunities for the making of diagrams, pictures and models, the keeping of class or individual record books and scrapbooks, dramatisation and role-playing, the setting-up of displays on the classroom walls or on a history table.

At this level the historical or geographical importance of the subject matter should be secondary to its appropriateness to the interest and capacity of the child, but by stage P IV topics and stories may usefully be grouped in order to illustrate selected aspects of our civilisation. The lives of great men and women, for example, might be grouped so as to show our Christian and Scottish traditions and our inheritance in all fields of activity—exploration, science, medicine, art, music, literature. Stories of other people will constantly throw up topics which show man's need, in all countries and in all ages, for shelter, food and fire, and which demonstrate his struggle to come to terms with his environment. At this stage the pupils should also be encouraged to take an interest in current events, and the teacher may occasionally use the "news" period to relate a discussion of current events to what the pupils have learned about life in the past or in other countries.

At the same time, the children are normally ready to examine the familiar features of their immediate environment in closer detail than before, and centres of interest can be developed in order to involve them in various kinds of investigation. The following are suggested as examples of the kind of topic which could appropriately be pursued by groups or by individual pupils at stages P III and P IV.

Weather

Initially all the work should be based on direct observation and should lead to simple recording. For example, wind force might be noted by its effect on leaves and on the branches of trees, by the behaviour of smoke and clouds. This might lead to the observation of cloud forms and associated weather conditions. The notes kept by the pupils should be such as to enable them to record, over a period, the number of wet or fine days, broad variations in temperature, the frequency and strength of the winds from various compass points, the variations in the length of daylight and darkness, the path of the sun in the sky. Conditions prevailing elsewhere, for example in deserts, monsoon regions and arctic wastes, might then be compared with local conditions. Observations of rainfall can readily lead to experiments using soil models and a watering-can to show how streams, rivers, islands and peninsulas are formed. The pupil might be encouraged to follow weather forecasts, and mention might be made of the value of, for example, frost warnings to the food grower and lorry driver, gale and fog warnings to aircraft and shipping.

Transport

The pupils might begin by keeping a count of the numbers and types of vehicles passing the school at different times of the day; at first this could be done, where it is practicable, by using matchboxes in columns to represent individual vehicles, and later by a column graph or histogram. They might also try to find out where the vehicles are going. Occasion might also be taken to stress road safety, and to explain, discuss and possibly dramatise some of the situations dealt with in the Highway Code.

Where there is a railway near the school the pupils might investigate where the trains go, what they carry, the functions of the various people who work on them, and why certain goods are transported by rail and not by road. Real or imagined journeys may lead to a discussion of the varying geographical features of the countryside en route, and of landmarks of historical importance.

If the school is situated near a port or an airport, the pupils might find out about the various types of ships and aircraft, the purposes for which they are used, and the routes they follow. This might lead them to seek up-to-date, factual information about the people they would meet and the things they would see in the course of particular journeys by sea or air. The pupils should be encouraged to gather relevant material in the form of pictures, diagrams, stamps, labels, brochures and specimens in order to build up their own impression of life in a particular place. The globe should be used to trace some of the routes in order that pupils may be introduced to the shape of the earth and the distribution of land and sea.

Clothing

The pupils might examine fabrics and compare in a simple, experimental way their strength and their capacity to absorb moisture. Their attention might be drawn to the combustibility of certain fabrics, and to the number of accidents in the home which are caused by the use of inflammable materials. Stain removal might also be attempted in a very elementary way. In dealing with natural fibres, reference can be made to their plant and animal origin and to the country from which they come. The pupils might also discuss the kinds of clothing worn at different seasons of the year, in our own and other climates, and by people in various types of occupation, for example doctors, miners, welders, firemen, and workers in shop and factory.

Local Studies

The locality will provide a variety of nature topics. Investigations should not deal in great detail with a particular object—for example the structure of a single flower—but should be based on a more general study of a pond, a hedgerow, or a garden. The children should be encouraged to observe, to think for themselves and to record their observations, mainly in the form of fair-sized drawings or models which may be built up as a group or class activity. For city children museums, parks and the contents of shops are good sources of material for study. When appropriate, attention might also be directed to animals, crops and other products of the farm. Thus if the teacher is focusing attention on the farmer and farming activities, different types of soil and the plants and animals found in them might be introduced in an elementary way. In rural areas the farm might be studied in closer detail. Investigations might include the cycle of operations throughout the year, the types and numbers of animals in particular farms, times when young are born, and the number of young per birth, animal foods in summer and winter, farm products and their marketing.

Quite short journeys can often provide opportunities for some investigation into the activities, industries and historical associations of the area, and further studies may furnish information about how the locality came to be as it is, how it got its name, how people lived there in the past, and how improvements have been effected.

It is an easy step from the rough outline drawings which at an earlier stage the young child has made of his school or his home or the nearby streets to the 50-inch and 25-inch plans of his immediate neighbourhood. On these he can recognise easily the streets and roads which are familiar to him and the houses in which he and his friends live. These plans, copied roughly by the teacher and the class, can be used as a basis for simple projects, for example on the distribution of different kinds of shops in a town, or crops in a rural area, or industries in an industrial region. Later, the pupils might proceed to an examination of the 6-inch map of their area, and should be encouraged to familiarise themselves with the district which it covers. Towards the end of stage P IV many children will be ready to be introduced to the convention of representing variations in the height of the landscape by the use of layer colouring, and to the $\frac{1}{4}$-inch map on which their own area figures. All the sheets of this map include part of the coastline of Scotland, and routes to and from the seaside can be worked out. Only then will the pupils be ready to move on to the map of Scotland. During this work there should be ample opportunity for the pupils to make their own

maps, initially to a scale of their own choice, and to become familiar
with some simple geographical terms.

Classes P V, P VI and P VII

When children have attained the age of about nine years, they
appear to enjoy collecting, classifying and arranging, and show
significant changes of attitude; their interests have widened and
they have reached a level of maturity as a result of their development
and experience when they can begin to embark on more systematic
subject studies. This does not imply a total separation into subjects
at these stages, nor that each will receive the same amount of
attention and time each week or even each month. Prominence
should still be given to the development of centres of interest. In
addition, the teacher should feel free to develop aspects of current
interest, and the emphasis will change from time to time according
to the centre of interest and the extent to which subjects are co-
ordinated. A balance, however, should be aimed at over a period
of time, possibly a term.

Real study is not passive absorption of facts from teacher and
textbook, to be tested by verbal answers at the end of term. One of
the teacher's main functions is to stimulate active investigation by
pupils, individually, in groups, or as a class, encouraging them to
collect, select, arrange and record material. In this work there are
many possible sources—parents and grandparents, biographies,
background books, encyclopaedias, textbooks, pictures, films, radio
and television programmes, museums, field studies. There are also
many possible ways of recording the results of research—by means
of diagrams, simple graphs, wall charts, handbooks, class magazines,
talks, plays, models. Each classroom should contain historical, geographical, mathematical and scientific books of appropriate levels
of difficulty which the pupils should be encouraged to use.

Apart from the cross references which the teacher continually
makes from one subject to another, there are various ways in which
subjects can be made to support one another. In class P VII a very
general study of a topic such as world food supply may be approached
from several points of view. Population trends in different countries
may be studied, and illustrated by means of histograms and other
types of graph. It may be appropriate to introduce experiments on
the preservation of food, on the germination and growth of crops,
and on the control of pests. Reference could also be made to the
World Health Organisation and the Food and Agriculture Organisation and to eminent men such as Ross and Fleming. A project on

coal might bring in the coalfields and mining towns in Britain and abroad, the miner, a discussion of past and present conditions of labour and housing, the industrial revolution, coal gas and its by-products, and imports and exports of coal represented graphically.

There is a very definite place for field studies at all stages in urban as well as in rural schools, provided that the places chosen for visits or investigation are appropriate to the age of the pupils. There might be:

(a) studies made in the pupils' own time, for example finding the answer to questions posed by the teacher or arising from their own interests;

(b) brief visits to the area round the school in school time, with possibly two or three longer excursions per term;

(c) studies based on a field centre within the county or beyond its limits.

Fact-gathering should not exclude other considerations. The pupils should be encouraged to pay heed at times to the sights and sounds of nature for the sheer pleasure they bring—the sounds of the shore or moorland, the graceful movements of animals and birds, the scents of woodland and meadow, and in the towns the kaleidoscope of colours in busy streets, the pattern of lights or the textures in walls and roofs. When the senses are alerted in this way, new impressions are stored, new phrases are found to describe them, and new thought is generated.

Field studies must be carefully planned and co-ordinated. The head teacher and his staff should know the possibilities offered by their pupils' environment and together should work out lines of approach appropriate to each stage. The pupils must be active and may be guided in their work by questionnaires. Preparation beforehand by teacher and pupils and follow-up after the field work are essential. Interpretation of what has been observed is as important as observing and recording. Log books, diaries, tape-recordings, and records of visits are valuable, and at all stages plans, sketches, diagrams and Ordnance Survey maps should be employed.

History

Education through history depends as much on how the child learns as on what he learns. Historical studies provide excellent opportunities for reading, looking and listening, for selecting, organising and recording information by various means, and for reviewing and discussing material. The important thing is that children should learn primarily by working for themselves.

History also provides subjects for imaginative work in drawing and painting. Children need little encouragement to draw and model their own conceptions of historical persons, events, places and things. Some of the illustrations, especially if made on the spot, for example during field work, may be quickly produced without attempts to secure accuracy of technical detail.

Those who learn about the past should be encouraged to talk, write and read about history. The oral contributions of the pupils can take many forms. In addition to brief factual answers to questions, there is the lively discussion which can be initiated by the study of a good illustration, a transparency, a filmstrip, a film, or a programme on radio or television. The pupils can dramatise an episode from history, identifying themselves with characters and scenes from the past. Dramatisation may start with miming, dialogue being introduced later, and afterwards the pupils may be interested to be told the actual words of the characters they have been playing. Puppetry can be used in the same way. The example of television should not be neglected: the techniques of programmes such as "Press Conference" can be usefully employed in the classroom.

Writing will start with "free" stories and brief explanatory captions to drawings, progressing through sentences which supplement pictures to imaginative reconstructions, eye witness accounts, diaries, and the production of class newspapers. Each pupil should have his own record book. This should be lively and colourful, illustrated with pencil and crayon drawings, cut-outs, maps and diagrams.

A good supply of reference books and other source material should be readily available in the classroom. Possible historical sources are poetry, music, pictures, filmstrips, films, radio and television programmes, museums, local antiquities, background books, biographies, historical novels and encyclopaedias. Though factual knowledge is the very stuff of history, facts themselves are of subsidiary importance in the primary school and should be used principally to build up in the child's mind a historical knowledge which makes him aware of the differing characteristics of life in the main historical periods.

FACING PAGE:

*The pupils will enquire, observe, experiment and perhaps even link cause
and effect* (page 141).

It is not possible to have pupil participation, which is essential to understanding, if the children hurry through an outline of the past which reduces the leading characters to stock figures. Only when children are on familiar terms with the people who lived in a particular period can they enter in imagination into the ideas and events of the past; and only then has history any value for them. They must be given the time and the opportunity to read what the people said and wrote, to look at the pictures which they painted of their houses, to share their domestic chores, to accompany them on their journeys. There is scope here for individual and group research, the children themselves looking for information in books, pictures, museums and other sources, and so becoming familiar in a simple way with the techniques of independent study.

If studies are to be made in such detail, then it is necessary for the teacher to make a radical selection of periods, and to adopt what has come to be called the "patch" method, where the study of history may be limited to three or four patches per year. This method consists of selecting and studying a series of periods so that a many-faceted and living portrait of each age or period—for example the Romans, the Stuarts, the Industrial Revolution—may be drawn by the pupils. Study can be arranged under different headings—great men and women, homes, social customs, food, dress, work, transport—in accordance with the abilities and interests of the pupils, and group or individual research projects on them can be developed. The patch method ensures a fuller appreciation of a past age than is otherwise possible; the pupil can to some extent reconstruct the period in his imagination. The child who really knows a past age vividly should be able, by making comparisons between "then" and "now", to look with some detachment at his own environment, making judgments which, though not wholly accurate, will be genuinely his own.

The fact that gaps are left in the child's knowledge of history is not important. Indeed, it is probable that too much thought has been given in the past to devising ways of inculcating in primary pupils a sense of historical time. Few of them are capable of fully appreciating historical time before they leave the primary school. It is more important at this stage that the word "Stuart", for example, should bring to mind, not a date, but a clear picture which

---

FACING PAGE:

The teaching of measurement might take pupils into the playground (page 63).

K

truthfully portrays the spirit of the period. The teacher can, however, try to create a sense of continuity by treating the patches mainly in chronological order, by outlining the contexts in which they occur, and by encouraging pupils to make their own time charts on which they can record main historical turning-points. It is also possible to link the patches by pursuing the study of specific topics such as dress, housing, exploration, transport and industry in the evolution of history. The interest which the patch method arouses will encourage pupils to read for themselves about periods which have not been studied in class, and suitable books should be available.

A convenient way of introducing children to the types of investigation associated with the patch study may be through a consideration of life fifty years ago. Here the sources to be exploited are obviously at hand. Most children have available to them photographs and the memories of their parents and grandparents. A firsthand list of changes in the neighbourhood can be built up which can be supplemented and corrected by books and newspapers, and the differences among the stories which the children collect may illustrate the need to question hearsay evidence. The history table can become the nucleus of a small folk-museum. A surprising collection of significant relics of the past can be brought by the pupils from home. When such relics have been found to have meaning, the pupils are ready to consider more remote periods. As a preliminary to the more intensive work at later stages, such an investigation can be easily blended with a general survey of the environment, showing how the present has grown out of the past.

The child will have a better understanding of his own world and his place in it if his historical studies attempt to add up to the story of mankind rather than of some smaller group. The Scottish teacher, however, would not wish her pupils to leave the primary school without some knowledge of their own country and its story. A period such as the Stuarts or the Industrial Revolution may form the basis of a patch in which a whole age can be looked at from the Scottish point of view. In other patches—the mediaeval period, for example —Scottish source material should be used as much as possible.

Wherever suitable, local history should be used to illustrate the national story. This practice gives life to facts which become meaningful to children by reason of their relation to their familiar environment. Not all localities are full of romantic interest or have links with historic events and personages, but even a mention of local places, persons or events can bring to many topics a heightened interest and a sense of reality. This should be exploited by organised visits to such places.

However valuable the intensive study of a remote period may be, the pupil should also have some understanding of his own times and the society in which he lives. The teacher should continually illustrate past by present and vice versa. She might begin from stage P V to encourage comparison between "then" and "now"; each "patch" might include elements which tie the present to the past, either as the most recent stages of an evolutionary process or as a subject for contrast. She should also encourage the children to take an interest in important events at home and abroad reported in newspapers, or on radio or television. The discussion which follows is the opportunity for the teacher to supply background facts and set the child on a search for pictures and information to be recorded in a twentieth century class news-sheet.

What pupils gain from the study of history in the primary school is difficult to assess. Their achievements may be to some extent intangible, but they are nevertheless very important. The pupils should have a keen interest in the past and in the present, and some grasp of the idea that the object of the study of history is to establish the truth. They should have begun to differentiate between fact and opinion, and to see that a question has more than one side. They should have some feeling for change and development, and a grasp of what is meant by such broad time divisions as B.C. and A.D., and ancient, mediaeval and modern times. They should also have become aware that we owe a debt to the endeavour, self-sacrifice, vision and intelligence of people in the past, and have begun to appreciate some of the problems that confront the world today.

Geography

Geography in the primary school is concerned with the description of places—natural, man-modified, and man-made—and of the different peoples throughout the world who in their sum make up humanity. The subject can be approached through the study either of places or of man himself and, provided both are eventually dealt with, it matters little which is the starting point. Any attempt at separation into physical and human geography should be avoided. This, however, does not deny the possibility of introducing lessons on physical features such as rivers, mountains, volcanoes and glaciers, especially if they have a topical interest for the pupils, but it does mean that such lessons are only a small part of a much more important and wider study.

Briefly, the aims of geography-teaching are to foster an interest in and an understanding of man's environment, and to help the pupils to acquire certain skills—the ability to write a straightforward description of an area, a place, a landscape, and to draw tentative conclusions, to draw, read and set a map, to read a photograph, to present information by word, diagram and map.

Certain general principles should be established—the dependence of man on water, food, clothing and shelter, and the interdependence of man throughout the world. It is necessary also for pupils to acquire a vocabulary of common geographical terms, for example hill, mountain, valley; village, town, city; quay, harbour, port; coalfield, oilfield.

Generalised regional geography should be replaced very largely by sample studies, which are particularly suited to young children because they make the subject matter real. A sample study is an examination and description of a particular feature, physical or human, of a region, chosen because it characterises the region or represents man's reaction to it. A fiord on the west coast of Norway, a Pacific atoll, a crofting community of north-west Scotland, the woollen industry of the Borders might each be the theme of a sample study. Eye-witness accounts, pictures, films, simple statistics, maps and diagrams provide some of the source material, and accurate verbal descriptions, diagrams, maps and plans are the tools. Generalisations, especially about people, should only be made at the end of a series of sample studies according to the age and ability of the pupils.

The treatment of an area should touch on aspects of its general culture such as its history, music, art and architecture. For example, if sample studies of France are being taken, then something of the culture of France as illustrated by the chosen samples will also be learned.

At stages P V, P VI and P VII, the pupils are ready to look beyond their local area to the homeland and to the rest of the world. They have already done so in a rather incidental fashion and a more systematic approach now seems appropriate; indeed the abler pupils at stage P IV may be ready to make this approach. Consequently the programme at these stages should cover a range of different kinds of environment, a range of standards of living, and a range of areas showing growth, change and development.

Pupils should be trained to work on their own or in groups. If an area such as North America is being studied, groups or individuals can investigate different aspects, and a general regional study by the whole class will preserve the unity of the work. Similarly, at the later stages, if a major grassland is being studied—the prairies of Canada or the Steppes of Russia—the teacher should encourage the pupils to integrate the work done on a number of similar areas into a systematic study of grasslands in general so that they appreciate that there are similar patterns of climate, land use, and human activities and developments in different parts of the world.

The Local Area

The local area is the appropriate starting point for wider geographical studies, illustrating geographical facts and principles— altitudinal zoning of vegetation, river erosion, rocks and soils, the seasonal rhythm of human activities, markets, route centres, urban expansion. It provides conditions and activities which can be used as yardsticks when dealing with other lands and it allows good geographical methods to be practised. In addition the local area should be the first regional survey. This choice helps to impress on the pupils the unity of a region or landscape, and avoids the idea that a landscape is made up of separate items—relief, climate, vegetation, land utilisation, industry, settlement. At this stage use should be made of the appropriate one-inch Ordnance Survey map and of air photographs.

The Homeland

The study of the homeland will include not only the local area as outlined in the previous paragraph but also other areas of Scotland for comparison and contrast with it, and a few general themes on Scotland such as holidays, routes, farming, power, imports and exports, manufacturers and important towns. It is probably advantageous to spread the studies of different aspects of Scotland over stages P V, P VI and P VII, in order to use them as links in the study of areas elsewhere.

The remainder of the British Isles should not be taught regionally. It is better to select a few topics or areas for study such as:

(a) towns of special historical, industrial or other significance;
(b) London; trade;
(c) sample studies of particular types of settlements and landscapes—a port, an iron and steel town, a Welsh mining valley, a Yorkshire Dale, the Vale of Kent, an Irish village;
(d) at least one national industry; sources of raw materials; markets and products.

A complete coverage of England, Wales and Ireland is not possible. As in the study of Scotland, the work should be spread over stages P V, P VI and P VII and linkages made wherever possible. For example, when the pupils are investigating the largest towns in Scotland, they might at the same time make a map of England showing all towns with a population of 100,000 or more, and then make some comparisons between the two countries. This type of study might be conveniently carried out at stage P VII.

The Remainder of the World

A complete coverage of the world is equally impossible. Areas or peoples should be selected because they illustrate certain geographical principles and not because they are in the Commonwealth, or U.S.A., or U.S.S.R. Very often, however, examples can be selected which satisfy both requirements.

Areas, peoples, topics and themes should therefore be chosen to illustrate a range of environments. These could be based on:

(a) major climatic and vegetation zones—desert, tropical grassland, Mediterranean;

(b) different kinds of terrain—mountains, plains, coasts, islands;

(c) different kinds of towns as agricultural, industrial, commercial and administrative centres.

A year devoted to "How People Live" would enable many of these environments to be included and would show the variety of ways of life, besides introducing the pupils to the influence which the environment exerts over man, the extent to which he has succeeded in controlling it, and the interdependence of peoples in different lands. Studies of physical features and phenomena—glaciers, rivers, volcanoes, waves—can also be made.

The topics chosen should involve a good deal of practical work and research by the pupils. If, for example, at stage P VII, cereal farming and the growth of wheat are studied, this might suggest a project on the Canadian prairies. The class can then be divided into groups working on separate topics—a wheat farm, Regina, Winnipeg, a cattle ranch, Edmonton, oil wells, communications and types of transport, a journey to the prairies from Scotland, settlement and the history of settlement, relief, climate and vegetation. This might be consolidated in a class display entitled "The Prairies of Canada Today", which should include written descriptions, pictures, diagrams, maps, and perhaps a tape-recording.

The pupils should be given opportunities to link geography with other subjects, in particular with current affairs. This linkage should lead, for example, to the study of the modern history and the geography, even if only on a very limited scale, of such areas of major importance as the U.S.S.R. and the U.S.A. and to some appreciation of the role they play in international affairs. Especially at stage P VII, the pupils should also acquire some knowledge of geography as a subject, and something of sound regional geography. In addition, they should acquire some knowledge of the basic skills and techniques peculiar to geography—map-reading and map-making—and of others common to several subjects, such as the art of description. On this knowledge and these skills will their future work in geography be built.

Science

The aim of science at these stages, as in other environmental studies, is to cultivate an attitude of mind as a result of which the pupils will enquire, observe, experiment and perhaps even link cause and effect. It cannot be too strongly emphasised that it is no part of the purpose of science in the primary school to cover a rigid syllabus as a preparation for the science of the secondary school, nor should there be any insistence on the memorising of a particular body of factual knowledge. A study may arise from a chance occurrence, from an interest expressed by the pupil in something he has seen or read about, from a desire for some explanation of how this works or why that has happened, or from an interest deliberately implanted by the teacher.

A pupil may bring an electro-magnet to school, or the teacher, because of other relevant work being done, may place one on the "discovery table". If pupils have enquiring minds, they will ask questions. "What does it lift?" "How much does it lift?" "How can you make another one?" There is no need to seek for any formal course of experiments or for any set of conclusions to complete the enquiry; the purpose is rather that the pupil may learn from playing with his magnet that he can, for example, lift more nails if he has more current or more turns of wire or if he keeps the turns closer together, and that the one he makes works better with an iron centre than with a wooden one. In his play he may have learned incidentally about conductors and non-conductors and how to join two batteries to double the current.

Again, questions may arise about, say, the use of "anti-freeze" in cars; such questions may lead to an investigation along the following lines. Two bottles, one filled with water and the other with a mixture of water and anti-freeze, are placed out of doors on a frosty night and examined the following morning. The experiment is then repeated, with a varying quantity of anti-freeze in the mixture, in order to find the minimum amount required to prevent freezing on a particular night. The bottles of mixture are now left on a window ledge and changes in colour are noted. This may prompt a further investigation of the effect on colour of exposure to light. This can readily be done by exposing one mixture to light and by keeping a comparable mixture in the dark, to show the use of a control in an experiment. Observation will also show that a sediment is formed, and so the reason for flushing the cooling system of cars may be understood.

In the investigation of a particular topic the teacher should be aware of the possible lines of development, but should be prepared to be guided in her actual choice by the pupils' response and thought. On one occasion, for example, the pupils may wish to know where tap water comes from and how it goes to the top of a tenement, and may go on to a study of the local water supply. On another occasion they may wonder why water in a pond or river is deeper than it looks. This may bring up the old parlour trick of the penny which cannot be seen at the bottom of a bowl until water is poured in, and subsequently the pupils may look at a pencil half immersed in water. When the question of sound is raised, some pupils may show particular interest in the speed at which sound travels. Others may be more interested in trying various ways of making a higher or a lower note, and may proceed to make and use simple monochord instruments. Some may explore other ways of producing notes and may make, for example, a set of chimes with tumblers containing different amounts of water.

At these stages pupils might be encouraged to demonstrate the working of their toys or their "experiments" to the rest of the class; the enthusiasts will soon encourage others to take their turn. Such demonstrations provide good training in preparation, in self-confidence, and in oral expression. If they are followed by comment, questions and discussion, prompted by the teacher if need be, further demonstrations may be given. For example, a boy may wish to show the class his new bicycle with a three-speed gear. What can he tell the class about cycling on the road with these different gears? How can the class find out what changing the gear really does? Such questions may induce the class to look at gears elsewhere, for example in a hand-turned egg-beater or a clockwork motor, and to experiment with "meccano" gear wheels.

Full advantage should be taken of the pupils' interest in living things. Classrooms should have, wherever possible, living plants and living animals in conditions as nearly approaching those found in nature as can be arranged. Vivaria of all kinds are particularly valuable for the development of sustained observation, and for training in the need for constant care if plants and animals are to be kept alive. There is no need to start with elaborate vivaria: one type of animal is sufficient at first. Spiders, lady-birds, snails, earthworms, stick insects, to name but a few, are easy to obtain and keep at home as well as in school. Modern plastic materials, cut with scissors and joined with sellotape, provide simply made transparent cases for observing, for example, a spider spinning its web on some twigs. A jam jar with some meat in it and a funnel fitted to the top will soon attract bluebottles. When several have entered, the funnel may be replaced by a fine gauze. Eggs will be laid and the full life history can be followed if a piece of paper is put in to allow the larvae to pupate.

Observation out of doors is essential. Advantage should be taken of the immediate surroundings, whether they be the fields adjoining a country school or the parks or wastegrounds of a city. It is not always practicable to take classes for nature rambles, particularly in an urban area. Much can be done, however, out of school hours if pupils are encouraged to look and to record their observations. What one pupil sees and reports to the class may arouse interest and encourage others to look for themselves. Sometimes the pupils may be set a specific task—to look for caterpillars in the garden or on wild plants and to bring in a caterpillar and a bit of the plant it was found on, or to find out the three most common weeds in their gardens. The first, with some attention to providing the conditions necessary for pupation, should allow pupils to see the insect which develops from the caterpillar; the second should lead to a study of the plants and their way of life and why they keep on reappearing.

Having observed which gardens have spring flowers first, which fields show germination first, the pupils may go on to study exposure, or to consider why some soils are cold soils, Failure of seeds to germinate in a particular plot may prompt further discussion. In the country the activities of rooks, lapwings, owls and sparrowhawks may be noted, and the pupils may seek information about their food and discuss whether or not they are beneficial to the farmer. In the town the starling or the sparrow might be the subject of study.

How far a particular pupil or group of pupils may go into any one study or topic will depend on the questions they ask and how they seek to answer them, or on the questions raised by the teacher if she wishes to direct attention to some particular point.

There is no need for elaborate, ready-made equipment. Much can be done through improvised apparatus, information about which is available in many books. The great advantages of improvising apparatus are that children have a part in the making of it, that they learn much in the actual making, that they will be encouraged to try other things at home and so extend their first-hand experience. Any child with a comb and a piece of cardboard on a sunny day can produce parallel rays of light and see for himself what happens when they go through his magnifying glass or meet a mirror. Further, when the working of a model depends on the accurate fitting of its different parts the making of apparatus may provide an additional incentive to careful measurement and construction. Much useful material can be acquired if pupils bring to school articles which are being discarded at home, such as plastic bottles, jam jars, old alarm clocks, clockwork toys, mirrors from handbags or powder compacts, torch batteries, egg-timers. In time schools will build up stocks of the tools and materials they need for making models or apparatus.

Among the most essential items is a good supply of reference books for the use of both teachers and pupils. Films and radio and television programmes also provide excellent material for experimental work and practical activity.

In all the work in science, reporting and discussion should be a basic part of the training. The pupils should also be given training in recording in various forms—by histograms, pie charts, graphs, coloured diagrams—and occasionally they might describe in writing experiments which they have performed. There is no place for notes dictated by the teacher or copied from the blackboard.

Some fields of interest which have already been explored in primary schools are outlined below. The items listed should not be regarded as a syllabus but rather as topics which in appropriate circumstances might be profitably pursued. The choice of topic should arise from the pupil's obvious interest in what is happening around him, both inside and outside the classroom.

Ourselves; hygiene; pulse; rate of respiration; body movement.

Other Living Things: insects and their life histories; direct observation from vivaria; spiders; snails.

Field Work: bird and other animal studies; tree and flower studies; exploration of habitat; extension of earlier studies of weather; weather lore; single observer forecasts; forecasts from weather maps.

Water: rain; water supply; solution; detergents; water power.

Heat: fuels; fire precautions; insulation; expansion; evaporation.

Air: breathing; burning; ventilation; air currents; flights.

Materials: examination and informal classification of objects, e.g. wood, metal, plastic, textile.

Machines: machines in the home; pulley, lever, gear wheel; the bicycle.

Electricity and Magnetism: electrification by friction; simple circuits; electro-magnet; mariner's compass.

Light and Colour: mirrors, lenses; the prism and colour.

Sound: production and speed; simple musical instruments.

Sky and Space: planets; sun and stars; conspicuous star groups.

Mathematics

In a broad sense education is the process of helping the child to understand his environment; consequently, it is essential that he should become aware of those aspects of it which are best expressed in terms of number or which show qualities of regularity, order, pattern, structure or form. Since these concepts are at the very core of mathematics, the use of the word "mathematics" in connection with the work of the primary school needs no justification. What remains, however, is to decide what elements are appropriate for the primary school child and by what methods they should be approached. This will undoubtedly involve the introduction of some topics and ideas which by tradition have been delayed until the secondary stage, but which, if properly presented, have real relevance and interest for pupils in the primary school.

At this point it may be well to give a word of reassurance. Teachers whose experience of mathematics has, since their own schooldays, consisted only of teaching arithmetic may at first sight be alarmed by some of the technical expressions used—Moebius strips, sets, bar graphs, triangular numbers. The matter is, however, not essentially one of difficulty but rather of unfamiliarity with current mathematical terms, and the interested teacher will find that even a short study of some of the many books available will give her all the information she requires.

For many years the teaching of mathematics in the primary school has been almost exclusively concerned with the development of skill in reckoning and the perfecting of routine methods of carrying out computations. Much of this work has little general educational value. Many topics, such as division of compound quantities, are introduced arbitrarily before the underlying concepts have been established, while others, such as profit and loss, are taught before the pupils have any need of them either in or out of school. The introduction of calculating machines, from the simplest desk calculator to the most complex electronic digital computer, in a rapidly increasing number of industrial and scientific fields has also weakened the vocational argument for intensive training in computation. Only those skills which the child requires in everyday life or which are essential to his understanding of elementary mathematics need be taught.

Material for the study of mathematics is to be found everywhere in the child's environment. Four cups require four saucers; three chairs are not enough for five visitors; Mary's four dolls and Jean's three dolls provide a family of seven for the Wendy House; John, who has five pennies, requires another three pennies to buy a toy costing eightpence; five cars have twenty wheels; twelve sweets can be shared equally among three girls; four boys cannot be given five marbles each from a bag containing fewer than twenty marbles. From situations such as these the child's concept of number is gradually developed. Ribbon has to be measured and fitted to an apron; flour has to be weighed for baking; the class aquarium has to be filled; a journey to the seaside has to be planned and the cost estimated. From a variety of such practical experiences an appreciation of the concept of quantity will emerge at different ages for different children, and the need for number in order to secure precision in measuring will be realised. If the child looks at his environment with an enquiring mind he will find a rich variety of shapes and a wealth of spatial relationships of fascinating interest. For example, he will see the triangle in leaf form, bridges and cranes, the spiral in springs and sea shells, the hexagon in snowflakes and honeycombs, the circle in wheels and hoops. By observing and working with such objects he should gradually discover their most obvious properties. Thus our concern in the primary school should be with number and quantity and shape and with the relationships which exist within these aspects of the environment.

The method of approach is of the utmost importance. If pupils are to be attracted to a mathematical mode of thinking, they must find their mathematics in as wide a range of meaningful experiences as possible. They must be given the opportunity to experience the joy and excitement of exploration and the thrill of discovery. Much of the pupils' time will be spent in counting, lifting and pulling, pouring, comparing, measuring, folding and cutting, arranging and re-arranging the materials of their environment, constructing models, making maps and plans, and all the time searching for new relationships and seeking ways of expressing them. Discussion among groups of pupils and with the teacher will be required to ensure that vaguely conceived ideas are clarified and that the pupils acquire the necessary vocabulary to understand and express these ideas. Essential skills must still be practised and basic facts mastered, but excessive repetitive drill in mechanical calculating and in learning standard methods of solving problems should not be allowed to dull the pupils' interest or cramp their initiative. Sufficient competence in the basic skills can be achieved with briefer periods of practice than were previously thought necessary. Problems should, as far as possible, arise from real situations and lead to activity, such as measuring or looking up a reference or carrying out an experiment; they should stimulate discussion and on occasion may require a variety of approaches before a final method of solution is reached.

There are important implications in this kind of approach. Firstly, there must be readily available in the classroom ample supplies of suitable material, the miscellaneous objects and stuff of the everyday environment, as well as appropriate structured apparatus, and there must also be the space in which to work with this material. Secondly, since pupils will progress at times by following their individual interests without regard for a preconceived logical sequence of development, programmes of work have to be flexible; they should not be drawn up on a day-to-day or week-by-week basis but should rather provide a broad and tentative framework of general development, listing the kind of activities and opportunities that may be expected over a fairly extensive period of time. In order to cope with this variety of activity the work of the class will have to be organised to allow a blend of individual, group and class learning, with the teacher frequently prepared to adopt the role of helper rather than of leader and instructor.

Number

Various kinds of practical work in number are normally tackled in modern infant rooms. Much more, however, requires to be done in the later stages of the school, where at present it is only too common for a child to develop skill in reckoning in a more or less abstract way, with little real understanding of the nature of the processes. Practical exercises should be used throughout so that the pupil can develop a proper understanding of notation and come to realise that each of the four operations is merely a re-grouping of the material; that addition and multiplication are methods of combining groups of different size and of the same size respectively, while subtraction and division are ways of sharing, the first into unequal and the second into equal groups. It is important that the teacher should so order her classroom that the pupils can discover as many as possible of the number relationships and processes for themselves. It should be accepted that children who have been allowed to develop in this way will at first use less orthodox and perhaps superficially less efficient computational techniques than those who have been trained in the traditional rules of reckoning.

The use of some form of structured apparatus will make it easier for the teacher to provide her pupils with the opportunity to discover many of the number relationships for themselves. At the same time it should help the pupils to a clearer understanding of the nature of the processes involved in computation, and give them useful experience of sequence and ratio. No one type of apparatus, however, should be considered sufficient in itself to meet all the needs of the child. For an adequate grasp of number the wider environment must be constantly exploited to provide essential experience.

Wherever possible, the teacher should help her pupils to develop an interest in other aspects of number such as pattern, and to look for special relationships between numbers. For example, in the multiplication tables arranged as a square array, the cells occupied by multiples of three or perhaps eight might be shaded and the pattern observed and discussed. Again, some children, when examining special sequences of numbers, might discover that the sum of consecutive odd numbers, beginning with unity, is always a square number, and that the sum of any two consecutive triangular numbers is also a square number.

A simple introduction to binary arithmetic might be attempted with the abler pupils. This can be done by making up weights ranging from one to 15 ounces and using only 1, 2, 4, 8 ounce weights. Later these pupils might translate numbers in decimal notation into binary notation, and vice versa, and carry out addition and subtraction in the binary scale. Experience of this kind will give the pupils a clearer understanding of the principles of place value.

In the top classes John Napier of Merchiston might be briefly mentioned and a set of his rods made and used. The more able pupils should be able to understand the principles underlying the construction and use of the rods.

Quantity and Measurement

The use of number for measurement, if it is to be meaningful to the developing child, must be closely related to his increasing grasp of such concepts of the physical world as quantity of matter, weight, length, area, volume and time. The varied experiences which help to develop these concepts should be included as part of the work at each stage and should be provided in a variety of situations both inside the classroom and out of doors. Each child must be actively involved in the process of discovery; demonstration is not enough. An outline of one way in which the topic of length can be developed is offered as an illustration of this method of approach.

The pupils are encouraged to compare two objects for length—pencils, for example, or pieces of coloured ribbon. This leads easily to the use of words implying comparison. Next, they put three or more objects in order according to length, and make a record by drawing coloured lines to correspond with the relative lengths of the objects compared. Questions such as "Which is wider, the classroom door or the cupboard?" take the development a stage further. This type of question should be left as a challenge to be solved as best the pupils can, but helpful apparatus—pieces of string, lengths of wood, and a ruler or measuring tape—should be available. Gradually the pupils realise the need to choose a unit as a basis of comparison. For some this may be the span or a pencil length, while others, because they have helped with measurements being made at home, may wish to use the inch or the foot, and should be encouraged to do so. The teacher should be aware of the arbitrary nature of the unit and should lead her pupils to solve the same practical problems using different units, for example spans, pencil lengths, or inches. Gradually the pupils come to appreciate the advantages of using the standard measures of the yard, foot, and inch, and do a good deal of measurement in the classroom, in the corridor and in the playground, using these standard measures. The length of curved as well as straight objects is measured. As a next step, the pupils draw lines to a prescribed length, beginning with fairly long lines in the playground or on the classroom floor. To develop the idea of growth, a record at regular intervals of the size of a fairly fast-growing plant might be kept, full scale, by means of strips of paper gummed to the wall. At this stage measurements are generally made in one unit, but children who are familiar with the use of a rule or a measuring tape at home should not be discouraged from attempting to use more than one unit. For increasing accuracy the use of fractional parts of a unit should be introduced.

Once the pupils have learned to measure in a variety of single units and to solve practical problems involving these units, the use of mixed units is established, and the techniques of written reckoning gradually developed. In general, this work should be confined to the yard, foot and inch, and to not more than two of these at any one time.

With the older pupils the most important aims are to develop the ability to measure and set out as accurately as the circumstances demand, to carry out simple practical and costing calculations involving length, and to appreciate the ideas of scale and of speed.

The other measures of quantity should be developed in the same exploratory and practical way as length. Weights should be lifted and balanced, water and sand poured, simple pendulums and water clocks made and experimented with, and grids used to compare areas.

At suitable points throughout the course, and more deeply with the able pupils, the appropriate and customary degree of accuracy of particular measurements might be discussed. In length the tolerances acceptable to the engineer, the joiner, and the builder vary greatly; in weight, the weighbridge, the shop scales, and the chemist's balance have similar functions but widely different standards of accuracy in measurement. Opportunities should be found for the pupils to make rough estimates and to work out solutions to practical problems with appropriate approximations.

A brief survey of measurement through the ages will help the pupils to understand the whole concept of measurement and the arbitrary nature of the standard units. Such a survey can be undertaken by the pupils themselves, and for this purpose books of reference should be available in the classroom.

Shape

The development of activities concerned with shape and spatial relationships is more recent and less well defined than that concerned with number and quantity, and there is still considerable scope for experiment to discover a sequence of development which will progressively increase the child's power to abstract spatial ideas from his environment and organise them meaningfully. The tentative approach described below is based on work already successfully carried out by pupils in various primary schools.

FACING PAGE:

Above: Art and craft play a part in other subjects (page 62).

Below: From the beginning the child is surrounded by books and by other printed material (page 109).

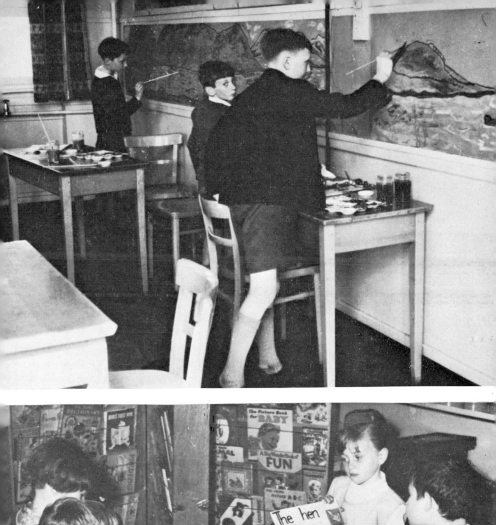

In the first instance the pupils are given the opportunity to work informally with boxes, bricks, and cartons of varied shapes and sizes; they are encouraged to build with them, to pack them into containers, and mould their shape in plasticine or other suitable material. The correct names for the solids, for example prism, cylinder, pyramid, cube, are used by the teacher, but not formally taught. Pupils cut and unfold containers to form their "nets", and then rebuild them. Later, when they have gained sufficient manual dexterity, they are given the opportunity to construct other shapes by first imagining the net for themselves and then drawing and folding it. At the outset the drawing is done on squared paper; later plain paper is used. Other aspects of shapes are investigated by constructing models in frame form with wire or drinking straws. From these exercises a great deal of knowledge of the common shapes and figures of geometry is built up in a practical way. To draw properly, for example, a square or an equilateral triangle as part of the construction of a pyramid, it is necessary to isolate certain of the essential properties of these figures. By discussion and experiment others are discovered, and the pupils begin to acquire a practical knowledge of the inter-relations of these properties. By packing cartons and boxes with bricks the concept of volume is developed gradually from the infant stage, to be progressively formalised in the later classes. The concept of area is also developed through practical exercises. The estimation of irregular areas, which later may have considerable practical value, is undertaken on squared paper. Again, by making models of simple solids, such as a cube or cuboid, with lengths of sides, say, twice or three times those of a given standard model, the ideas of ratio, proportion and scale are developed in relation to length, area and volume.

Attention is drawn to symmetry where it occurs in nature or in man-made objects, and the concept further illustrated and clarified by folding and cutting patterns on paper and by experimenting with ink blots. Many facts about, say, the square, the rectangle, or the isosceles triangle are discovered by folding these shapes in as many ways as possible into two coincident parts. Designs effected by translation, reflection, and rotation, such as can be seen on wallpaper, are also studied. It is interesting to find out which geometrical

---

FACING PAGE:

A variety of activities involving groups of different size and composition
(page 67).

figures fit together to tile a plane surface and to make designs with a set of such shapes.

Through puzzles and games spatial relationships which do not involve size and measurement or shape and ratio may be investigated informally. Maps which show only the order of places on a network of rail or air routes can be compared with normal maps which incorporate information about distances and directions. Moebius strips can be made and experimented with. The drawing up of a table and listing the number of faces F, edges E, and vertices V in solid figures might give the ablest pupils the opportunity to discover the general relation $F + V - E = 2$. Attempts to discover the minimum number of colours required for a political map which has different colours in adjacent areas will lead to much interesting speculation.

Relationships and their Expression

In the foregoing paragraphs many relationships between numbers, between quantities and between shapes have been mentioned. Pupils are on the threshold of appreciating the nature of mathematics when they themselves begin to search for and recognise such relationships, think about and discuss them, and try to express them in the most appropriate way.

When pupils begin to classify and group things together the teacher should recognise that they are making contact with the mathematically important concept of a set. This may arise when the set of pupils in the class is divided into the subsets of boys and girls. Later, by consideration of other characteristics such as colour of eye or hair different subsets can be formed. The idea of the union of subsets will arise naturally when, for example, those members of the class who have either dark hair or brown eyes are listed, while that of intersection will arise when those members with both dark hair and brown eyes are listed.

Although relationships of inequality and equality may be effectively stated in words, pupils should come to realise that symbolic expressions such as $10 > 6$ are more concise and succinct. Again, although formal algebra will not be taught, able pupils should be helped to progress from particular examples to such a generalisation as $P = 2(L + B)$ for the perimeter of a rectangle.

It will be found that certain relationships such as those of size, position and direction can sometimes be best expressed by drawing pictures, plans and maps or by making models. For example, the route from home to school might be most easily communicated by drawing a map, while the relative size and the position of school buildings would show up most clearly in a model.

The pupils should be gradually introduced to as wide a variety of graphical representation as possible. Actual outline drawings of children, at first full size and later to scale, might be used to demonstrate their relative heights. Progress towards a target for a charity might be shown on the classroom wall by a bar graph. Later, statistical counts such as the number of cars, vans and lorries passing the school in a given time could be made and the data shown in a graph. Abler pupils might progress to using line graphs to represent functional relationships such as that between the area of a square and the length of its side.

Links with Other Subjects

The ideas and concepts of mathematics should not only arise from other aspects of primary work but should also serve to illuminate them. This will be easily possible in geography, where maps and plans are used and the ideas of distance, direction and scale are met. In science the results of experiments will sometimes involve numerical data which might be best expressed as a formula or in graphical form. History will be involved when the origin and development of our methods of measuring quantities are investigated or when a time scale is drawn. Skill in measuring and drawing will contribute to the pupils' satisfaction in craft work and an appreciation of mathematical shapes may add to his understanding of design in art.

Programmes of Work

As suggested earlier, programmes of work should provide a broad framework of general development and a list of the kind of activities and opportunities that may be expected over a fairly extended period of time. Head teachers, with their knowledge of the potential of their pupils, will be able to give general guidance to their staff as to what formal work should be tackled and systematised at each stage and to what degree of difficulty it should be taken.

The abler pupils should be given the opportunity to delve more deeply and roam more widely in the mathematical field; much of this work can be done independently if a collection of popular books on elementary mathematics is available. It is equally important to make allowances for those who find even the normal course too exacting. For those whose ability falls just short of the average, there should be a definite policy of priorities and omissions. The list of deletions, for example, might be led by long division and work with all but the very simplest of vulgar and decimal fractions. For the weakest pupils, the priority should operate in the other direction, and a list of the items to be included should be established. Mere restriction to the early stages of the normal syllabus is stultifying and rarely proves satisfactory. The approach should be realistic, based on the pupils' requirements in daily life, and should aim at developing competence in dealing, at a practical level, with money, weights and measures. This should be done even if they have little skill in computation; ready reckoners should be available for these pupils. Whatever modifications are made in the syllabus to meet the needs of the less able pupils, the school should on no account curtail practical activities in order to provide more time for computation.

The scope of the work in number in which it appears reasonable to expect the ordinary pupil to be competent is indicated below in three broad over-lapping stages. An indication of the content of the course in quantity and shape is also given; some of this is appropriate to the average pupil, some to the more able. The programme suggested is neither exhaustive nor definitive, and the importance of keeping programmes of work as flexible as possible is again stressed. The essence of the approach is an appeal to initiative and discovery. The pupils' progress, which depends so much on their personal involvement, will be best encouraged by a programme which allows them opportunity to pursue their own interests.

STAGES P I TO P IV

Number

Count objects and events. Record these counts pictorially and graphically.

Ordinal numbers; sequence.

Number rhymes, songs, games.

Notations; place value. Multiplication by 10, 100, etc. Some schools may wish to introduce their pupils to more than one number scale.

The number line; position of zero, whole numbers and fractions. Illustrate addition and subtraction, using one number line, or two number lines in the form of a simple slide rule.

The four operations. Relate to practical work with objects and quantities. The extent of informal work will be determined by the discoveries which the pupils make. The facts discovered should be systematised to give the pupils an exact knowledge of the basic number bonds. Formal written work might be developed in addition and subtraction as far as hundreds, tens and units, and in multiplication and division as far as the bonds to 9×9. Use of brackets to indicate precedence: $(3 \times 4) + 2 = 14$. Equations such as $\frac{2}{3}n = 18$ without recourse to formal rules.

Pattern and relationship: rectangular, square, triangular numbers; odd and even numbers, addition and multiplication tables, odd + odd = even, even $\times$ odd = even, etc.

Quantity

Length, weight, capacity, time and money introduced by means of practical exercises involving measuring, counting, classifying, ordering, adding, subtracting, multiplying and dividing; grocer's shop, sweet shop, bank, Post Office, etc. For most of this stage single units of quantity should be based.

Graphs of relationship, e.g. bar graph of relative value of coins up to half-crowns; graphs to illustrate cost/weight relationships.

Introduction to the formal setting down of addition and subtraction of money. Formal exercises with the other measures may be delayed.

Shape

Make a collection of solids and shapes, natural and man-made, and use them in play and work. Classify, using correct names. Copy shapes using plasticine and by drawing. Change shapes using clay and plasticine, e.g. sphere to ring.

Construct jig-saws.

Pack cartons into containers. Tile with a variety of shapes. Ideas of volume and area.

Make plans and models using solids and shapes, e.g. church from cuboids and pyramids.

Make symmetrical shapes by folding and cutting. Make ink blot figures. Make collection of symmetrical shapes.

STAGES P IV TO P VI

Number

Environmental surveys, e.g. size of family. Tabulate and record results graphically.

Notation; brief historical treatment; introduction to another number scale.

The number line; position of decimal fractions.

The four operations. Continue informal and practical work. Continue formal written work in multiplication to multiplication by two figures, and in division to division by a single figure and by 12. Illustrate associative, commutative and distributive laws of addition and multiplication. Use these laws to ease computation.

Vulgar fractions—only the most common; equivalence; order by size; fraction of a number, of a quantity; ratio; the four operations.

Decimal fractions; notation; order by size; fraction of a number, of a quantity; addition and subtraction, multiplication and division with whole number multiplier or divisor.

Example of decimal coinage; practical work in measuring on metric system.

Equations such as $3n + 5 = 14$ and $p + q = 5$, without recourse to formal rules.

Pattern and relationship; factors, sequences and series, prime numbers, average, ratio, proportion.

Quantity

More exact use of ruler, balance, clock, measuring jar, etc.

Estimation of length, weight, capacity, etc.

Make models and plans to scale on plain paper.

Draw patterns involving measurement.

Experiment with extension of springs and improvised steelyard. Draw graphs of relationships, e.g. the extension of a spring under different loads.

Costing and shopping. Construct and use graphs and ready reckoners.

Time. Calculations need only be of the type which arise, for example, from the use of time tables or holiday brochures. The stop watch; the pendulum.

Concept of speed; measurement of speed.

Formal written work to addition, subtraction, short multiplication and short division of two units of length, weight, capacity, with application to problems which might involve measuring inside the classroom and out of doors. Continue formal work in money to short multiplication and short division of pounds, shillings and pence.

Shape

Extend collection of solids and shapes.

Make models from their nets. Make frame models using wire, straws, perforated metal strips, etc.

Ratio of length, area and volume in similar solids, e.g. in cubes built from unit cubes; graphical representation of relationships between length and area, length and volume.

Draw outlines of the shape of the surface of water in various containers as these are tilted; sections of solids.

An angle as a shape and as a rotation; right angle; 3-4-5 triangle.

Level and plumb line; horizontal and vertical.

Directions; compass bearings.

Symmetry; kite, rhombus, rectangle, square, circle, etc.

Heights of buildings by means of similar triangles.

Area of irregular and regular shapes by counting squares.

Simple topology; informal approach through puzzles.

Sets

Idea of a set of objects; set of children in the class; the subsets of boys and girls; sets of shapes, etc.; complement, intersection and union of sets.

STAGES P VI AND P VII

Number

Environmental surveys. Tabulate and record results graphically.

The four operations. Continue informal and practical work. Continue formal written work to multiplication and division by two figures. Pupils might be given experience in the use of an adding machine and a desk calculating machine.

Vulgar fractions as required in practical work. In formal work brackets should be used to avoid the need for elaborate rules of precedence.

Decimal fractions as required in practical work. Multiplication and division by decimal fractions. Decimal coinage. Equivalence of vulgar and decimal fractions.

Percentages; applications.

Equations, without recourse to formal rules.

Direct and inverse proportion.

Powers.

Sequences and series.

Construction and use of Napier's Rods.

Quantity

More exact use of a wide variety of measuring instruments, e.g. micrometer.

Models and plans to scale; construction of maps; distances from maps; area on maps.

Concept of speed.

Balance, leverage.

Costing problems involving all the measures of quantity including area and volume; costing of excursions; value for money; graphs and ready reckoners.

Continue formal written work to addition, subtraction, short multiplication and short division of two units of length, weight, capacity; long multiplication of money by two figures.

Ratio and proportion.

Shape

Extend collection of solids and shapes, e.g. crystals, spirals, shells, leaf forms.

Angles of a triangle; rigidity of triangular frames.

Triangle, square, rectangle, rhombus, etc.; fitting and folding to discover properties.

Measurement of angle; use of protractor in design and map work; position on the earth's surface.

Stitch patterns.

Area and volume: $A = 1 \times b$, $V = 1 \times b \times h$.

Graphs of relationships, e.g. circumference of circle to diameter, area of circle to radius.

Topological puzzles; Moebius strips; topological maps; networks.

Sets

Further use of set notation; Venn diagrams.

Chapter 21

Art and Craft Activities

DRAWING, handwork and needlework were for long regarded as separate skills in the primary school. More recently, however, "art" has been established as a convenient omnibus term to include painting, modelling, pattern printing and a variety of work in three dimensions. The former conception of handwork as a training in accurate measuring and shaping has given way to a broader view which encourages each pupil to experiment with a variety of materials to express ideas developing in his own mind. In the same way needlework, which was formerly conceived solely as a technical skill detached from other aspects of the curriculum, is now seen as a field of activity which is closely linked with others and in which lively invention, wider interests and discriminating judgment can develop alongside pride of craftsmanship. Separation of art, handwork and needlework no longer seems desirable, and the three are therefore brought together here under the title "Art and Craft Activities".

The beginnings of these activities appear in the spontaneous play of childhood, through which children unconsciously initiate their own ways of learning. Their habit of investigating materials and objects and of shaping or assembling them to represent images in the mind has proved to be a more effective educational method than that of requiring them to produce, step by step, what has been thought out in advance by an adult. Similarly their whole-hearted enjoyment of sensory experience, visual and tactile, is the source from which their pleasure in the arts grows and matures.

Recognition of these characteristics has brought changes in classroom practice. Colour has come into its own, the scale of the work has increased, and a variety of materials of different consistencies and textures has been brought into use. All these have proved more challenging to imagination and skill than stereotyped exercises using a restricted range of materials. This change of approach, however, does not exclude practice in working closely to a specification.

Art and craft activities can have many links with other aspects of the curriculum. The expression of meaning and emotion through mime, movement and drama helps to invigorate painting, modelling and puppetry. The excitement aroused by narrative, the imagery

159

evoked by description, and the moods suggested by music have similar value. Study of the local environment and of plants and animals lends another source of inspiration. If vividly presented, story, legend and history offer a wealth of material for interpretation in visual terms. In return the art and craft activities help to develop the keenly observant eye on which so much learning depends and contribute directly in the making of costumes, settings, illustrations, diagrams, folios and models.

A striking feature of children's creative work is the great diversity of ability and experience shown by children of the same age. Pupils with wide experience can outshine some with more ability but less experience. Some may show considerable imitative skill but little imagination or aesthetic feeling, while for others the reverse may be true. These differences make it impossible to state categorically what attainment should be expected at each stage. Fortunately pupils of widely differing ability can find equal pleasure in interpreting the same theme. The fact that Michelangelo has already chosen David as a subject need not deter class P V from doing likewise.

The Early Years

When children first come to school they enjoy manipulating different materials to find out how they feel and what can be done with them. Sand, water, clay and dough are materials for this kind of experimenting, to be poured through the hands, squeezed, sifted, pulled and rolled. This happens spontaneously, without suggestion from the teacher. Solid forms from nature, such as pebbles, shells, cones, twigs, can be added, and also man-made things like bobbins, boxes, dowels, cartons, tins, flexible wire and cloth. Toy bricks, pieces of hardboard and offcuts of wood are valuable for building. Large sheets of newsprint or kitchen paper, blocks of tempera colour and bristle brushes for painting are needed, as well as stout wax crayons for drawing. The materials should be readily accessible so that each pupil can choose for himself.

At first full satisfaction comes simply from exploration and manipulation, descriptive words being learned incidentally. Soon, however, efforts at conscious arrangement or shaping appear. Objects or lumps of material become, at least to the child, representations of real things. The box becomes a house, a bus or a ship according to the idea forming in his mind. Lumps of clay acquire identifiable characteristics, perhaps two eyes and a mouth or a body and a head, and pebbles or rolls of clay are formed into outlines of rooms or aeroplanes. Out of unidentifiable squiggles with the brush come rudimentary symbols for people, houses, motor cars and the like.

These first efforts to express personal ideas are the small beginnings which point the road for pupil and teacher to follow. If she is sensitive to the child's way of thought the teacher can do much by a word, a query, or the offer of other materials, to extend the thought further. But she must beware of sweeping aside the pupil's vision to make way for her own, in the hope of a more polished result. Imaginative energy in primary school children has to be released rather than implanted; without wise guidance it cannot achieve its full potential.

The guidance that is given must take account of the child's way of thought. The symbols which children create, so that they can set the stage for their own fantasies, are most clearly seen in their drawings. Generalisation is their most obvious characteristic, and the younger or less able the child, the wider is his application of the symbol he has evolved. One symbol is made to serve many purposes. The figure in the drawing may be Mummy or the child himself. Emphasis by size is usually given to whatever features seem most important to him, as, for example, the face in symbols for people. It is all too easy at this stage to apply wrong criteria and ask for more detail or better proportion when his thoughts may be occupied quite properly with events or ideas rather than with the appearance of things.

Relationships of position are at first ignored, symbols being drawn anywhere on the paper. It is not long, however, before a base line appears on which the various items are set out—the house, the tree, the man. Above, another horizontal band serves for the sky. Between ground and sky is a great space which keeps them permanently apart—a very reasonable statement of the child's idea of sky above and earth beneath. This is not a landscape picture as visualised by an adult. It is a setting of the stage for the action taking place in the child's imagination. The child may also use a kind of sectional or "X-ray" drawing to show what is happening inside and outside at the same time—another admirable device for explaining a situation and one for which he is more often criticised than praised. Another feature typical of his way of thought at this stage is that each item is drawn as a separate entity, standing firmly on the ground but otherwise surrounded by space. People do not pass in front of each other or trees grow in front of houses. All is arranged horizontally from left to right.

The teacher's most valuable contribution in these early years is to see that the pupils are free to pursue their own imaginings but are assured of her genuine interest and appreciation. Sooner or later a moment comes when the effort of imagination is spent and the child seeks confirmation of his sense of achievement. At this point he will explain as best he can the significance of his painting or model, and if he finds an appreciative listener his satisfaction is complete. So much more is in his mind than the result itself conveys. Often a word, a phrase or a new experience is all that is needed to start a new train of thought and a fresh burst of activity.

The images on which imagination depends are gained through first-hand experience. The classroom must serve as a reception centre for all manner of interesting things. Visits with the teacher to the park, the zoo, the woods, the seashore or the farm also help to enlarge the pupils' store of impressions.

Acting a part also stimulates imagination and expression. Children take delight in going through the motions of pulling crackers, setting off fireworks, playing cowboys and Indians, bathing the baby or pouring out tea for the visitors. Their play interests in home and shop can suggest various forms of modelling, painting and cutting out. For the baker's shop many items are within the young pupils' modelling power. The fruiterer's, the fishmonger's, the florist's, the pet shop and the aquarium offer similar opportunities. With paper, paint, paste, cartons and other discarded materials many items can be produced to stock the shop. Paper bags can be decorated and newsprint painted in gay stripes for wrapping paper. The shop sign can be painted in bold, if unskilled, letters.

Stories and poems, if well chosen, can also inspire visual forms of expression. The content, however, should not be so remote from the children's experience that they cannot visualise it in terms of what they themselves have seen. Tales and poems which quicken the emotions help to bring imagination to the point of vivid expression. Sometimes they can be chosen or invented to suit particular characteristics in the children's drawings. When sectional drawings appear, the story may be about the family that lived over the shop or the train that stopped in a tunnel.

Colour is itself a powerful stimulus, to be enjoyed and used with increasing confidence. This involves finding out what happens when paints run together and form new hues, how each colour has many "relations" lighter and darker, nearer and further from the parent colour, how some are warm and bright and others cold or gloomy, how light colours stand out well against dark and vice versa. This experience comes when the children are given a limited range of colours, for example red, yellow, blue, white and black, and are allowed to mix them freely. It is also helped by the use of oddments of coloured papers and fabrics gathered from many sources. The usual coloured gummed squares are too limited in hue, texture and pattern to provide the experience needed. Printing with cotton reels, clothes pegs, flat pieces of wood, rubber, cork, potato, strawboard and blocks of wood to which string, felt, rubber or strawboard has been stuck gives experience of the overprinting of colour upon colour and texture upon texture which sets imagination to work in several new directions.

At first each colour is appreciated on its own, the most vivid or the most assertive—black, for example—having the strongest appeal. Cutting out and sticking down pieces of fabric, paper, yarn or sequins can result in inventions which may be free arrangements, or more regular patterns, or pictures with a recognisable theme. Three-dimensional work can take the form of making very simple dolls, puppets, animals, or doll's furniture, or, on a larger scale, party hats and the various items for "dressing up" which are needed for simple forms of dramatisation. Some children revel in the sheer pleasure of putting materials together, without thought of producing an identifiable object. Such enjoyment of colour and form for its own sake is obviously to be welcomed.

Making decorations for festive occasions has a strong appeal and encourages children to think about the attractiveness as well as the function of what they and others produce. If the teacher dictates the precise forms which are to appear, the results will inevitably be stereotyped. Encouragement to invent gives a livelier, if cruder, result and is more beneficial educationally.

In the past the tendency throughout the primary school has been to work on a miniature scale. The jotter size is probably the smallest at which most children in the younger classes can work satisfactorily, but it should not be used to the exclusion of larger sizes which are more appropriate to their stage of development. There should be easels or wall boards at which the pupils can paint standing up and using the full movement of the arm. Painting on large sheets of paper on the floor is also satisfying to little children, who are accustomed to move freely in this position. Similarly, constructional and inventive work with materials should vary from large scale, as in building with boxes and cartons, offcuts of wood and hardboard, corrugated paper, garden canes and old sheets, to finer work with clay, stones, matchboxes, bobbins and shells. All cannot work on a large scale at the same time, but all should have the opportunity from time to time.

Although a larger scale is physically satisfying to the pupils, as well as exciting by reason of its more spectacular appearance, they take pleasure also in drawing freely in outline on a miniature scale. For this the work-books or jotters in which they make their own illustrations of words, sentences or stories are appropriate. Pencils, wax crayons of good quality and ball-point pens are very suitable. Gradually they realise that there is a connection between the thickness of the drawing or painting instrument and the scale on which it is to be used. Disappointment comes when they try to do on a small scale with a broad brush or soft chalk crayon what is appropriate to a thinner instrument such as pencil or pen. Conversely it is a mistake to begin a large painting by drawing in fine outline with a pencil. The brush is the appropriate drawing implement in this case. In due course the children will be able to select for themselves the right materials and the right scale for the purpose they have in mind.

The Middle Years

As children advance through the primary school their ways of thought show a gradual change which is reflected in their manner of drawing, painting and modelling. They are more confident in placing figures and other items along a base line. Symbols for different categories of people are broadly distinguished by differences of size and dress. Limbs may be bent to show simple actions. Realistic proportion means little to the pupils at this stage: heads are usually as wide as bodies; arms and legs may have length but no thickness. "X-ray" drawings are still typical and, where the setting is thought of as a plan or a map, objects are made perpendicular to opposite base lines. Thus the trees on each side of the road lie flat, their trunks at right angles to the side of the road and those on the nearer or lower side appearing to be upside down. Objects still have their own separate identity and are seldom combined in a group; rarely do any appear to overlap. Colour may have no connection with the colours of nature, or may be purely symbolic, as in a diagram.

Although such drawings may seem stiff and crude to the adult, they in fact provide a much more flexible medium of expression for the child than the fixed viewpoint perspective which adult vision demands. At age nine, most children still do not imitate what they see, although some of them can do this if it is required of them. Instead they represent the things they are thinking about by drawing recognisable symbols for them, and they arrange these symbols in elevation or plan, or in a combination of both, to illustrate their position in space. Much confusion has arisen in the past because this was not understood. It would be a mistake to assume that drawing of this kind is necessarily incompetent. In fact many such pictures by children reveal a delightful sense of colour or spatial arrangement, and express the theme more powerfully than any photographically accurate version. At all times they convey more directly the thoughts in the child's mind than his attempts at imitative drawing can do. Some children, including some of high intelligence, continue to visualise in this way throughout their school days.

For many pupils, however, a gradual transition takes place towards objective seeing. The symbol is compared with actuality and found wanting; from this point onwards there is a desire to make the drawn or modelled form "more like the real thing". This trend towards realism is usually limited at first to separate items such as people, animals or houses, while the setting itself retains its diagrammatic quality, relying on base lines and plan views to explain the location. Themes can now be suggested which involve the grouping of items which the child would previously have treated consecutively and in isolation. Impromptu acting helps in this, as in dramatising simple themes such as "Pulling together on a rope", "The barber at work", "Carrying the boy who was hurt", "Mummy brushing my hair". Sometimes the process develops more quickly through modelling. Boys wrestling are more convincingly inter-twined in the modelled version than in the drawn. On occasions the same theme may be attempted in paint after it has been modelled. Those who achieve realism in their work are admired by their class-mates, while others, often with more creative potential, may begin to feel sadly incompetent. A sympathetic teacher can do much to restore the balance, explaining that ability to imitate is a very useful skill but not always the most important one in art and craft activities.

If left to themselves to find inspiration, many children do not discover their latent powers of expression. In such cases the teacher should be able to supply the stimulus which sets imagination to work. Emotional associations are often helpful. Strong feeling can also influence the shape and colour of what is produced and so lead to a more forceful and coherent result. The memory of a gale driving through trees evokes shapes which bend and sway in rhythm, or the blazing heat of a forest fire conjures up yellows, oranges and reds and eliminates or subdues the cool greys and blues. A theme such as "Boys blue with cold after a sea bathe" brings together another set of colours. In this way the pupils may become aware of the two main expressive groupings, warm and cool. Although at this age children are usually delighted to interpret

a story, incident or poem vividly told by the teacher, they should
be encouraged to develop ideas of their own. Pure fantasy of their
own creation is the true field of some children. Items from the news
can also offer a starting point, as when the Queen pays a ceremonial
visit or fire destroys a school.

In constructional work emotion gives way to ingenuity. There is
also scope for developing the sense of order and inter-relationship
which is needed in projects such as a model of a harbour, a farm
steading, a pit-head or an airport.

In such efforts, whether by individuals or groups, the aim is
descriptive rather than functional. The technical skill which produces a lasting piece of craftsmanship is not required, although the
beginning of skill in the use of simple tools may emerge incidentally.
By choosing from the scrap-box, the piece-bag and other sources
the pupils become familiar with the nature of different materials,
learning what they are suitable for and how they can be worked.

Meanwhile everything tends towards rough approximation, precision being a quality that comes by degrees, and to some more
than to others. No absolute standard should be applied at this
age. Stitches will be more erratic than the teacher would wish; joins
in wood or cardboard will inspire little confidence; but she will find
herself deeply involved as the adviser to whom the children go when
they cannot see their way round a difficulty.

Making arrangements of form and colour for their own interest,
with no descriptive or functional thought in mind, has always held
an attraction for children, and indicates their growing awareness of
aesthetic considerations. Conscious efforts to make decorative
arrangements of colour and shape are much enjoyed. Free invention
with the brush, clippings of coloured paper or cloth, printing
blocks, paint over wax, string, needle and coloured wool teaches the
pupils to consider the general effect more than the individual items.
Low relief experiments can be made by incising slabs of clay or one
of its substitutes, or by pressing buttons, beads, shells, matchsticks
or string into the soft surface. The sense of arrangement differs
from pupil to pupil, some tending towards a rigid symmetry, others
inventing more freely, and a few making little attempt at recognisable
organisation. Pattern-making by repetition can be introduced, the
pupils relying on eye-judgment rather than mechanical aids to
achieve a degree of regularity. The idea of seeing two or more
colours together making either a harmonious or a strident chord
develops only slowly, although pleasing and unusual harmonies are
to be found in the work of some pupils. The expressive associations
of colour and shape can often inspire new invention, as in a warm,

sunny pattern or a wintry one, or in a rippling, flowing pattern all in greens.

Attention should be drawn to the patterns in nature—frost on the windows, daisy-heads on the grass, cobwebs in the hedges, the grain in shells, pebbles and polished wood. The pupils should be encouraged to discover others for themselves, sometimes with a magnifying glass, so that the wonder and beauty of nature become a reality for them.

In pattern-making as in pictorial work, practice on different scales is important. Sometimes a ball-point pen can be used, on a tiny scale, perhaps after looking at the delicate tracery on an insect's wing. Or the full sweep of the arm may be brought into play, with the pupil working on a large sheet of paper pinned to the wall and using a broad brush. Some of these patterns can be composite efforts by a group or by the whole class.

Invention of the kind described is worthwhile on its own account, but it also has practical applications. School parties, concerts and dramatic performances can benefit from the exercise of this talent. Fantastic forms of flora and fauna can be invented and embellished to decorate the classroom or school hall, florist's wire being used as foundation when larger creatures are involved. Coloured yarn or shapes cut from fabric remnants can be used as surface decoration on the curtains of a puppet stage or on full-size garments for a class play. Reference to Celtic, African or Polynesian sources will suggest the making and embellishing of war shields, canoe paddles or tribal drums, or of simple thumb pots in clay. In this way the pupils gain an insight into the nature of materials and the uses to which they can be put. This helps them to understand the reasons for the great variety of forms which the crafts of man have taken, in distant times and places as well as within recent experience.

The Later Years

In the later years the trend towards greater realism and objectivity is noticeable in an increasing number of pupils. When drawing or painting, many now show a desire to represent distance and solidity. The base line becomes a plane on which objects are set in depth as well as to right and left. A sense of foreground and background is evident, with a receding plane between, though rarely expressed in normal perspective. Few depict the scene as it would appear to a spectator looking from a fixed viewpoint. Those who do so will of their own accord draw with astonishingly accurate perspective, but they are not necessarily the artists of the class. Their strength lies in

M

their cool objective vision; others may have greater creative force, a keener sense of colour or livelier decorative invention.

Sharper and more widely ranging observation can bring a fund of new material to stimulate creative thought. Environmental studies, school excursions, dramatic performances, local events of special interest, indeed any experience that brings fresh visual information and stirs feeling can provide subject matter. But the interpretation should be the pupil's own. His drawing idiom at this age is more akin to that of the Bayeux Tapestry than to that of Victorian studio painting; the vigour and directness of the one should never be sacrificed in order to attempt the imitative realism of the other.

Although much of the pictorial work of childhood is concerned with telling a story, children also take pleasure in producing what is attractive in its own right. Satisfaction in a picture as a pleasing object in itself is widespread at ten or eleven and can be encouraged by looking for subject-matter which lends itself to pictorial rather than narrative enjoyment. Flowers, sprays of leaves, pot plants, fruits, attractive objects and fabrics can be brought to school, arranged by the pupils and freely interpreted to create pleasing pictures. Children are often astonished to discover what attractive paintings they can make from what is to be seen from the classroom window or the playground, especially when they note the changes of light and colour in different weathers and seasons. The pupils themselves can serve as models for portraits, sometimes in costume or fancy dress. These portraits usually show an interest in details of dress and in the main features of the face but little in the light and shade which give the effect of volume.

In pictorial work it is better to draw attention to the elements which give aesthetic pleasure than to strive after effects of shadow or linear perspective. This means giving thought to how colours look together, how contrasting tones of colour enliven the picture and similar tones make it dull, how "busy", textured or decorated areas can look well against plain, how scale and arrangement should suit the size and shape of the picture space, how balance can be achieved without geometric symmetry, how attention can be focused, and how the pupil himself can edit his picture by cutting to remove unwanted padding. It should be remembered, of course, that the child, like the artist, often sketches his ideas without thought of arrangement within boundaries; this is a process to be encouraged.

At this stage many pupils begin to show an awareness of subtleties of movement, especially in animals and plants, and to express them sensitively with pencil, paint or clay. Some of this emerges in imaginative work, as in depicting a stalking cat or a frisking puppy.

Or it may come from direct observation, as when pets are brought to school or trees are seen bending to the gale. Not all children react in this way; some will always record piece by piece, building up a static picture which is without trace of animation but may be satisfying in a different way.

Modelling now takes on greater realism, and the tendency to group items naturalistically can be seen in the work of some children. Themes such as "Family sheltering", "Circus riders", "Adrift in a storm" give scope for this development. For some subjects it will be necessary to support the clay with a skeleton core of wire fixed to a base board.

Papier mâché or pasted newspaper strip is effective for making figures and animals, masks, puppets, dolls for dressing, hulls for model ships, landscapes for projects or model railways, armour and other properties for dramatic activities. Carving can be done in damp blocks of plaster, hardened clay, block salt, soap or soft wood, with the simplest of tools. Carving in low relief as well as in the round can be tried. In both modelling and carving there should be experiments at times in making "abstract" forms which please the eye on their own account. If encouraged to do so, some pupils will discover for themselves water-worn stones or roots which satisfy by means of shape and texture alone.

At this stage descriptive model-making also becomes more ambitious, though still depending largely on discarded materials. With these materials boys and girls can create buildings, furniture, costume, most forms of transport, working models of cranes, lifts, cable cars, indeed a limitless variety of descriptive models. Simple musical instruments can be made from the same sources. In model-making most pupils find it easier to develop their ideas from existing three-dimensional objects than from a flat sheet of cardboard. In these ventures the teacher should not be dictating what is to be made or detailing every stage and dimension in its production; rather she must allow the pupils, working individually or in groups, to exercise their own initiative and ingenuity.

The practical approach to other subjects such as science, mathematics, geography and history calls for the making of simple pieces of apparatus and the use of various types of measurement. This promotes ingenuity and an appreciation of the value of mathematical accuracy in situations where this is appropriate.

The collation of written and illustrative material also offers a challenge. Wall charts, folios, albums, loose-leaf and stitched books provide scope for planning and construction by the pupils. The storing, annotating and cataloguing of coloured transparencies, filmstrips, tape-recordings, gramophone records, assignment cards, instruction sheets, scripts of plays, stories, poems and songs composed by the pupils, give other opportunities. Many pupils of this age are capable of penmanship of real beauty and can use this on different scales, whether for a wall diagram or for an illustrated page of text. In the process they can learn how to make writing instruments suited to each need.

Personal hobbies give rise to other legitimate requirements such as albums and boxes for various collecting enthusiasms. Railway and aeroplane modelling has a strong appeal for many boys, as does doll's house furnishing for girls. In some situations it is possible to build on a larger scale. A sledge, a four-wheeled trolley, a rabbit hutch, a totem pole, a wigwam, a footbridge, a rustic shelter are all appropriate possibilities.

The craftsmanship which produces finely made articles of good design involves more knowledge and skill, more time and patience than can be expected of most primary school children. Nevertheless the foundations of the craftsman's attitude to his work can be laid. It is soon appreciated that lessons can be learned from good examples and that, if the article is to serve its purpose, the proper materials must be chosen, the best shape and size decided, and the method of construction thought out. For some pupils the neat appearance of the final result may seem more important than the initial planning, which they may be content to leave to others, but they should be encouraged to undertake or at least participate in thinking out what shape and size the article should be. Much will also depend on the teacher's knowledge of the craft processes involved; children cannot be expected to find these out for themselves. At the planning stage it is important that they should be concerned with making aesthetic decisions as well as with purely functional problems.

It is not possible here to deal in detail with the various crafts which can be offered. Processes which occupy a great deal of time in unthinking repetition, such as the making of knotted rugs and some forms of raffia and cane work, are better avoided, and the tendency to deal mainly or entirely with needle or shuttle crafts should be resisted, especially in the case of boys. Choice must obviously be affected by the teacher's experience and the conditions obtaining in the school. Constructional work in wood may be possible in one classroom and out of the question in another. There is no reason other than that of expediency why all the members of the class should be occupied on similar tasks. As in other forms of learning, adjustment to individual ability and interest is the ideal. This leads to the formation of groups whose members have interests in common.

Crafts which give scope for imagination, aesthetic judgment and skill include clay-modelling, carving in wood or plaster, doll-making and doll-dressing, puppetry, toymaking in various materials, embroidery and appliqué, pottery, fabric dyeing and printing, and bookcraft, including handwriting, lettering and pattern-printing.

It cannot be too strongly emphasised that at all stages display of the pupils' work is one of the best incentives that the teacher has at her disposal. The weaker members in particular are in constant need of reassurance. In their case often a part of the picture can be cut out, mounted and praised for its success, or two products by one child can be put on view, showing clearly how the second has improved on the first. Credit should be given as much for development as for innate talent, and for ideas as well as execution. Corridors and entrance hall, as well as classrooms, should be used for display. The temptation to honour only "the best" should be resisted.

The enjoyment of beauty in art and nature should be a part of life for children as well as for adults. Great progress has been made in designing attractive school buildings, and the pupils' response to this is widely recognised. The typography and illustration of school books have brought these also into the category of pleasing objects. Pot plants in corridors and classrooms add a grace of their own. Prints and original paintings can bring genuine pleasure or mere desultory acknowledgement according to the choice and the manner of presentation. There is no need to be timidly conservative. Young children are often more ready than adults to enjoy the impact of some forms of modern art, meeting "abstract" painting on its own terms and enjoying or rejecting it according to its immediate visual appeal. This does not prevent them from taking equal or greater interest in work which has a straightforward story to tell. Opportunities of seeing craftsmen at work or hearing them talk about their craft are also valuable. The potter, the weaver, the wood-turner, the stone-carver, the blacksmith, the silversmith and the printer have much to give through their attitude to craftsmanship as well as through their skill.

Needlework at the Later Stages

In the previous paragraphs reference has been made mainly to the less familiar roles which needlework can play in primary school education. Suggestions have been made for activities in which boys and girls may join, emphasis being laid on invention and on uses for sewing which might not occur in an orthodox needlework course.

Making costumes for dramatic work, making and dressing puppets, using fabrics to create pictures, patterns or items for projects in environmental studies are examples of activities in which needle and thread play an important part, if to a less exacting standard than more permanent articles require.

This section deals, therefore, with the complementary aspect of needlework which provides practice in the basic skills of the craft through making serviceable articles of pleasing design, taking into account what may appropriately be expected of pupils of different age, aptitudes and interests. Needlework in this sense is not only a skill honoured by tradition and by its continuing usefulness; it is also a craft which is peculiarly fitted to help imaginative expression in many directions and to develop a feeling for the beauty inherent in the materials used.

By age nine the girls will have gained experience in choosing, shaping and joining fabrics through free experiment in which other materials have also been called into service. With the teacher at hand to advise and demonstrate, they will already be familiar with the advantages of stitching when cloth is the medium. They will have learned the sensible way of securing the thread at start and finish, how to hold the cloth and needle, how to make a short hem and how to join one piece to another. They may already have made paper patterns in arriving at the shape to cut for a sail, or for a dirndl skirt for a costume doll. They will have met some of the problems of shaping and finishing, for example, in fashioning the neck and armholes of a doll's garment. They may also have tried combined ventures such as a dolls' fashion parade or a menagerie of fanciful animals.

The decorative qualities inherent in the materials they use will also be familiar to them—how darker fabric contrasts effectively with lighter, and how thread darker or lighter than the background can be stitched to give a decorative effect. They will already have done appliqué work, in paper as well as fabric, though mainly stuck down rather than sewn, and will have discovered the fascination of choosing from an assortment of lace, ribbon, net, sequins, beads and similar materials the wherewithal for decorative invention.

In the work so far technique may have been of little account by adult standards, although some pupils may have shown great care in all that they have done. In the main, however, stitching has been rather rough and ready; indeed much has been attempted which no child could expect to complete in a craftsmanlike way. A sudden advance to precise needlework should not be expected. Around age nine the pupils themselves begin to see the need for better technique if invention is not to end in frustration. When articles are to be made for use, this need is still more obvious, whether in hemming a place mat or in making a beach bag.

From this age onwards greater heed should be paid to the use of appropriate processes, and the teacher should try to ensure that in the remaining primary school years the girls have practice in the basic techniques of sewing and knitting. This does not imply that every girl should now be issued with a standard piece of material and required to produce an article identical with that of her neighbour. Each of them should be given opportunities for deciding what is to be made, what size and shape it will be and what kind and colour of material should be used.

Obviously this is more practicable in some situations than in others; difficulties arise when an article demands considerable expenditure on materials. Compromise is often necessary, but the ideal in the teacher's mind should be to involve the pupil in the whole process of planning and making, including finding out the cost of materials and their suitability for different purposes. Some of this information is worth collating in class folios or individual notebooks, with cuttings of material as illustrations and with brief notes on origins, characteristics, uses and price. Any experiments in the dyeing of wool, yarn or fabric should be recorded in the same way.

No fixed list of the articles to be made should be prepared, but a wide list of suggestions helps some pupils to decide where their interests lie. The teacher should discuss with the pupils the possibilities in the ideas they have put forward, drawing upon her superior knowledge to avoid the pitfalls attached to an unsuitable choice and simplifying the more difficult processes as she thinks necessary. For example, in the early stages the difficulties of hemming can be overcome by turning the hem to the right side of the article or garment and attaching it with an embroidery stitch.

Special attention should now be given to techniques as they arise. Tacking, running, hemming, oversewing and the making of simple seams will inevitably be needed. In knitting, garter stitch and stocking stitch will be used. "Increasing" and "decreasing" should also be taught. The pupils should gradually become accustomed to refer to teaching aids and instructional diagrams instead of relying wholly on the teacher for demonstration. This reduces time-consuming repetition by the teacher and helps to develop the pupils' self-reliance. Time spent by the teacher on the preparation of such aids very quickly repays itself. Books of reference for teacher and pupils should also be readily accessible.

As the pupils advance through classes P VI and P VII they become more ambitious and capable of better workmanship. Some set themselves standards which are surprisingly high for their age; others still have great difficulty with techniques. The teacher's problem is to draw the line between over-fussiness about neatness, with its consequent reduction of time spent on planning, and acceptance of slip-shod work which gives satisfaction to nobody. Only the teacher on the spot knows her pupils well enough to judge who needs to pay more attention to technique and who should be encouraged to think more adventurously. A display of fine examples of needlework often acts as an incentive. These should be chosen with an eye to their design as well as their craftsmanship. In addition, photographic illustrations should be available to show the great variety of uses to which skill and good taste can be put.

Techniques in classes P VI and P VII will involve more difficult shaping. The cutting and adjusting of material to fit the human form will already have been solved, in rough and ready fashion, through the practice which the pupils have had earlier in making dresses for dolls. Now the use of bought patterns, the careful cutting out of full-sized garments and the following of printed instructions should be encouraged. The techniques of finishing edges, making simple openings and attaching buttons and other fasteners can be taught as the occasion arises. An efficient sewing machine should be available at this stage, for use when prolonged seaming is involved.

Knitting can now include ribbing and the use of four wires. Imagination should be encouraged in the choice of article: a knitted glove puppet or a gay ski-ing bonnet or scarf may give more pleasure and variety than the traditional pair of socks. The pupils should be encouraged to follow printed instructions as an essential part of their experience.

Some pupils have a stronger decorative sense than others and are more attracted to decorative needlework than to plain sewing. This should be encouraged, even at the loss of some experience of constructional work. At this stage attention should be paid to the traditional range of embroidery stitches. From the outset practice should include the combining of a few stitches of contrasting width, form, texture and tone to form simple decorative motifs. When cut out, each of these can be tried out against backgrounds of different colour or tone so that the most satisfying relationship and spacing can be found. This directs attention to the overriding need for balance between decorated and plain surfaces. Subsequently the placing of decoration within the surface area of a variety of articles can be considered. In this way the pupils begin to see the object and its decorative detail as one and not simply as a dull thing to be made pretty by superimposing some form of ornament.

Similar considerations arise in the use of appliqué. Freer rein to fancy can be given in decorating stuffed animal toys and in making dress accessories. In this work bought patterns and transfers should on the whole be avoided, as they deprive the pupils of the inventive opportunities from which they stand to gain so much.

It will be found that some pupils retain or develop an interest in the miniature scale associated with making dolls and dolls' furnishings or marionettes and their stage settings. The experience and skill gained in this way can be set against loss of practice in more orthodox garment-making. Dressing dolls in historic or modern costume has proved a fascinating exercise for girls with this interest and an eye for small-scale work. Doll-sized millinery and its display provide an imaginative project for a group working together. Other opportunities arise from time to time, as when a lectern fall is needed for the school hall, place mats for a dining table, a large appliqué panel as decoration in the entrance, or banners, pennants and flags for various occasions.

From the suggestions which have been made for needlework in the older classes, it should be clear that the girls for most of the time are concerned with the normal applications of the craft, making articles and garments which each has planned. Those with special interests are encouraged to pursue them, and all on occasion may be expected to attempt something less familiar, such as the weaving of a tie or belt or the printing of a light scarf.

It is obviously essential that the tools of the craft, including facilities for ironing, should be available and in first-class condition. In particular, the standard of lighting should be fully adequate. Consideration should also be given to eyesight and the pupil's degree of motor control, if unreasonable demands are not to be made on girls for whom fine work is an impossibility.

Selection and Organisation

It might well be thought that the suggestions made in this chapter demand that an inordinately large part of the school week be given over to art and craft activities. The intention is to make clear the wide range that is educationally fruitful and to allow choice according to the pupils' abilities and interests. The suggestions also provide for change and revitalisation, without which most subjects risk lapsing into routine practice. When the unfamiliar is being tried for the first time, it is usually advisable to attempt it with only a small group, or even a single member of the class. The fact that no separation has been made here between art and craft or between boys' and girls' activities—except at the later stages—indicates that changes of organisation affecting timetables and curriculum may be necessary in many schools.

Chapter 22
Music

By the time children come to school most of them have had considerable musical experience, since music, in various forms, is a familiar feature of their environment. They have probably heard an extensive range of vocal and instrumental music on radio, television and perhaps on records; they may have learned to distinguish the different chimes of the ice-cream vans that serve their areas; on visits to shops and restaurants they may have heard the recorded background music which is increasingly common in such places; and they will certainly be aware of the popular songs of the day, sung by their elders at home and elsewhere, or purveyed through one or other of the mass media. Some may have been brought up in families where music-making is part of everyday life, where songs are sung and instruments played, and may have learned from their mothers some of the traditional nursery rhymes and songs. Most of them will have made music themselves; for there are few five-year-olds who will not have attempted to reproduce snatches of a song or tune, or who have not in moments of exhilaration passed apparently unconsciously from speech to song. They may also have become aware of differences in the quality and volume of sound which can be produced by striking or plucking various objects, and may have discovered the satisfaction of improvising rhythms by these means. In their play they may also have participated in the singing games which are still part of the local culture of some areas. A few may come from homes where among their playthings are musical toys, or where they have been allowed access to a piano or other musical instrument which has given them scope for experimentation.

Music is thus an integral part of the life of most young children, and the majority are ready and willing when they come to school to participate in the making of music, and to respond actively to the stimulus it provides. It is part of the function of the primary school to ensure that music enters as freely as possible into their lives, and that the scope of their musical experience is enlarged and their powers of perception and performance developed. Throughout the school, therefore, music should be a recognised part of their daily life, and opportunities for musical activity, whether it be singing, playing, listening or moving to music, should be as regular and as enjoyable as the teacher can make them.

At the early stages musical activities should be free and informal, occurring at points in the day when the teacher feels that they are appropriate, and involving the pupils in singing, playing instruments, listening, and moving to rhythms and melodies. Active participation should be the means by which they find pleasure and at the same time incidentally become aware of the varying patterns of rhythm and pitch that make up music. As they move up the school, enjoyment and satisfaction through participation should remain the principal objectives; for the first aim of music-teaching is to foster an enthusiasm and love for music. However, if children are to be able to develop as listeners or as participants, they should be encouraged to realise that music as an art has its own disciplines. The older they become, therefore, the more the teacher should encourage discrimination in listening and skill in performance, and the more she should seek to develop their ability to perceive and reproduce accurately the conventional patterns of rhythm and pitch. Uniform attainment is not to be expected in music any more than in other branches of the curriculum, but every pupil should be given opportunities to progress as far as his capacity will allow in the acquisition of musical skills.

The Singing of Songs

Singing will provide the main experience of music-making for the majority of pupils. In the youngest classes the pupils should be introduced to a wealth of simple songs, such as nursery rhymes —including Scottish rhymes—action songs, singing games and hymns, and opportunities for singing them should be frequent. As they grow older, the songs they are capable of learning will become melodically and rhythmically more complex, and the teacher's aim should be to cover as many songs as time and her own ability will allow, chosen from a wide variety of styles and periods. The repertoire should include folk-song, especially Scottish folk-song, and songs by classical and modern composers, in both simple and compound time and in both major and minor mode. At all stages there should be a place for a few examples of "occasional" music, such as the National Anthem. "Auld Lang Syne", and music for worship—carols, psalms, hymns, paraphrases—selected for the suitability of the words and music. Opportunities should also be taken to teach songs in association with other branches of the curriculum, such as number, history, geography, poetry, drama, and projects of various kinds. The national and folk-songs of various countries, for example, can complement work in geography;

a historical "patch" on a particular period can involve suitably chosen songs of that period; "work" songs can provide a glimpse into the social conditions of the past. The pupils should also have some experience of part-singing, beginning quite simply with nursery rhymes and rounds like "Frère Jacques", and proceeding later to more demanding rounds, canons and descants.

The methods which the teacher uses in introducing a new song will vary according to the nature of the song and the degree of its difficulty. All songs, however, must be taught methodically, and should always be presented first as a whole. In all but the oldest classes, the melodies of most songs will require to be taught by pattern and imitation. Whatever method the teacher employs, the object should be to teach the whole song quickly so that the pupils have a sense of achievement, and that interest is not lost. In the learning of new songs the pupils should be encouraged to use any skill they have gained in reading musical notation. In the primary school few will be able to read a complete song at sight, but song-books with the tunes in staff notation should be used extensively and the pupils trained to observe the music as well as the words. At first they may merely follow the notation as the song is played or sung to them; later their attention may be drawn to the appearance in notation of certain features of the music they are singing; the mastery of a difficult phrase can often be aided by reference to notation.

As pupils gain experience, the teacher should aim at gradually improving the standard of their performance, so that they may know the satisfaction that can be derived from singing well, and learn to discriminate between what is good and what is bad in vocal technique. To achieve this she will have to consider accuracy of pitch and time values, security of tuning, clear articulation, the production of vowel sounds, beauty of tone, observation of phrase lengths, rhythmic flow, observation of expression marks, and realisation of mood. Vocal exercises may be used to develop un-forced sweet tone, good production of vowel sounds, and the clear enunciation of consonants. These exercises should always be purposeful, and should be designed or selected with the vocal faults of a class or group in view. They should not become mere routine, and may not require to be undertaken frequently, especially if good vocal technique is encouraged whenever the voice is used. Many teachers find it useful to "tune up" the voices of their pupils at the beginning of a music lesson by spending a few minutes on purposeful voice exercises.

Not all songs will be treated with the same thoroughness. Some may be quickly learned and sung for a short time only; some may be sung often over a long period; some may be polished for performance in a concert or a music festival; each session a number should be learned sufficiently well for the pupils to be able to sing them from memory, and without the aid of the teacher. It is particularly important that the pupils should be encouraged to sing without accompaniment, having been given the correct pitch of the key-note of the song on an instrument—a piano, a tuning fork or a pitch-pipe. Apart from the pleasure which it affords to the singers and to the listener, unaccompanied singing is valuable because it helps children to become musically self-reliant, especially if part-singing is encouraged, and gives both the pupils and the teacher opportunities to listen carefully to their own vocal technique.

The Playing of Instruments

Pupils should also be given opportunities to play instruments, and to this end instruments of appropriate kinds should be available at all stages. The pupils themselves can make a variety of simple percussion and wind instruments with little difficulty, and will derive a great deal of pleasure from playing them. In the youngest classes instruments might be used in the first instance by individual pupils during periods of free play, when they can explore for themselves the possibilities of the various instruments, and improvise their own rhythms and melodies. By this means the musical experiences afforded by the home can be complemented, and the pupils can begin to develop a feeling for rhythm, pitch, and tone colour. Thereafter they can be gradually introduced to the discipline of playing in a group, a form of music-making which can give them a great deal of enjoyment and satisfaction and at the same time encourage team-work. Improvisation continues to have a place throughout the school, but increasingly, as the children develop, instrumental work can be used as a means of encouraging reading from musical notation, particularly if the teacher makes use of compositions and arrangements which cater for different levels of ability and attainment. The playing of instruments need not involve the whole class at one time: the imaginative teacher will be able to devise a variety of activities in which some pupils will play, some sing, and some move to the music.

The non-pitch instruments of the percussion band can be used throughout the primary school. The literature on the percussion band is wide, and study of one or two of the many books which are available will enable a teacher to take her pupils with confidence from the stage of spontaneous playing to that of reading from notation. The playing of percussion instruments helps to develop a sense of rhythm, a feeling for phrase length, awareness of variety of tone, and self-reliance in reading music. Opportunities can be given to pupils to make their own rhythmic arrangements to accompany recorded music, music played by the teacher or by other pupils, or the choral speaking of suitable poems. Published arrangements of accompaniments to standard works may also be used. These demand from the pupils both active participation and concentrated listening, and enable them to become familiar with well-known compositions, but they can be used effectively only when the pupils have some skill in reading music.

Melodic percussion instruments such as the dulcimer, the xylophone and chime-bars, if well constructed, produce attractive tone colours which make an immediate appeal to children. They do not require advanced technical skill, they provide opportunities for playing simple tunes, and they are suitable media for extemporisation. Playing these instruments may also help pupils who are unable to sing in tune to develop a sense of pitch. An increasing repertoire is available for these instruments alone, and for these in combination with voices, recorders, and other instruments.

The recorder has a long history and an extensive repertoire. It can be taught to fairly large classes provided the music taught is simple, and provided the pupils can practise at home. Before attempting to teach the recorder, a teacher should be able to play a simple piece confidently and artistically, and so be able to commend the instrument and its repertoire to her class. The study of the recorder develops appreciation of good tuning, especially if experience of part-playing is obtained, and gives an added purpose to learning to read from music.

If expert teachers are available, pupils with special musical abilities should be given instruction individually or in groups in the playing of orchestral or brass-band instruments or the piano. A development of this may be the formation of ensembles or of an orchestra.

Creative Work

It is desirable that, in addition to playing and singing tunes learned by pattern and imitation or from musical notation, pupils should be given scope to invent their own rhythms and melodies, and perhaps to record them on tape or to write them down. Some teachers have quite successfully encouraged their pupils to "compose" simple rhythmic or melodic figures, for example, to accompany folk-song, using non-pitch and melodic percussion instruments, recorders, pianos and violins. Others have stimulated oral improvisation by asking pupils to speak a word, a phrase or a line of verse rhythmically and then to sing it, supplying their own musical inflexions.

Much more experimentation is required in this aspect of music-making before it can be known how many children are capable of pursuing such activities with profit. Certainly it should be possible to take advantage of the urge which many pre-school children show to make their own music. How this can be done, and the extent to which it can be developed, must be matters for experimentation by the schools.

Listening to Music

Throughout the school the pupils should have frequent opportunities to listen to music and to respond to the stimulus it can provide. Listening, of course, is involved in many of the other musical activities which the pupils will undertake. They must listen during the teaching of a song as the teacher plays or sings it; they must listen with attention and concentration to music, played on piano or gramophone, to which they are providing a percussion accompaniment; they may be required to listen to the singing or playing of a group of their fellow pupils in class or on some school occasion. In addition, however, time should be set aside for periods of listening to recordings of suitably chosen music, to broadcast lessons which provide guidance in listening to music, and to "live" performances, so that the pupils may have experience of a wide range of different kinds, produced in a variety of ways.

The approach will vary according to the music which is chosen. At times the teacher may draw the attention of the pupils beforehand to features or instruments for which they should listen. Often the class will afterwards wish to talk about the music they have heard, and discuss their reactions to it. Occasionally they may be stimulated to express their reactions in writing, in pictorial terms, or in movement. Sometimes listening to unfamiliar music can be made more interesting and meaningful if there is something to look at: films and filmstrips, with the pictures appropriately synchronised with the music, can be useful in presenting for the first time a descriptive piece, or music associated with a story; in the older classes the pupils might be encouraged to follow from staff notation the principal themes of the piece to which they are listening. Whatever approach the teacher decides to adopt, she must ensure that the pieces she chooses are not so long as to demand an unduly long span of attention from the pupils, and she must allow each pupil a measure of freedom to react in his own way. Not all of them should be expected to sit and listen quietly.

The teacher may from time to time suggest to her pupils that they should listen at home to suitable pieces of music which are to be sung or played on radio or television. She may also find it worthwhile to discuss with them the music they hear out of school, so that she may learn more about their musical background and perhaps help them in the development of their own standards. The "pop" tunes of the day must be accepted as part of their musical environment; the wise teacher will not condemn them, but will encourage her pupils to listen to them critically, and will supplement them with a sufficient range of music of quality to enable them to form their own judgments.

Aural Training

Through the opportunities which they are given to sing, play and listen to music, some children quickly develop an awareness of rhythmic patterns and pitch relationships and an ability to imitate them. For most pupils, however, other supplementary activities are necessary which are specifically directed at training the ear to perceive these basic elements of music, and at helping the pupils to reproduce them accurately and confidently in their singing or playing.

The development of the child's sense of rhythm should begin in the youngest classes, and can be most easily done through the rhythms of his natural bodily movements and of his speech. At first the pupils might be encouraged to walk, run, and skip, to music in which the ♩, the group ♫, and the group ♩♪ predominate. Thereafter they might be encouraged to fit steps to simple marches and waltz-tunes, and so be made aware of the difference between duple and triple time, which are the basic groupings of the pulse. The teacher may also draw their attention to the rhythms of their speech, and to words and phrases which illustrate the use of the pulse, combined pulses, and subdivisions of the pulse. The pupils may be asked to imitate rhythmic figures, devised and presented by the teacher, by clapping or other movements, or on percussion instruments. When the imitation of rhythmic figures of this kind is secure, they

N

can be introduced to the French rhythm names, and will enjoy expressing the rhythms of speech and of well-known tunes in this new vocabulary.

Children differ widely in the development of their ability to perceive pitch relationships, but from an early stage the teacher can help this development, by illustrating the ideas of "high" and "low", "going up" and "coming down" in her singing or playing of appropriate fragments of melody. She may also ask the pupils to sing one note, then two-note, three-note and longer melodic figures in imitation of her own singing or playing. Once they are able to imitate these figures accurately, it is useful to introduce the solfa pitch names, and to use these in association with easy phrases from tunes with which the pupils are familiar. The notes of the scale can then be introduced gradually, and perception of the intervals between them reinforced by songs which include them, by the use of the "hand-signs", and by purposeful exercises on the solfa modulator. Books are available which provide guidance on the most appropriate sequence to be followed in teaching the notes and intervals of the scale. How far training of this kind can be taken depends on the ability of the pupils, but it is desirable that they should become familiar with the intervals between the notes of the minor scale as well as those of the major.

Teachers must understand the purpose of such aids as the rhythm and pitch names. Basically, their purpose is to clarify relationships between sounds, and, incidentally, to provide the foundations on which an understanding of staff notation can be built. They must never be taught as ends in themselves. Exercises in which they are used may be frequent, but should also be brief, and presented as an enjoyable game. The teacher should always make the purpose of the rhythm and pitch names clear to the pupils by using them in the teaching of songs, and, at the later stages, in helping the pupils to find their way in musical notation.

Musical Notation

The ability to read music is a valuable skill, which will enable the child in later years to take a full part in music-making as an individual or as a member of a group, and will allow him access to a vast store of music which might otherwise be closed to him. Pupils vary considerably in the extent to which they can progress towards the acquisition of this skill. Some may be able to learn to read simple melodies quite fluently, especially if they receive instrumental instruction in school or outside. Indeed, if creative work, instrumental ensemble and part-singing are developed on the lines suggested above, the abler pupils may soon feel the need for notation, either to record their "compositions" or to ensure accuracy in their playing or singing. The achievement of others may be much more modest. Nevertheless, it is desirable that all pupils, before they leave the primary school, should at least become accustomed to the appearance of a page of music, have an elementary understanding of the conventional symbols and their arrangement on the staff, and be able to follow generally the notation of simple pieces.

There are various ways in which familiarity with notation can be encouraged. Even in the youngest classes the pupils' curiosity may be aroused by including in the class library a few books containing simple tunes. During creative work the teacher may be able to write down for the pupil a melody or a rhythm which the pupil has invented. When the pupils begin to use song-books, it is helpful if they contain the melodies in staff notation, so that the pupils may follow the notation while a song is played or sung by the teacher.

In most cases, however, more specific and progressive instruction is necessary, if any degree of skill is to be acquired. Generally, this can best be done by making use of the experience which the pupils have gained of rhythm and pitch, and the oral proficiency which they have acquired in the use of the rhythm and pitch names. At first the symbols corresponding to the rhythm names can be intro-duced, and the pupils can be given opportunities to read these symbols to the rhythm names, and to read them for the playing of percussion instruments. As soon as they have developed some confidence in the use of the basic sol-fa pitch names, the teacher can demonstrate how these can be indicated on the staff, by using the fingers of her hand, or by gradually building up a staff modulator on the blackboard, and can encourage the pupils to sing simple tunes involving at first only a few notes of the scale. The process of reading rhythm and pitch simultaneously may then be attempted. There is no need at any stage in the primary school for technical explanations of flats and sharps, alphabetical names of notes, key signatures, time signatures, or even such names as "crotchet" or "minim". Exercises which are used for practice should at first be based on very simple tunes, some of which are already familiar to the pupils. Later, excerpts from the works of the great composers or from folk-songs, incorporating examples in simple and compound time and in major and minor mode, may be used. At all stages exercises should be purposeful, tuneful and enjoyable.

Use should be made as soon as is practicable of the pupils' knowledge of notation and of their skills in reading. Otherwise the

teaching of notation has little purpose. As mentioned above, when
a song is being learned the pupils might at least follow the melody
in staff notation during the teacher's playing or singing. They might
read a suitably selected part of a song. If the content of a whole
song lies within the scope of their experience in reading—and many
of the songs included in school song books do—they might be given
the challenge of finding their way through the whole song from
notation. At the same time, every encouragement should be given
to the pupils to read for instrumental playing. Very often children
see more point in learning to read music if they are doing so in
order to play an instrument, and they frequently make more rapid
progress in reading by this means.

Differences of Ability

Much of the music course can be appropriately taught on a class
basis, but teachers must be aware of the differences in musical
ability which exist amongst their pupils, and must as far as possible
make allowances for them. Children with a better than average
perception of rhythm and pitch, with good singing voices, or with
skill in reading music may be asked to illustrate or to lead the class
in songs and musical exercises; in instrumental ensemble they may
be given the more difficult parts; in creative work their ability to
extemporise should be given every encouragement. Opportunities
might also be given to gifted pupils to sing or to play, individually
or in groups, at assemblies or other school occasions. It is not
possible, however, to cater adequately for exceptional ability in
the classroom situation, and teachers should encourage gifted
pupils to take advantage of the instrumental instruction which is
offered by the education authority or by private tutors, and might
also make the parents of such children aware of the desirability of
developing their talents to the full.

Musically backward pupils are equally deserving of consideration.
Many pupils have difficulty in controlling their voices; it is inexact
and unfair to classify them as "tone deaf", or to label them with
any term which leaves them with the impression that they are
lacking in some faculty possessed by their fellows. These pupils,
slower in developing pitch sense or vocal control, should never be
silenced, nor should attention be drawn to them, even although
their efforts may tend to spoil the general effect of class singing. In
the first instance a pupil who is musically backward should be
encouraged to sing easily and gently and to listen with concentration.
If it is possible for him to be taken individually, remarkable improve-

ment can often be expected. Experience in the playing of a simple melodic percussion instrument may also help him to acquire vocal skill.

In general the question of the most suitable ways of catering for differences of ability in music should be given more thought than hitherto, and could well be the subject of experimentation. Imaginative teachers can very often devise activities which enable pupils of varying degrees of skill within the same class to contribute something at their own level; but it may be that certain aspects of music —for example, aural training and reading—are best taught to groups formed on the basis of the ability of the pupils and that those who are particularly gifted or interested in music would be more adequately catered for if they were grouped together under teachers with a special contribution to make in this direction. Experiments would be welcome in which various forms of grouping and "setting" according to ability and interest, and various ways of utilising the talents of the teaching staff can be tried.

Chapter 23

Physical Education

AT one time physical education in the primary school was almost wholly concerned with the exercising of various parts of the body and the teaching of prescribed skills, emphasising conformity with uniform standards. The "Syllabus of Physical Education for Primary Schools", published by the Department in 1960, reflected a change of emphasis, taking account of individual differences among children, stressing the need to allow for individual rates of progress in the acquisition of skills, and introducing the idea of movement as a means of expression. The guidance given in the Syllabus has been very useful to teachers, but in some respects the approaches suggested in it require to be supplemented so as to take account of the most up-to-date thinking on physical education.

The activities covered by the Syllabus are of two kinds—those which involve functional movement and are aimed at the co-ordination of the body for use in such activities as gymnastics, games, national dancing and athletics, and those which are concerned with movement as a means of expression. It may be useful to consider each of these two aspects—functional movement and expressive movement—and to describe briefly the approaches which are now being recommended.

The various types of functional movement suggested in the Syllabus are in general still appropriate. Through the work listed as "gymnastics" children are given opportunities to run, jump, climb and swing when the will to such activities is at its height. The handling of balls, hoops, bean bags and ropes helps to develop hand and eye co-ordination. If, as is suggested, the pupils are organised informally in small groups and the accent is on varied activity and individual effort, the work is enjoyable and each pupil can progress at an appropriate pace, competing against himself rather than others. Emphasis is rightly laid on the learning and practice of a variety of techniques which ensure safety in landing and stopping, and in the use of apparatus. In the section on games a wide range of individual, partner, group and team activities is recommended for various stages, and through these the unathletic as well as the athletically gifted can find pleasure and satisfaction and learn something of co-operation and competition in play without developing undesirable attitudes of team rivalry. The national

188

dances which are included in the section on "dance" provide opportunities for the development of poise, grace and variety of movement.

Much of the functional movement contained in the Syllabus, therefore, is still of value. The current trend, however, in gymnastics goes beyond the teaching of prescribed skills and towards what has sometimes been called "inventive movement". The emphasis has moved from set exercises with pre-determined results to an approach which allows scope for the pupil's ingenuity and individual ability and enables him to discover for himself the range and quality of movement of which his body is capable. The aim is to ensure that each pupil explores as far as he is capable the many possibilities of movement, using at different times and in various ways every part of his body, and experiencing movements that range from quick to slow, from large to small, from gentle to vigorous, as occasion demands. The teacher's part is to present the pupils with situations or challenges to which they are to respond in their own way, to assess the response of each pupil in terms of his own individual potential, and to help him to discover ways of improving or varying his performance. A few examples of this new approach may be helpful by way of illustration.

The teacher may ask the pupils to move over the floor in as many ways as possible, and different pupils may respond to this challenge by walking, running, skipping, leaping or hopping. The teacher may then suggest that parts of the body other than the feet might be used, and the pupils will explore other possibilities, such as moving on feet and hands or knees and hands, or using the body to roll. On other occasions she may encourage them to think about moving with different body shapes, at different speeds or in different directions.

If even the simplest of apparatus is available, a wide range of inventive movement is possible. The pupils may be asked, for example, to go from one end of a bench to the other using hands and feet. Some may travel along the bench moving both hands together and then both feet together; some may move hands and feet one at a time; some may stay on the bench, others move hands or feet alternately on and off; some may move forward, some backwards; there will be small, quick movements and long, slow movements; there will also be pupils who fail to comply with the teacher's instructions by running or lying and pulling their bodies along. The teacher must try in this situation to assess each child's performance in terms of its acceptability as a solution to the problem, the degree of his confidence and the variety of movements he has discovered, to suggest ways in which greater variety may be achieved, and to give him opportunities to practise, improve and repeat those of his movements which have been most effective.

The more complex the apparatus, the greater the range of possibilities. Once pupils have been given sufficient time to explore all the ways of moving on and around a climbing frame, for example, and have discovered ways of gripping and of taking their weight on different parts of the body, the teacher can begin to guide their exploration by setting problems in movement. She may attach a bench and a ladder to the frame and indicate a track which is to be followed—for example, up the bench, through the frame, along the ladder and down the far side—without specifying what types of movement may be necessary. The pupils' initial responses to the challenge will then, as suggested above, be assessed and developed, and opportunities given for consolidation of the most successful movements.

The examples of this approach to gymnastics which have been given above may be sufficient to indicate the principles underlying it and the part the teacher has to play. Its essential feature is the freedom which each pupil is afforded to develop at his own pace and as far as his capacity will allow. There is ample scope for effort, ample opportunity for him to learn from others; but there is no uniform standard at which he must aim, no suggestion of competition with others whose stage of development may well be different from his own.

One further activity which must be mentioned under the general heading of "functional movement" is swimming. It is highly desirable that all children should learn to swim. Besides its obvious utilitarian value, swimming is useful as another kind of movement, calling for a different kind of effort, and as a means whereby children can achieve enjoyment and satisfaction by extending their versatility and their mastery over their environment. Primary schools, therefore, should take advantage of any facilities that are available locally so as to ensure that every pupil who needs it receives instruction.

Expressive movement, elements of which appear in the Syllabus in the section on "Dance", takes its place alongside art and craft activities, oral and written language, drama and music, as a medium in which children can express feelings, moods and ideas. In this, as in inventive movement, encouragement is given to each pupil to explore the many possible ways of moving, not in this case to solve a problem or answer a challenge, but to express his own individual response to a stimulus—a rhythm, a melody, a story, a dramatic idea. The teacher's function in this aspect of physical education is to provide a wide variety of material, situations and ideas which will kindle the imagination, to help the pupils to evolve their own ideas and give them form and shape, and to open out for them fresh possibilities in movement.

Teachers who have successfully developed expressive movement have found that some lessons can be planned round a theme which suggests many different types of movement and allows for many different interpretations. Suitable themes for various stages are recommended in the Syllabus. Others may be suggested by the pupils themselves from their own interests; science fiction and television programmes may be popular sources of ideas. Or ideas may emerge from the work of the class in other fields—from history, from the Bible, from mythology, from poetry or from pieces of music with contrasting speeds, rhythms and moods. The themes should be selected so as to ensure, over a period, as great a variety as possible. On each occasion the pupils should be given opportunity and time to work out their own responses to the stimulus, their own interpretations of the theme, perhaps with suggestions from the teacher. The younger the pupils, the more individual will be the response, but as children develop they enjoy working out their ideas with partners, in small groups, or as a class.

No more than an outline of the modern approach to physical education has been attempted. Enough, however, has been said to refute the traditional view that the subject affects the physical well-being of the child only in the narrowest sense, and to show that it has other valuable contributions to make to his personal and social development.

Chapter 24

Health Education

DURING the primary school years the school shares with the home the responsibilities of promoting the child's health and forming in him attitudes and habits which will result in healthy living and high standards of personal hygiene. Close co-operation between home and school is essential. Parents should feel free to visit the school in order to talk over the general welfare of their children, and should be encouraged to attend routine or specially arranged medical inspections and avail themselves of the advice of the school doctor. By such means the importance for the general well-being of the child of sleep, cleanliness, a balanced diet and suitable clothing can be emphasised when necessary, and the school can bring to the notice of the parents aspects of the child's physical condition of which they may be unaware.

In addition, the head teacher and his staff must ensure that the conditions in the school are conducive to the physical, emotional and social well-being of the pupils. The value of a school environment which is bright, attractive, comfortable and stimulating, and of an organisation and methods which offer security, satisfaction, and opportunities for co-operation and individual development has already been indicated in earlier chapters. Classroom furniture and its arrangement, the use of the facilities for heating, lighting and ventilation, the provision of flowers, plants and visual material, the tone and atmosphere of classroom and school, the personal relations the teacher establishes with her pupils and fosters among them, and the demands she makes of each of them are all factors which affect their general well-being.

The primary school also has the more specific tasks of making its pupils aware of the importance of good health, of giving them some understanding of how the body works, and of forming in them habits which will help them to promote and maintain their own health. The head teacher must have a clear policy on these matters, and must ensure that each teacher knows what is expected of her. It is not suggested that health education should be treated as a separate subject in the curriculum or that there should be a prescribed syllabus for each class. It is best treated incidentally and informally, not by means of specific lessons. Nevertheless, each teacher must be aware of the school's aims, the broad lines on which

192

they are to be implemented, and the scope of her personal responsibility in this aspect of school life.

In classes P I to P IV the approach should be largely practical. Attention should be given, perhaps daily at first, to details of personal hygiene so that the pupils may acquire habits of cleanliness at an impressionable period of their lives. Training may have to be given, for example, in the use of the lavatory, wash-hand basins, handkerchiefs, litter-bins, doormats. Regular attention will have to be paid to such things as hand-washing after using the lavatory and before meals, and guidance given about caring for the skin, the hair, the teeth, the nails and the feet. School meals should provide opportunities for the encouragement of good eating habits and for informal talks about the choice of food and the need for a nutritious and varied diet. By practical lessons in the playground and the environs of the school the pupils can be trained in habits of carefulness and good behaviour on the roads.

The teacher should also take advantage of opportunities for incidental references to health and welfare. A fall, a cut finger, the care of a classroom pet, a topic thrown up during work on a centre of interest, a visit by the dentist or the doctor, a national or local campaign for dental health, road safety or accident prevention may all be exploited to bring home to the pupils some aspect of health education and to increase their appreciation of good habits and healthy living.

In the older classes attention must still be given to personal hygiene and the continuation of routines established in the earlier stages. Older pupils, however, are more able to grasp the reasons underlying these and the advantages of exercise, fresh air, sunlight, sleep and rest, and the teacher may find it useful to encourage them to investigate and discuss these matters more fully than before. The subjects of the curriculum, particularly history, geography and science, will include topics with a bearing on health which can be followed up by groups or individual pupils or which may lead to profitable investigation of contemporary problems. Food, clothing, the care of the body, safety and accident prevention can be more fully considered by means of practical lessons, discussion, reading, films and talks. More can be learned about the people concerned in the prevention and treatment of disease—the doctor, the dentist, the nurse, the sanitary inspector—and the work which is done in clinics and hospitals. Special consideration should be given in the oldest classes to the dangers of smoking.

So far as conditions in the school allow, the teacher should aim at the highest possible standards of hygiene. She should, however, guard against the dangers of an over-emphasis on health and hygiene, which may produce feelings of anxiety in sensitive children. She must in an unobtrusive way be constantly observant of the physical and emotional condition of her pupils, recognising their differing rates of maturation and prepared to make allowance for them. She must, too, be on the watch not only for emotional upsets which she can solve within her own classroom situation but also for those problems which may require expert medical or psychological help or sympathetic investigation of the child's home background.

Since many girls and some boys, now reach puberty before the age of 12, it is desirable that the primary school should give some instruction in physical growth and development. The questions also which pupils, both boys and girls, ask about sex suggest the very real need for guidance while they are still in the primary school. Whether systematic instruction in sex should be given in the primary school is still a controversial issue. What form sex education should take, if it is to be introduced, at what stage it should be begun, which pupils should be involved, and who should be given responsibility for dealing with it are matters for very serious consideration. Some head teachers and teachers say frankly that they do not regard themselves as competent to deal with sex education and that they would feel embarrassed if asked to do so. Mixed classes containing pupils of different levels of maturity present a further problem. Moreover, not all parents would agree to their children being given sex instruction in school.

It is difficult, therefore, to make firm recommendations with regard to sex education in the primary school. Perhaps the most important question which has to be answered is how sex education in schools can deal adequately with the emotional as well as the physical aspects of sexual development. Some points, however, appear to be beyond reasonable dispute. Whatever the school attempts should have the consent of the parents concerned. Menstrual hygiene must now be the concern of the primary as well as the secondary school, and there should be facilities for the provision and disposal of sanitary towels. Girls approaching puberty should be given instruction individually or in small groups on menstruation, and they should know to whom to turn for help and advice. Any questions which the pupils themselves ask about sex should be answered factually and without elaboration, and if possible without embarrassment.

Chapter 25

Handwriting

HANDWRITING is for most people an important means of communication and expression. While the development of mechanical
devices has done away with the need for a good deal of manuscript
writing, there are still many occasions on which manuscript is
appropriate or convenient. On almost all occasions, too, the element
of speed is a factor, which becomes more important the more
writing an individual has to do, for example in the secondary school
and in all forms of further and higher education. Despite the advent
of mechanical aids, therefore, there is still need for all who are
likely to have to set anything down on paper to acquire a form of
handwriting which can be written at speed and still retain a high
degree of legibility. It is also desirable that what is written should
not be unattractive. The development of aesthetic qualities in handwriting, however, is a secondary consideration in the primary school,
where the main aim in the teaching of the skill must be to lay,
through appropriate training and practice, the foundations of a
style that is, above all, clear and fluent.

The resurgence of interest in handwriting which has recently taken
place has resulted in the publication of several books on the subject,
and the issue by some education authorities of new schemes of
work. In general these books, and the suggestions to teachers which
usually accompany the schemes, give sound and detailed guidance
on most teaching points, and as this helpful information is already
available little would be gained by covering the same ground in the
same detail here. One general point, however, requires particular
emphasis: the policy adopted throughout the school must be
consistent.

In the youngest classes, where one of the teacher's main aims is
to give her pupils a wide sensory training, nearly everything that
contributes to this basic training contributes also to the development
of the skills necessary for handwriting. For example, play with
water, clay, paints, crayons, scissors, improves the pupil's muscular
control, and games involving counting, matching and grading help
to foster awareness of size and shape. Nowadays, too, since handwriting can play a part in the learning of reading, children eager to
learn to read not only have a powerful incentive to try to write,
but also the chance of seeing examples of the teacher's written work
—often executed in front of them—in the form of captions, news

items, pupils' names, or labels for objects of interest. Often a child's earliest attempts in handwriting are pure "make believe": uninhibitedly he sets down on paper shapes which in his eyes show some resemblance to adult handwriting and to which he can pretend to attach a meaning. Quite soon, these attempts may be followed by efforts to reproduce some words he has seen in the classroom or which have been written for him by the teacher—for example, his name or a caption for one of his drawings. The most appropriate form of writing will be a simple script print.

In these activities, because he is thinking of what he is writing rather than how the letter shapes are to be formed, he tends to be relaxed and free from muscular strain or tension. His crayon or thick pencil is held comfortably, the blank sheets of newsprint he uses imposes no premature restrictions on size, shape, or position, and he makes his letters of a size in keeping with the degree of control he has attained. As early as class P II or the end of class P I a pupil requires some guidance in the formation of letters; otherwise he may have difficulty later in acquiring the necessary skill. At the subsequent stages the teacher has to help him improve his basic handwriting skills—a process which demands attention to particular elements such as formation, size, spacing and alignment—without losing the spontaneity and fluency with which he "wrote" the free patterns, the "pretend letters" and the captions which made up his early informal practice.

There is a good deal of evidence that progress is most rapid when the pupils understand the purpose of the exercises they are asked to do, and when short periods, perhaps ten minutes at a time, are given to intensive practice on particular points, the pupils being reminded that though they should write with a due measure of care, yet they should try to maintain fluency at all times. The experienced teacher knows in advance where difficulties are likely to arise and can plan her instruction accordingly. Almost all her pupils will require considerable practice in certain elements, for example the formation and linking of letters, but the amount of practice needed may vary greatly from one child to another. As at the early stages, the pupils should continue to use materials which give them the maximum freedom to develop the movements most suited to their own hand —a writing instrument which allows easy handling, and blank paper or paper ruled at most with one guide line in preference to multi-lined sheets. In her own handwriting, whether on the blackboard, on cards, or as a model for copying, the teacher must exemplify the patterns and the fluency of movement which she is trying to develop in the writing of her pupils.

Left-handed pupils require special consideration. By the time children come to school, most have a clearly preferred hand, but some use either. There is no advantage in a child's using his left hand if he can use his right, but he should not be forced to use his right. If there is doubt, a simple throwing test with a ball of paper or a cutting test with scissors will usually indicate which is his true hand. When pupils are clearly left-handed, it is necessary to eliminate as far as possible any physical difficulties which may lead to awkward posture and bad writing habits. They should sit where they have free movement on the left and should tilt their jotters downwards to the right. Ball-point pens and pens with flexible nibs are particularly suitable for left-handed writers.

Since ultimately the value of what is written lies in its substance and not in its appearance, the writer must be able to give as much of his conscious attention as possible to the content of the task in hand. He cannot do this fully unless the processes involved in handwriting have become so much a part of himself as to be almost automatic—a ready response on paper, as it were, to the thoughts he has in his head. Mastery of this kind depends on his acquiring an easy, fluent style which he can write with confidence, and this in turn depends on continuity of development—the shapes and movements required at each stage being based on those learned earlier— and on the establishing of certain muscular habits in regard to the making and joining of the letters. Modern handwriting has simplified many of the letter forms, especially the capitals and the "ligatures" which join letters, largely discarding such intricacies as loops— often a cause of illegibility in careless or unskilled hands—and linking letters only when this is necessary to preserve or facilitate fluency of movement. The resulting gain to legibility has been considerable.

Enthusiasts for handwriting as an art have expressed the fears that a style shorn of loops and using the simplified capital forms now advocated would lead to an unwelcome uniformity and to a lack of individuality. This has not proved to be so. Even from the first, small differences make themselves noticeable, and as the pupils' mastery grows they tend, on their own, to introduce the minor modifications which cumulatively make up a personal and clearly identifiable style. Such variations, which often add to the aesthetic appeal of a script, are to be encouraged so long as they do not adversely affect legibility or speed.

The modern approach to written English gives the pupil many more opportunities than ever before to use his handwriting so that by the time he leaves the primary school he should be equipped in handwriting technique for the demands of secondary education. In the recent past, however, it would appear that a number of secondary schools have shown themselves reluctant to accept the less traditional forms now offered by some of their pupils. There is no justification for this attitude: any form of handwriting which is legible and can be written comfortably at speed should be acceptable anywhere.

Chapter 26

Gaelic

THE areas within which Gaelic is spoken continue to become fewer. It is also true that even in some Gaelic-speaking areas the use of the language for conversation by children of school age is declining steadily. Nevertheless there are still areas where Gaelic maintains its vigour and is not only the normal means of conversation for adults but is also the language which the children speak when they come to school. These children have to be taught English. Since, however, they have little or no understanding of it in the early stages, it is the duty of the primary school to maintain and develop Gaelic as a living means of communication and expression. And if the primary school is to discharge its function fully in providing an education in keeping with the needs and interests of the pupils it will not only teach the mother tongue as a subject in its own right but also use it functionally when appropriate as a means of instructing Gaelic-speaking pupils in other subjects.

In the infant classes the main aim is to encourage the pupils to speak confidently and fluently in Gaelic. News periods, talks and conversations about familiar places, people and things, traditional Gaelic songs and stories, rhymes and games play a not inconsiderable part in achieving this aim, and since they form thus early an important part of the curriculum, the pupils come to regard their own language with respect.

The initial stages of reading and number present their own problems in any circumstances, and it would be absurd that children who come to school speaking only Gaelic should have their early lessons in reading and number in English. For such pupils, therefore, since understanding is an essential of learning, reading and number should be in Gaelic until such time as the pupils have gained a working knowledge of English. Understandably, teachers in bilingual areas are reluctant to postpone reading in English, but even in such areas it has been found that once the pupils have acquired some skill in reading through the medium of Gaelic, they readily go on to master the mechanics of reading in English, and both languages can be used to support each other in enabling the pupils to understand the content of their reading.

At the subsequent stages of the primary school reading and comprehension should be taken regularly in Gaelic and reading

o

skills developed on lines similar to those recommended in the chapter on "Language Arts". It is important that in the conduct of the lessons Gaelic should be treated as a living language. Formal translations into English should be avoided. Ideally, discussion on the content, vocabulary, and idiom of the passages read should be in Gaelic. The extent to which this is practicable is likely to vary from school to school. Where there is a number of pupils who do not speak fluent Gaelic the teacher inevitably will have on occasion to resort to the medium of English. She should, however, resist the temptation to overdo this practice and rather encourage such pupils to speak in Gaelic as often as possible during the Gaelic lesson.

The range of reading material in Gaelic is very limited and lacking in variety as compared with what is available in English. The recent publication of a series of interesting and colourful readers for the younger pupils has, however, been a welcome development, but the provision is still quite inadequate. Under the guidance of the organisers of Gaelic who have been appointed by two education authorities, individual teachers have prepared selections of reading material suited to the particular needs of their own pupils. The display of this material and of other teaching aids at conferences on the teaching of Gaelic has encouraged others to follow this example. So far, however, this material is not available in printed form and consequently lacks permanence. The efforts being made by groups of teachers to select and edit this material with a view to publication are commended.

Although the main emphasis will be on oral proficiency and on reading and comprehension, written work will also have a place in the course. In the infant classes, while written exercises should at first be closely linked with reading activities, opportunities for free writing should be given. This approach should be continued in the subsequent stages. Undue emphasis should not be placed on spelling, since it has been found that insistence on correct spelling tends to inhibit originality and freedom in composition and that the best results are achieved where pupils are encouraged to read widely and thus become familiar with the printed word. From class P III onwards pupils whose ability and attainment warrant it should be encouraged to improve their proficiency by various means, for example, by writing the answers to simple questions on interpretation lessons, by writing letters, by keeping individual work books and diaries which may include descriptions of topics of personal interest. Older pupils might produce a small magazine.

It is of paramount importance that pupils should have the opportunity at all stages of improving their oral proficiency. Recitation, singing, dramatic work, and oral interpretation are useful for this purpose, but the teacher should also make a point of utilising the less formal occasions which often present themselves in the course of the school day. Since Gaelic is a living language, progress in it cannot be regarded as satisfactory unless it can be freely used as the normal medium of communication and expression. How far pupils will be able to use it in this way will depend on their linguistic background and their stage of development, but as far as the circumstances of the school will permit, Gaelic should be integrated with the other subjects of the curriculum. Some subjects lend themselves to such treatment more than others, particularly those which have an obvious connection with the school environment, and some schools have already proved that Gaelic can be successfully used at least for part of the lesson in religious education, natural science, local history and local geography.

Much has to be done to stimulate interest in the language and enhance its prestige in the schools. Reference has already been made to the need to increase the supply of suitable reading matter. Within recent years considerable attention has been devoted by Jordanhill College of Education to discovering the most effective methods of using Gaelic as a medium of instruction and of improving teaching technique in the schools. Teachers who have attended vacation courses have exchanged ideas on teaching practice and have been encouraged to experiment with methods of presentation. Two education committees, as already indicated, have appointed supervisors of Gaelic, and after an experimental period in which recommendations made by panels of teachers were tried out Inverness-shire Education Committee has issued a "Scheme of Instruction" for the guidance of teachers in its bilingual areas. If the Gaelic language and culture are to be preserved, it is important that teachers should adopt the methods which have been found effective in arousing and maintaining the interest of the pupils.

Chapter 27

Modern Languages

In the last twenty years there has been in almost every country in the world a great upsurge of interest in the teaching of modern foreign languages.

Much thought has been given to ways of enabling as many people as possible to develop a command of the spoken language, and the belief has grown that the most promising way of attaining this goal lies in an earlier start to the learning of a foreign language.

Recent linguistic research has produced a very potent argument in favour of an early start, namely, that young children apparently have a great capacity for assimilating language. They possess powers of mimicry and memorisation which enable them to acquire with relative ease new sounds and new language structures and these powers decrease as they grow older. The vocal cords and face muscles are less set than in adolescence, and boys in particular are not handicapped by breaking voices which at the age of entry to the secondary school make them self-conscious and easily embarrassed. Furthermore, the spontaneity and lack of inhibitions which characterise the behaviour of young children make it easier for them to acquire another language and to accept it as a natural medium of expression.

It can therefore be accepted that the early introduction of a foreign language is desirable both from a utilitarian and from an educational point of view. But the question still remains whether it is advisable to introduce the teaching of modern languages into the primary cycle of education in view of the problems which such an undertaking must bring in its train and the burden it may place on the resources of the primary school. Before any decision can be reached, a number of questions must be carefully considered. The answers to some of these questions may be comparatively easy; some will require a great deal of research and experimentation before an answer can be found; to others there may be no satisfactory answer. The controlled experiments which are already taking place are therefore to be welcomed and should yield valuable knowledge. Research in other countries will also undoubtedly be a fruitful source of information.

The main questions for consideration are indicated below. Is there, or can there be, an adequate supply of suitable teachers? What is the optimum age for starting a second language? How much time is required? Should all pupils in an age group study a foreign language? If not, how is selection to be made? How can continuity of instruction within the primary school be assured, and adequate liaison be effected with the receiving secondary school? What methods of language teaching are appropriate for young children?

Supply of Suitable Teachers

The task of teaching a foreign language to pupils in the primary school is one which requires both an understanding of young children and a reasonable command of the language, especially the spoken language. The teacher's pronunciation must provide a good model for imitation; if it does not, the pupils will acquire a poor pronunciation which it will be extremely difficult to eradicate later. Just as it is relatively easy for young children to acquire good linguistic habits, it is equally easy for them to acquire bad habits. In addition to possessing a satisfactory degree of linguistic competence, the teacher should be familiar with primary school methods and should be able to create in her class a friendly, sympathetic atmosphere, which is essential if children are to be encouraged to express themselves freely and willingly.

It has been suggested that native speakers—"exchange" assistants, for example—might be used. Usually, however, they are not trained to teach in the primary school and do not appreciate the difficulties of young learners. Consequently they are likely to be less successful than the competent primary teacher.

Secondary school specialists, although competent linguistically, are often unfamiliar with the aims and methods of primary school teaching and many would find it difficult to adapt themselves to the needs of younger pupils. Moreover, the increasing shortage of modern language teachers in the secondary school makes it undesirable to divert any to the primary school where the main requirements in a teacher are not so much high academic qualifications as an adequate command of the language combined with the ability to create the right atmosphere.

There are, of course, already in the primary schools many teachers who are qualified to teach a modern language although they have previously had no occasion to teach it. Those of them who have adopted modern methods of teaching and have been willing to brush up their knowledge of the spoken language are at present the most successful teachers of a foreign language in the primary schools.

It is obvious that the supply of primary school teachers possessing the necessary qualities will in the first instance be very limited. Mechanical aids such as films, audio-visual courses, gramophone records and teachers' manuals can, however, do much to help a teacher to compensate for any deficiencies in her linguistic equipment. In some schools teachers with only a limited knowledge of a language have achieved surprisingly good results by a systematic and intelligent use of mechanical aids. A special organiser for an area, with real linguistic competence and a proper conception of both aims and methods, can likewise offer valuable guidance and advice to primary school teachers who are inexperienced in language work.

If the introduction of modern languages into the primary school becomes general, a supply of suitably qualified teachers will be necessary. The colleges of education are already taking account of this by giving to selected students in their diploma courses opportunities of developing their proficiency in a foreign language and also some instruction in the techniques of teaching it to young children.

Starting Age

The age at which it is most profitable for children to start to learn a second language has been, and continues to be, the subject of intensive research. Experiments have shown that, given suitable instruction, children can begin to learn another language at a very early age; there is evidence that a promising start can be made at the age of four or five.

Although the practicability of beginning a second language at a very early age is beyond question, the psychological effects on the general development of the young beginner have not yet been fully investigated. The controlled experiments which are going on with the introduction of a foreign language at all stages from classes P I to P VII may yield an answer to this problem. There will also have to be careful assessment of the advantages or disadvantages for the pupils once they reach the secondary school.

Allocation of Time

The amount of time which should be devoted to teaching a foreign language in the primary school is not yet known, but there is general agreement about certain conditions. The time allocated must be sufficient to allow of steady progress. The desultory teaching of a few French songs and of some odd words and phrases is rarely worth while and may have the effect of robbing the study of the language in the secondary school of its freshness and interest. It is certainly desirable that the time given to the foreign language should be regularly spaced out. If possible, a little should be done every day. Again, the younger the child the shorter the periods of actual instruction should be. Lessons lasting longer than 30 minutes put too great a strain on the attention of even the older pupils and achieve no useful purpose. With some classes two short lessons might be more profitable than one longer one. Further opportunities can be taken during the course of the day to use the foreign language for routine greetings, commands, and everyday expressions.

Selection of Pupils

Whether it is profitable to teach a second language to all children in the primary school, irrespective of the level of their intelligence, is a question which has not yet been resolved. Results of investigations seem to indicate that even young children display different degrees of linguistic aptitude and that this aptitude declares itself at a very early age. It is also a fact that some children have difficulty in learning to speak their mother tongue. While it is therefore dangerous to assume that children who do not possess this innate ability cannot learn a second language, the question whether a second language ought to be taught to pupils below a certain level of linguistic aptitude requires careful investigation.

Until reliable information is available, it must be left to head teachers who propose to introduce a language to decide, in the light of all the circumstances of their schools, whether it should be taught to all the pupils in particular classes or only to a proportion of them. Experiments which include all the pupils in any age-group must be carefully studied from the viewpoint of the less able pupils, both in the early stages and later. Only when this has been done and the results assessed will it be possible to offer really valid advice.

Choice of Language

There has been a good deal of criticism of the preponderance of French over all other languages taught in this country. There is here something of a vicious circle: more pupils learn French; therefore more teachers have a command of this language; therefore more French is taught. While it is obviously desirable that opportunities of learning languages other than French should be made available for pupils, it would be impossible for the secondary schools which receive them at the age of transfer to cope with a wide variety of languages begun in the primary schools. Moreover, any pupils transferred from a school in which one language was taught to another in which a different language was favoured would find themselves faced with additional difficulties.

In the present experimental period it is probable that French will be the language most frequently introduced, and this has certain advantages. Experiments will be more easily compared with one another than would be experiments with a variety of languages. Also, more research into the basic requirements of the native language has been done in France than elsewhere and this information is at the disposal of teachers. Moreover, one of the main obstacles to the learning of French is the difficulty of pronunciation and intonation, and this is exactly the aspect of language learning which is most easily assimilated at the primary stage. While, therefore, schools should not be discouraged from sensible experiments with the introduction of other languages, any serious efforts to encourage the teaching of a reasonable range of languages throughout the country might be postponed meantime.

Continuity

If it is proposed to introduce a foreign language at any stage of the primary school, every effort must be made to see that the course can be carried on without interruption in succeeding years. Similarly, it is important to ensure that, as far as possible, instruction can be carried on in the secondary school. It is also necessary to consider the position of the receiving secondary school which may have to deal both with pupils who have had no previous language teaching and with pupils who have followed courses of language instruction which differ from one another in type, length, depth and treatment. For this reason it is essential that experimental courses in the primary school should not be started in isolation but according to a systematic plan for the area. It is very desirable that the teachers of receiving secondary schools should be consulted at the planning stage and should be represented on any panels formed to consider modern language teaching in the primary schools in their catchment areas. This does not mean that the secondary school teachers should dictate content and method, but that there should be full co-operation between receiving and sending schools.

Methods

A good deal of the difficulty experienced in this country in organising the teaching of a foreign language to primary school children arises from the fact that this is an entirely new field and that there is no body of experience on which to draw. Information, however, is gradually accumulating from experiments which are being carried out at present. In addition, linguistic experts have given much thought to the problem of how a child learns his first language, and research has been initiated in an endeavour to establish to what extent the learning of a second language follows the same pattern. While it is still a matter of controversy whether the process of learning a first language is identical with that of learning a second one, it is widely accepted that the younger the child the more closely the two are linked. Just as in learning the first language listening comes before speech, so in learning a second language listening should precede speech and both should come long before reading and writing. Experiments based on this view of language learning have proved that it is a fruitful approach. But care must be taken that a too ready acceptance of this assumption does not lead teachers to underestimate the difficulties involved in teaching a second language to young children. Conditions in school are markedly different from those found in the home environment. In school the language is used only for a short time daily, and though the teacher may show great resource and ingenuity in creating situations which stimulate the pupils to use the foreign language, it is difficult for her to reproduce the totally functional context of, for example, the home or the family.

If instruction is to be based in the first instance on listening, then it is essential that a good speech model should be provided, either by the teacher herself or by means of a mechanical aid, or preferably by both. It is also very important that pupils should be trained to listen carefully, and young children often show remarkable powers of accurate hearing. The pupils should, therefore, listen and imitate what they hear. The material should be presented in a lively and interesting manner, with as much variety as possible, by means of informal play, dramatisation, singing, puppets, competitions and games.

Pronunciation and intonation should receive close and constant attention. While too high standards of accuracy should not be demanded at the expense of free and uninhibited expression, it should be borne in mind that it is as easy for the pupils to learn the correct pronunciation of a word or phrase as it is to learn the wrong one.

Obviously it is important that they should understand what they hear, and to ensure this the teacher should pronounce new words or phrases clearly within a context that leaves no room for doubt as to their meaning, using mime, actions, pictures, or in the last resort the mother tongue. In order that the pupils may establish an association between words, ideas and behaviour, the repetition of newly learned material should be accompanied by some form of activity—action songs, pointing out and naming objects, carrying out commands.

An approach through play and activity methods does not mean, however, that language learning at the primary school stage is a mere toying with language. Formal grammar, translation disconnected lists of words and verb drill have no place in the teaching of a foreign language to younger children, but the teacher should have a clear idea of what she is doing and must build up a systematic and progressive course of instruction.

The linguistic material used by the teacher must be restricted to what the pupils can assimilate and use with ease. Quality and not quantity should be the criterion. The course should progress, not in terms of grammatical points but in terms of topics which interest the pupils, such as the school, the home, the family, and situations such as shopping, making a telephone call, going for a walk or a bus journey, in which certain basic words and phrases are needed. Thus a body of speech patterns based on normal language usage will be built up and gradually extended.

The amount of ground covered will, of course, depend on the time allocated and on the ability of the pupils. In the early stages the approach will be purely aural and oral. If the course lasts several years reading and writing may well be introduced, but not until good speech habits have been firmly established.

Whatever is taught must be thoroughly and accurately assimilated, and whatever their age the pupils should be encouraged to express themselves as freely as possible in the language within the limits of their linguistic knowledge. The teacher's chief aim should be to train the pupils to use the language with confidence and to apply what they have learned to different situations which approximate as closely as possible to those of real life situations. The pupils are thus given an experience of the language arising from its use in everyday situations, and it becomes part of their normal behaviour to express themselves through the medium of the foreign language. Development of the creative use of language is undoubtedly the most difficult part of the teacher's task, but if language teaching is to be worth while this part must not be neglected and should form an essential element of every unit of work. Every opportunity should also be taken to make the pupils aware of the background, culture and customs of the people whose language they are learning.

If the language course is systematically planned and the methods applied are appropriate to their age and interests, the pupils will have acquired at the end of their primary schooling a knowledge of the foreign language on which they can later build because it will have been gradually and progressively acquired in accordance with sound principles of language learning.

Part 4

Chapter 28

The Small School

In recent years there has been a trend towards the closing of small rural schools. To some extent this has resulted from a belief that the pupils may gain additional social and educational advantages from being taught in a larger school community. Other factors that have contributed to the trend are the decline in the roll of small schools as a result of the depopulation of the areas which they serve, and a reluctance on the part of education authorities to incur expenditure on the replacement or modernisation and extension of old buildings when the pupils can be adequately catered for in larger central units within reasonable travelling distance. Even where small schools have not been closed, similar educational and economic considerations have led in some instances to the centralisation of the older pupils in large schools to which transport can easily be arranged.

Although the number of small schools is decreasing, many will continue to exist in areas where geographical factors make centralisation difficult or even impossible. Indeed, at the present time more than half the primary schools in Scotland have fewer than 100 pupils on their roll, and approximately a thousand of these are one-teacher or two-teacher schools. These small schools vary considerably in character. The great majority are rural schools, some serving village communities, others drawing their pupils from scattered farms and crofts. A few, however, are in or near urban centres, and are not "rural" in any real sense. Special problems which rural schools, unlike their urban counterparts, may have to face are the comings and goings of migratory families, the shyness and comparative inarticulateness of some country children, and the professional isolation in which the teachers have to live. One problem which all of them share, however, is that presented by the grouping of children of various ages and stages under one teacher.

Difficulties such as these make it essential that small schools, and particularly those staffed only by one or two teachers, should be generously treated by authorities. The inevitable emphasis in such schools on group and individual work calls for liberal supplies of books and equipment suitable for a wide range of ages and levels of ability; material for individual work, a comprehensive library, and a frequent turn-over of books from a central source are particularly important. Aural and visual aids, too, are invaluable to the teacher in supplementing her own resources; even if each school cannot be provided with a full range of these, it should be possible in most areas for groups of small schools to share some of the more expensive items of equipment.

Every effort should also be made to provide guidance and help for the teacher who is faced with teaching every branch of the curriculum to pupils not only of widely differing ability but also of different ages. Subjects such as music and physical education, art and craft activities, and drama present difficulties to teachers who have little talent in these directions; the backward child and the able child make demands on the teacher which she may need help in meeting; the isolation in which many of the teachers work makes it difficult for them to form realistic standards and keep abreast of modern developments in curricula and methods; even the day-to-day organisation of the work and life of the school may over-tax the teacher's resources. Arrangements should be made, therefore, for visits by the teachers to other schools of various sizes, for courses of in-service training, and for meetings at which teachers from schools with similar characteristics can discuss their common problems. Visits from organisers and specialist teachers should be as frequent as circumstances permit. Consideration should also be given to the possibility of appointing auxiliaries to small schools, especially those where the number of pupils in each classroom is very near the maximum permitted by the Code.

In spite of the problems and difficulties which are peculiar to the small school, there is nothing in the recommendations of this memorandum with regard to the curriculum, organisation and methods which does not apply with equal force to schools of all sizes. Indeed, the approaches which some teachers in small schools have adopted for years, with their emphasis on activity methods, initiative, individual and group methods and assignments, are very much on the lines now being suggested for all primary schools. There is, therefore, little that can be offered in the way of advice to teachers in small schools which is not already adequately covered in othre chapters. The small school, in fact, presents unique opportunities for education in keeping with the aptitude and ability of its pupils, and the methods recommended elsewhere in, for example, language arts, environmental studies, and art and craft activities are well suited to its circumstances. For instance, centres of interest, "patches" in history, sample studies in geography, observation and experiments in science, and projects in art and crafts can all involve pupils of various ages and stages, each contributing something at his own level. Moreover, the country environment offers plentiful opportunities for field work in geography, science and perhaps local history, provided the teacher knows its possibilities.

One of the advantages that the small school has over the large school lies in the greater possibilities which it holds for flexibility of organisation. In grouping the pupils for work in various branches of the curriculum, age can largely be ignored and groups can be formed on the basis of ability and "readiness"; individual teaching is more easily arranged than in larger schools; each pupil is thus able to progress, in each subject, at a rate appropriate to his capacity. In large schools older pupils might be upset or even resentful if brought together for instruction with younger pupils, but in the small school, where they have grown up with the situation, they tend to accept it more readily. Difficulty of this kind can be avoided if the teacher handles the situation tactfully and if the material which is used is varied enough to cater for the range of maturity and interests among the children.

The suggestions made in other chapters for group and individual activities, therefore, are particularly applicable to the small school, where the range of age and ability makes grouping inevitable, and where it is essential for the pupils to learn to work independently while the teacher is occupied with another group. The teacher, however, must be aware of the dangers which can arise when the pupils have to spend a considerable amount of time working on their own. Opportunities for spoken English, for example, may be fewer than in large schools, unless the teacher encourages conversation and discussion during group work. On occasion material produced by the pupils in connection with projects might be recorded orally on tape rather than in writing. A further danger is that the children may work their way profitlessly through course-books in English and arithmetic. The teacher must ensure that exercises are carefully selected for the appropriateness and usefulness, that individual activities cover an adequate range of subjects, and that practical work, purposeful reading and continuous writing are given their proper place.

It is particularly important that the needs of the youngest children should be catered for and that the teacher should not concentrate unduly on the older pupils. She must resist the temptation to introduce the five-year-olds to formal reading before they are ready for it, even though she is anxious to make them capable of working independently. Country children, very often to a greater extent than town children, need initially opportunities for play, informal activity and language development in a rich environment, and the teacher

P

must plan her day so as to enable her to give her beginners sufficient attention and an appropriate start.

One of the features of the small school is the extent to which the pupil can be involved in every aspect of school life. Because the total number on the roll may be very small, he is likely to be one of an intimate family group in which the older members help and look after the younger ones. He also has opportunities for participation in the organisation and management of school affairs to a degree which is rarely possible in larger schools. In many rural schools, for example, the pupils not only perform the usual routine tasks of the classroom, but also assist the teacher by answering the telephone, organising the library, collecting and recording money for school meals and other purposes, and undertaking a variety of simple clerical duties. In such a situation the children feel that they "belong" in the school community and that they have a useful contribution to make. Moreover, the opportunities they are given to exercise responsibility and initiative play an important part in their personal and social development.

Chapter 29

The Duration of Primary Education

THE duration of primary education has of late been the subject of much discussion and study, and the suitability of the present lower and upper age limits has been questioned by some people. It may be useful to review briefly the arguments that have been put forward, and to draw some tentative conclusions.

There are those who advocate the raising of the age of entry to six years, on the grounds that this is the general practice in most other countries and would go some way to offset the shortage of teachers. It is likely, however, that any raising of the statutory age of entry would be followed by an increased demand for nursery schools, and as these require more generous staffing than most primary schools, the result might be that fewer teachers would be available for primary education. Moreover, the proposal to raise the age of entry is difficult to accept in view of what is now known about the earlier maturation of children and the benefits which the rich environment of the school can offer them. There is in fact much to be said for the contrary view that the age of entry might be lowered to allow all children to receive the benefit of an environment and experiences similar to those which can be provided in a good nursery school. At present, however, economic and staffing considerations prevent the implementation of such a policy. There seems, therefore, to be little possibility of departing from age five as the lower age limit for primary education. Experience has shown that this is a suitable age for children to start school, so long as teachers recognise the individual differences among five-year-old children and provide for them an appropriate environment and a suitable range of experiences and activities.

Arguments for lowering the age of transfer to secondary education are based mainly on the fact that children are maturing earlier and on the belief that the primary school in consequence may be unable to meet the needs of twelve-year-old children, who are more mature, more sophisticated and more advanced than those of previous generations. In addition it is claimed that the wide range of needs and interests exhibited by pupils at about age twelve, particularly in subjects such as modern languages, mathematics and science, is imposing a considerable strain on the resources of the class teacher, and that this situation could be relieved by transfer to secondary

217

education at age eleven. Against these views, however, must be set the fact that in terms of Scottish experience many pupils at the age of eleven are still to immature to adjust themselves to life in a large secondary school. Moreover, the small amount of research that has been carried out in Scotland on the age of transfer has demonstrated that there is no one age which can be regarded as suitable for all children to move into the secondary schools, and that the wide variations in children's development make it impossible to say with certainty that earlier transfer for all should be the natural consequence of generally earlier maturation.

The conclusion from all the available evidence must be that as yet no good reason has been adduced for changing the age of transfer in Scotland. What is required is flexibility in the application of the present age limit, to allow for accelerated transfer for pupils who, having followed an accelerated course through the primary school and completed stage P VII ahead of their age group, are seen to be intellectually, physically and emotionally ready to move into the secondary school. In some areas it has been traditional for individual pupils of marked promise to be transferred early. Their numbers, however, have been relatively small, and no general evaluation of the merits of this practice has been possible. One education authority is experimenting with the early transfer of groups of the ablest pupils, but the experiment has not been in operation long enough for reliable conclusions to be drawn. More experimentation is needed to discover ways in which transfer arrangements can be adapted to cater for the variation in children's development.

At the same time, the primary schools must be prepared to adjust their organisation, curricula and methods in the older classes to meet the expanding needs and interests of the pupils. If these make too many demands on the all-round ability of the class teacher, other ways must be found of using the special gifts which she and her colleagues possess to the advantage of the older pupils. Chapter 7 on "The Deployment of Teaching Resources" suggests how this might be done.

Chapter 30

Research and Experiment

It will be obvious from references that have been made throughout this memorandum that an increasing amount of educational research is being carried out, and that much of it is having an effect on curricula and methods in the schools. In Scotland most of the research which has been undertaken has been under the aegis of the Scottish Council for Research in Education, and it seems likely that this will continue to be so.

Research projects on a smaller scale are carried out from time to time by the universities, the colleges of education and some education authorities. In one area a development unit has been set up in which the university, the college of education and the education authority are co-operating in the study of programmed learning and its application to the work of the schools. It may be, however, that local co-operation of this kind is not sufficient to meet present-day needs, and that much more requires to be done to investigate questions of curricula and methods on a national scale. In any such undertaking the education authorities and the schools have a vital role, both in collecting information and in trying out syllabuses and methods.

It is important that education authorities and schools should be aware of the research that is in progress and the findings of completed research, and should also conduct experiments of their own. It is the education authority's responsibility to ensure that information about research is available to the schools, to give them opportunities and facilities to implement research findings, and to stimulate and sponsor experimentation by the teachers within its area. The teacher in her turn must be prepared to examine and assess new ideas and methods, to give them trial, and to incorporate them in her teaching if she finds them appropriate to her own circumstances. At the same time she herself must be willing to experiment in order to find what is best for her own pupils. Through experimentation of this kind the teacher may become aware of problems which could well form the subject of a research project. By making such problems known to an appropriate body the schools can make a further contribution to research.

Important as it is for teachers to have a progressive and experimental outlook, it is essential that experimentation should not be

219

undertaken without careful thought and planning. Experimentation for its own sake is of little value. No school should be so involved in trying out new ideas that it fails to develop a consistent policy or loses sight of its main aims. Moreover, there is little point in experimentation along lines on which information is already available in abundance from previous research and experiment. Above all, it is vital that the time and energy of teachers and pupils should not be wasted in misguided efforts undertaken without adequate knowledge or skill. Within each school, therefore, the head teacher, while encouraging experimentation, must ensure that it is purposeful and conducted on educationally sound lines. Each education authority too must guard against haphazard experimentation and unnecessary duplication of effort by controlling and co-ordinating new developments in the schools, and ensuring that their results are carefully evaluated. Valuable advice on experimental procedures is available from the Scottish Council for Research in Education.

Chapter 31

In-Service Training

IN recent years there has been a considerable development of courses of in-service training in the colleges of education and in some education authority areas. This has come about partly because of a growing realisation that the teacher's pre-service training is not sufficient in itself. During the initial college course, theoretical studies and classroom practice can be related only to a limited extent, and it is essential that teachers should have opportunities later to reconsider educational theory and practice and see their relevance against the background of their actual experience in the schools. In addition, it is being increasingly acknowledged that further professional training is particularly important in the present era of educational change, if teachers are to be familiar with developments in methodology and the content of the curriculum and be able to adjust their teaching accordingly. If such training is needed for serving teachers, it is all the more essential for those who return to the profession after some years' absence, and should be mandatory for head teachers and others in posts of responsibility whose duty it is to inspire and guide practice in the schools.

The efforts that have so far been made by the colleges and the education authorities merit the warmest commendation; but the number of teachers who have been able to benefit from these facilities represents only a small proportion of the teachers in the primary schools of Scotland. An expansion of refresher courses and courses of in-service training at national, regional and local levels is needed if the provision is to be adequate for present requirements.

The colleges of education have already recognised that the organisation of national and regional in-service courses is a major part of their function, and are taking steps to increase their provision. There is also room for a much greater development of courses on all aspects of primary education conducted by authorities both on an area basis and at local centres with the co-operation of the colleges of education and the inspectorate, and staffed by organisers, college lecturers, head teachers and teachers within and outwith the authority area. Consideration should also be given to the possibility of making more of these courses residential. There is a need, too, for conferences and local study groups at which ideas and experience can be interchanged, particularly by head teachers and teachers involved in similar tasks—for example, head teachers of small rural schools or large town schools, infant teachers, teachers of senior classes, teachers engaged in similar forms of experimentation, teachers with interests in particular branches of the curriculum. Through courses and conferences such as these, teachers have opportunities to listen to the views of those who have made a special contribution in their own field, and are able to participate in discussion and activity related to their own classroom situation.

There is also a need to overcome the reluctance which many teachers feel about having other teachers in their classrooms or about observing the work of their colleagues. Teachers must be given opportunities and encouragement to visit other classrooms and other schools where enterprising and successful work is being done. This may be done quite informally by arrangement between head teachers, but it should be actively encouraged by education authorities, whose contribution might include keeping their teachers informed of interesting developments within their own area.

Within the school the head teacher can ensure that his staff keep up to date by holding meetings at which specific educational matters are discussed and talks are given by teachers or invited speakers, by encouraging and organising visits by teachers to one another's classrooms, and by making appropriate books and periodicals available to them.

One final and important point must be made. Most of the in-service courses that have so far been organised have been held during school holidays, on Saturday mornings or on week-day evenings. If, however, it is accepted that teachers as professional people must be willing throughout their career to adapt themselves to new ideas, then it must be recognised that attendance at courses and visits to other schools should be a normal part of their work, to be undertaken during working hours. It is strongly recommended therefore, that teachers should be released during school time for these purposes, and seconded if need be for a week or more at a time to attend residential courses and conferences. Only in this way will it be possible to achieve the full-scale development of in-service training which is necessary if primary education in Scotland is to be relevant to the age we live in.

Index

Index

Printed in Scotland for Her Majesty's Stationery Office by Morrison and Gibb Ltd., Edinburgh
Dd. 957932/1864 K80 2/75